T0323786

TSARS AND IMPOSTERS

Russia's Time of Troubles

TSARS AND IMPOSTERS

Russia's Time of Troubles

Daniel H. Shubin

Algora Publishing
New York

Library of Congress Cataloging-in-Publication Data —

Shubin, Daniel H.
    Tsars and Imposters: Russia's Time of Troubles / Daniel H. Shubin.
        p. cm.
    Includes bibliographical references and index.
    ISBN 978-0-87586-687-1 (trade paper: alk. paper) — ISBN 978-0-87586-688-8 (hard cover: alk. paper) — ISBN 978-0-87586-689-5 (eBook) 1. Russia—History—Time of Troubles, 1598-1613. 2. Russia—History—Fyodor I, 1584-1598. 3. Boris Fyodorovich Godunov, Czar of Russia, 1551 or 2-1605. 4. Russia—History—Boris Fyodorovich Godunov, 1598-1605. 5. Russia—Kings and rulers—Biography. 6. Pretenders to the throne—Russia—Biography. I. Title.

    DK111.S513 2009
    947.045—dc22

                        2009005551

Front Cover:

Printed in the United States

TABLE OF CONTENTS

1. INTRODUCTION

In the entirety of Russia's tumultuous history, no era compares to the turbulent period that began March 18, 1584, the day of Tsar Ivan the Terrible's death, and ended July 11, 1613, the day Mikhail Feodorovich Romanov was crowned as tsar. During the first half of this 30-year period Russia endured more success and prosperity, and then during the second half endured more devastation, havoc and upheaval, than in any other period of the same length. This book is its record.

Sources

This history is the author's translation and adaptation into English of selections from the following texts, all in Russian.

Karamzin, Nikolai Mikhailovich, *Istoria Gosudarstva Rossiiskogo*, volumes 10, 11 and 12, St. Petersburg 1892; Moscow, 2004.

Kostomarov, Nikolai Ivanovich, *Russkaya Istoria v Zhizneopisaniyakh ee Glavneishikh Deyatelei*, Ves: St. Petersburg, 2005. Originally published 1873–1888.

Skrynnikov, Ruslan Grigoryevich, *Ivan Grozni, Boris Godunov, Vasili Shuisky*, Izdatel'stvo Nauka: Moscow, 2005.

Skrynnikov, Ruslan Grigoryevich, *Smutnoye Vremya*, Moscow, 1995.

Solovyov, Sergei Mikhailovich, *Istoriia Rossii s drevneishikh vremen*, volumes 7 and 8, first published in St. Petersburg, 1851–1879; Moscow, 2005.

Tatishchev, Vasili, *Istoria Rossiiskaya*, volume 3, Part 4, Moscow, 1962, 2004.

Names, Places, and Dates

All names in the text are shown in their Russian form, transliterated from the Cyrillic alphabet. In Russian, the middle name is the patronymic, derived from the father's name, with different endings for sons and daughters. For males, the ending is generally -ovich or -evich or a variation thereof. For females, the usual ending is -ovna or -evna. For males, the family name ends in -sky or a consonant, while for female family members the name usually ends with -a or -ya. For example, the full names of Boris and his sister Irina are Boris Feodorovich Godunov ("Boris, son of Feodor, Godunov), and Irina Feodorovna Godunova ("Irina, daughter of Feodor, Godunov").

The names of Poles are given the Russian forms in this text, with the Polish form in parenthesis.

The son of the tsar was referred to as the tsarevich; the wife of the tsar was the tsaritza; and the daughter was the tsarevna. Hereditary nobles were princes. A special class of non-hereditary nobles promoted by the tsar were the boyars.

In the Russian Orthodox Church men who are tonsured and become monks, and women who take the veil and become nuns, abandon their birth names and assume new names for the duration of their monastic careers. Those names are usually selected from a list of Russian saints and other holy people of the ages. The new name is mentioned in the text whenever a person becomes a monk or nun.

Dates cited are quoted directly from their sources. Ancient Russia used a calendar that assumed the creation of the world on September 1, year 1, while most of the population celebrated New Year's Day on March 25, the holiday of the Annunciation. The Julian calendar was not introduced into Russia until 1700 by decree of Tsar Peter the Great, although it was utilized prior to that time by tradesmen, government officials and others who had international contacts. Dates for events prior to Peter the Great's decree were converted to the Julian calendar by Russian historians. Since Russia continued to use the Julian calendar until 1918, and Russian Orthodoxy continues to do so at the present, all dates in early Russian sources are based on it. In any event, many or most of the specific dates were either fabricated by the early Russian chroniclers or are approximations, so that historians rarely bother to update them to match the Gregorian Calendar currently used in the West.

The population of Russia during the era under consideration is difficult to ascertain, and any figure is at best a conjecture. In 1550, a few years before our history begins, the population of Russia was estimated at 6 to 6.5 million. The nearest figure for the city Moscow is 130,000 in the year 1750. In most early histories, figures relating to military campaign armies and sizes of cities have been significantly inflated by the chroniclers. This tendency will also be apparent in this history, which gives the statistics exactly as provided by early Russian chroniclers. Estimates of the proportion by which the population decreased during the period of our history likewise can only be based on conjecture, although about 20% of the population, or about 1.5 million people, would be a good approximation.

Abbreviations

Patr.	Patriarch
Metr.	Metropolitan
Pr.	Prince
ROC	Russian Orthodox Church

2. The Era of Tsar Ivan IV the Terrible

Early Prominent Russian Families

A few prominent families with dramatic histories form the backbone of the narrative that follows. They were the core of the tsar's council, the Boyar Duma and led or influenced events during the reign of Tsar Ivan IV Vasilyevich (the Terrible).

The supreme assembly of noblemen, or Boyar Duma, was created by the tsars as an advisory and legislative body, although any of its decisions could be annulled or modified at the whim of the tsar, whose authority was dictatorial. This was especially true under Tsar Ivan IV. The boyars who comprised the Duma during the subject era were primarily members of the Shuisky, Mstislavski, Belski and Romanov families or closely related or associated with them.

The feudal or hereditary princes claimed descent from Yuri Dolgoruki, son of Vladimir II Monomakh, who migrated to northern Russia about AD 1155 as the first prince of Suzdal and Vladimir to begin a new dynasty and development of Russia apart from the Kievan princes. The royal line was the line of princes who descended through his great-grandson Alexander Yaroslavich Nevski (1220–1263). The Moscow posterity, through Nevski's grandson Ivan I Danilovich Kalita, was considered to have the supremacy over all other descendents of Vladimir II Monomakh.

The Vladimir–Suzdal princes were descendants of Andrei Yaroslavich, brother of Alexander Nevski mentioned above, but as time progressed and the importance of Moscow increased, the Moscow princes eventually gained preeminence over the Vladimir–Suzdal princes. Beginning with the reign of Ivan Danilovich the Vladimir–Suzdal princes were no longer considered part of the royal lineage and became Moscow's vassals, although they were still wealthy landowners with large estates and many serfs. The early tsars of Moscow further suppressed the significance of the Vladimir–Suzdal princes when they began to assign the title of "prince" to Russian noblemen migrating and settling in northern Russia from Lithuania, such as the Belski clan, or from the Caucasus, or even Russians whose ancestors had intermarried with the Mongols during the occupation period, 1240–1480.

Among the posterity of the Vladimir–Suzdal princes, the primary family of the 16th century was the Shuisky. Their progenitor was Pr. Andrei Yaroslavich of Vladimir, mentioned above. The representative of the family during the era of this history was Peter Feodorovich Shuisky, a distinguished military commander. His son Ivan Petrovich inherited the good reputation of his father and became one of the most respected figures of the era and was known as the hero of Pskov, having defended the city against a siege in 1581 during the Livonian war against Sweden under Tsar Ivan IV. His cousin Ivan Andreevich was likewise a hero in the war against the Swedes in 1582, attacking the city Oreshek (later known as Schlesselburg), although the Swedes were not defeated. Ivan Andreevich Shuisky had five sons: Vasili, Andrei, Dmitri, Alexandr and Ivan, who are all prominent in this history. The eldest son, later a tsar of Russia, Vasili, began his military career in the army of Pr. Ivan Mstislavski in the war against the Tatars (Crimean Mongols) in April 1583. During the Time of Troubles Vasili Shuisky would take advantage of his genealogy to justify his ascension to the throne of Russia. Another cousin of Ivan Petrovich was Vasili Feodorovich Skopin-Shuisky, whose son Mikhail Vasilyevich would become a hero during the Time of Troubles.

The Mstislavski family also claimed royal descent through Andrei Yaroslavich. Of the Mstislavski family, Pr. Ivan Feodorovich is the patriarch of the family in this history. His maternal grandmother was Evdokia, the daughter of Tsar Ivan III, and this connection drew him close to the royal family line. He distinguished himself as the eldest boyar of the Duma during the reign of Tsar Ivan IV, commander of Russia's military force and the most respected of the noblemen, as well as having several daughters who married into prominent families. After his imprisonment, his son Feodor Mstislavski continued the family tradition as a bulwark in Russian politics and distinguished himself as guiding the course for Russia during the civil wars and invasions.

Closely related to the Mstislavski family were the Golitsyns, whose representative during this era was Vasili Vasilyevich, who would later seek the throne of Russia after the defeat of False Dmitri Otrepyev in 1606, and his brother Ivan, another valiant military commander.[1] Both the Mstislavski and Golitsyn families migrated to Lithuania during the Mongol occupation and then returned to Russia after their defeat.

The next most respected member was Nikita Romanov Yuryev-Zakharin, the progenitor of the future royal Romanov line of Russian tsars, whose wife was Evdokia Alexandrovna, a descendent of the Shuisky princes. His sister Anastasia Romanova was the first and favorite wife of Tsar Ivan IV and mother of the next tsar, Feodor Ivanovich; their marriage lasted 14 years before her premature death from illness. Nikita Romanov was one of the few who was able to keep himself unstained by the bloodshed during the reign of his brother-in-law Tsar Ivan IV, and he was able to survive the purges and inquisitions of the Oprichnin during his reign of terror. Nikita Romanov was respected as an elder, a man of magnanimous character and kind heart. He passed away in April 1586. Nikita's son Feodor is prominent in this history and his daughters married into several aristocratic families.

There were two Belski families who were also influential during this era. The Lithuanian Belskis included Maluta Skuratov-Belski and his nephews Bogdan and Semeon. The other Belski family was the

---

1 Three major figures and several minor ones successfully, if briefly, posed as Tsarevich Dmitri.

Vladimir clan, who tried to gain control of Russia after the death of Tsar Vasili III, father of Tsar Ivan IV.

Semeon Bekbulatovich appears regular in the history, although incidentally, but he was often considered a threat to whomever was on the throne of Russia at the time. He was originally a Mongol Khan with the name of Sain-Bulat. After the defeat of his tribe during Tsar Ivan IV's campaign against Kazan, he converted to Russian Orthodoxy, was given a new name similar to his old but with a Russian identification, and was assigned the honorary title of Prince of Tver and Torzhok. For a short while he also carried the title Tsar of Moscow.

The Lyapunov family, represented by two brothers, Zachari Petrovich and Prokopi Petrovich, were also descendents of the line of Vladimir–Suzdal princes, although from Ryazan. They were the largest landowners of the region.

Marriage between prominent families was typical of Russian aristocracy and played an important role in loyalties. Maluta Skuratov-Belski had two daughters: Maria married Boris Godunov and Ekaterina married Dmitri Shuisky. With the two Cherkassky brothers, Vasili Mikhailovich married a sister of Feodor Mstislavski, while Boris Mikhailovich married a sister of Feodor Nikitich Romanov. The wife of Ivan Ivanovich Godunov (cousin to Boris) was another sister to Feodor Romanov. Another Mstislavski sister married Semeon Bekbulatovich. Vasili Shuisky and Ivan Vorotinski were married to sisters, the daughters of Pr. Peter Ivanovich Buinosov of Rostov, and they were cousins to Vasili Golitzyn's wife. The endogamy will be obvious as sides are taken in family aspirations for advancement and survival.

Marriage between prominent families was typical of Russian aristocracy and played an important role in loyalties. Maluta Skuratov-Belski had two daughters: Maria married Boris Godunov and Ekaterina married Dmitri Shuisky. With the two Cherkassky brothers, Vasili Mikhailovich married a sister of Feodor Mstislavski, while Boris Mikhailovich married a sister of Feodor Nikitich Romanov. The wife of Ivan Ivanovich Godunov (cousin to Boris) was another sister to Feodor Romanov. Another Mstislavski sister married Semeon Bekbulatovich. Vasili Shuisky and Ivan Vorotinsky were married to sisters, the daughters of Pr. Peter Ivanovich Buinosov of Rostov, and they were cousins to

Vasili Golitsyn's wife. The endogamy will be obvious as sides are taken in family aspirations for advancement and survival.

History of the Godunov Family

The progenitor of the Godunov clan was the Mongol Chet Murza, a prince of the Golden Horde who arrived in Moscow during the reign of Grand Prince Ivan Danilovich Kalita (1328–1341) from Sarai, the Mongol capital on the lower Volga River during the occupation era. He married a native Russian girl and settled to live in Kostroma. According to the traditional account, Chet Murza was baptized into the Russian Orthodox faith by Metr. Peter who assigned him the new Christian name of Zakariah. The grandson of Chet Murza was nicknamed Ivan the Godun, which evolved into Godunov, and he was the great-grandfather of Boris. The Russian ancestors of Godunov since that marriage were neither Mongol nor slaves, but residents of Kostroma province and servants of noblemen and princes. Later they became wealthy landowners of Vyazem province, while some distinguished themselves in the military. Chet Murza contributed charity to the local Kostroma Ipatiyevski Monastery and was buried there.

Boris Feodorovich Godunov was born 1552. His father Feodor Ivanovich was a landowner of moderate income, with another son Dmitri and a daughter Irina. The family patrimony in Kostroma served brothers Boris and Dmitri well, especially after the death of their father. The three youngsters then joined the family of their uncle Dmitri Ivanovich Godunov, who took a special interest and concern in the welfare of his nephews and niece. Nothing is known of their mother.

Not being of the class of wealthy landowners saved the Godunovs from the terror of Tsar Ivan the Terrible's Oprichnin, his gang of brownshirt henchmen, which was directed at nationalizing the property of the large estates. Nonetheless uncle Dmitri Godunov was recruited into the Oprichnin, but only as long as it took for him to display his administrative capabilities to Tsar Ivan, who was looking for fresh and young talented men. Then he was promoted to an officer of the palace court. The service of uncle Dmitri at the palace gave him the opportunity to involve nephew Boris and niece Irina in palace functions, including acquiring for them a good education and part of the many social activities of the Princes and their families. Boris was a teenager and Irina was seven years old when uncle Dmitri entered service at the Kremlin palace (no more is known about their brother Dmitri). Irina was the same age as Tsarevich Feodor Ivanovich, the second son of Tsar Ivan IV, both born in 1557. The event that brought uncle Dmitri to the forefront of political affairs was the death of Vasili Naumov, Tsar Ivan IV's chamberlain, and uncle Dmitri was selected as successor.

About this time the terror of the Oprichnin was under way and Maluta (his nickname, although his real name was Grigori) Skuratov-Belski joined the Oprichnin and rose to become one of Tsar Ivan's most reliable and trusted henchmen. In the summer of 1570, for example, Skuratov personally strangled Metr. Fillip to death in his cell by order of Tsar Ivan. Skuratov was also the architect of the decimation of Novgorod in 1570, where every day for six weeks between 1,000 and 1,500 corpses were thrown into the Volkhov River flowing into Lake Ilmen. Skuratov then turned against his own confederates and ordered the execution of Aleksei Basmanov, senior member of the Boyar Duma, and other state officials such as Afanasi Vyazemski and Peter Zaitzov. All of this was done to advance his power in the realm of Tsar Ivan. But the Godunovs survived, not being high enough in the ranks for Skuratov to remove, but in fact, a friendship evolved between Skuratov and Dmitri Godunov in the years 1571–1572. Skuratov realized that Dmitri Godunov — as royal steward and personal adviser to Tsar Ivan — could be utilized to his benefit.

The service of Boris Godunov began in the campaign against Novgorod in 1571, and he was also part of a military campaign against Mongols in 1572 and in the same regiment as Tsarevich Ivan Ivanovich, the eldest son of Tsar Ivan IV. After the campaigns and returning to the palace Boris and Tsarevich Ivan also became friends. Seeing the political advantage in an association with Dmitri Godunov, Skuratov gave his daughter Maria Grigorievna in marriage to Dmitri's nephew Boris. A son-in-law such as Boris was definitely to the benefit of someone like Maluta Skuratov. Subsequently both Dmitri Godunov and Skuratov endeavored by any means to gain a family relationship with the royal family. The first attempt was the marriage of Tsar Ivan's son Ivan to Evdokia Saburova, who was a cousin of Dmitri Godunov. But after two years, Tsar Ivan exiled his daughter-in-law to a convent and forced her to take a vow as a nun.

To advance himself in Tsar Ivan's government, Boris Godunov did not hesitate to wear the brown shirts of the Oprichnin as soon as he became an adult, and as a result of his uncle's influence in the royal court he was promoted to the rank of attorney, which was a type of palace steward. While in the Oprichnin campaigns of Tsar Ivan, Godunov was a witness to much horror and cruelty. The verdicts of the pseudo-courts and the executions of the Oprichnin were interwoven with extreme feasting and revelry and then ascetic vigils at various monasteries. This environment of extremes had an unhealthy influence on the mind of young Godunov. His turbulent service in the Oprichnin did little for Godunov's formal education, and he was considered illiterate by his contemporaries in the royal court. The official Ivan Timofeev recorded that Godunov never grasped literacy beyond the alphabet. Other accounts state that Godunov was capable of reading and writing, but as a person in his position, he preferred to have servants and secretaries do his reading and writing, that for him to have to read or write something on his own was beneath his dignity.

The first child of Boris Feodorovich and Maria Grigorievna was a boy, but his birth year and name are not recorded. He died in 1588 of some unrecorded illness in infancy. As superstitious as Godunov was, when his first son became ill he refused to listen to doctors. Instead, and in the winter cold, he took the boy to the Khram Vasiliya Blazhennovo (Cathedral of St. Basil the Blessed) in Red Square, hoping for a healing from one of the ascetic monks residing there. But the trip was of no avail. Daughter Ksenia was born about 1580, and a second son Feodor Borisovich in 1589.

Palace intrigues that the Godunovs were able to survive only propelled them further in the government of Tsar Ivan the Terrible, but they still lacked a blood tie to the royal court. In 1573, during war against Sweden for control of Livonia, Maluta Skuratov was killed by a bullet from a Swedish soldier and Boris lost the single person who had benefited him most in his political career. The widow Skuratova received 400 rubles compensation for the death of her husband, nephew Bogdan Yaroslavich Belski received 250 rubles, while son-in-law Boris received

50. Now with Boris severed from the Oprichnin and his father-in-law passed away, he prepared for worst times, although success would be granted him again. Godunov was no real friend to his wife's cousin Bogdan Belski, but only pretended so for purposes of self-preservation during Tsar Ivan IV's reign of terror.

Tsar Ivan, after his 5th marriage, decided it was time to marry his younger son Feodor. Uncle Dmitri Godunov jumped into action and offered the hand of his niece Irina Feodorovna, who accepted her fate being an orphan, yet with the promise of future security as the daughter-in-law of the tsar, even though she was well aware of Feodor's mental and physical shortcomings. But as many flaws that the tsarevich may have had, none of them were significant enough as far as uncle Dmitri and niece Irina were concerned. They married in 1574.

In time, by 1575, uncle Dmitri rose to the rank of Boyar, a non-hereditary nobleman, by order of Tsar Ivan. In 1577, when Tsar Ivan departed on his campaign against Livonia, he left son Feodor under the care of another uncle, Grigori Vasilyevich Godunov, the family making more inroads into the palace court. By 1579, Boris was listed in court records as part of the retinue of Tsar Ivan and listed above his wife's cousin Bogdan Belski.

After his murder of son Ivan in November 1581, Tsar Ivan began to dismantle the Oprichnin, which was to the benefit of Boris, now in government service close to the tsar and brother-in-law to the tsarevich. One matter that annoyed Tsar Ivan was that after some 8 years of marriage, Tsarevich Feodor and Tsarevna Irina were childless, and Tsar Ivan meditated whether this was perhaps God's judgment on him for his years of terror in order to terminate his dynasty. Tsar Ivan considered divorce for his son and remarriage, but it never came to his mind that perhaps it was his son and not Irina with the problem of procreation. Boris, viewing a divorce as a threat to his personal position, immediately became involved and also to protect his sister. Feodor's borderline retardation was apparent to everybody except his father Tsar Ivan, who seemed to be blind to it. Feodor was repulsed at the idea of a divorce and Tsar Ivan eventually concluded to leave matters alone lest they become like his late-son Tsarevich Ivan and his three wives. Tsar Ivan, learning from his mistakes with son Ivan, proceeded to designated Feodor as heir to the throne, but with reservations. Another son was born to Tsar Ivan on October 19, 1583, Dmitri Ivanovich. The mother was Tsar Ivan's sixth or seventh wife, Marina (or Maria) Alexandrovna Nagoi, from the city Uglich near Yaroslavl, which was also not far from the Romanov estate at Kostroma.

The testament of Tsar Ivan included four regents who would assist Feodor in his role as Tsar of Russia: Boris Feodorovich Godunov, Ivan Feodorovich Mstislavski, Ivan Petrovich Shuisky, and Nikita Romanov Yuryev-Zakharin.

3. The Era of Tsar Feodor Ivanovich

Power Struggle after the Death of Ivan the Terrible

Tsar Ivan IV the Terrible died March 18, 1584. Heir to the throne Feodor Ivanovich did not inherit any qualities of statesmanship, nor even the appearance of dignity or awe, or any traits of courage or integrity, which his grandfathers and the previous tsars of Russia possessed. He was short and stocky, overweight and physically weak, and hardly mobile. Feodor had a large body disproportionate to his small head. His face was pale and he always wore an incessant and pathetic smile. He moved slowly, shuffling his feet as he walked and could never seem to step in a straight line. Feodor's shallow mentality and lack of intelligence easily placed him on the borderline of retardation. Perhaps as an unconscious distraction to his inability to comprehend and grasp reality, Feodor was preoccupied by the rites and liturgy of the Orthodox Church, and so would dedicate his time to observance of pilgrimages and the company of clergy. As a result of his religious inclinations, the new tsar had a fear of authority, because to him it was a dangerous path to sin. Many boyars and other state officials, having concluded that the 27-year old heir to the throne was fated by nature to an infantile mind and dependant on others for his survival, could not rejoice at his ascension, even with the termination of the tyranny under his father. It was a tough choice whether the moral weakness and incapacity of Tsar Feodor would be more of a disaster for Moscovite Russia than the harsh rule of Tsar Ivan IV. Feodor was convinced that his own reign, although not alien to crime and sullied by the worst of brutality and malice and drive for power, would become a prosperous golden age for Moscovite Russia, and would appear to all his contemporaries as the materialization of God's mercy after the horrors of his father's reign. Many boyars and officials even doubted if Feodor was aware of, or could even comprehend, the gruesome inquisitions, tortures and mass murders committed by his father and his ruthless henchmen, the Oprichnin.

That evening, the Boyar Duma took control of state affairs and immediately banished from the capital city infamous servants of the wrath of Tsar Ivan — the Oprichnin officials — while the more threatening were immediately incarcerated. The relatives of Tsar Ivan's final wife Marina Nagoi were placed in custody, accused of an attempt to declare the year-old Dmitri Ivanovich as official heir to the throne. Moscow was agitated, but the boyars were able to quell the agitation. They gave their oath to the new tsar, Feodor Ivanovich, while regiments of soldiers walked the streets during the night and cannons and artillerymen were stationed at the city squares.

By morning, messengers were sent to the provinces with a directive to pray for the soul of Tsar Ivan and for the prosperous reign of Tsar Feodor. The new governing officials summoned a Zemski (Estate) Duma of provincial boyars, ROC prelates, hereditary princes, and other important figures, in order to take the necessary measures to rebuild the state after the detriment caused over the years of Tsar Ivan IV's reign of terror. A day for the coronation of Feodor Ivanovich was selected, May 31, 1584, to occur after the traditional 40-day mourning period for the late-tsar and a requiem. The assembly would also deal with the issue of most importance: to curb state oppression of the populace.

That day the widow-tsaritza Marina Nagoi with her young son Dmitri Ivanovich, her father, brothers, and the entire Nagoi clan were accompanied out of Moscow and to Uglich, a city on the Volga River near Yaroslavl, to the family estate. She was assigned servants, cooks, maids and butlers as her attendants and to furnish her house, and a private nursemaid for the child Dmitri, to make her royal exile fit for a queen. The cheerful Feodor bid farewell to his half-brother Dmitri, shedding a few tears in the process, as if involuntarily fulfilling the demands of the boyars now in control of political and palace affairs. Bogdan Belski, the person selected initially by Tsar Ivan as tutor and mentor of son Dmitri, remained in Moscow, claiming that he would be of more benefit with his participation in the Duma. The exiles left Moscow in a splendid display of royal elegance.

Meanwhile, as Russia's population was blessing the good intentions of the new governments envy and the lawless drive for power was subtly gaining momentum in Moscow. Bogdan Belski ordered the gates of the Kremlin closed. He hoped to use the Royal Guards (Streltzi) and his previous command of the Oprichnin to wrestle authority from the Boyar Duma and Godunov, and be able to govern Russia in the name of Tsar Feodor. Rumors spread throughout the city that the heir to the throne was in grave danger, and the name that spread about was Bogdan Belski (he was earlier rumored to have poisoned Tsar Ivan's son Ivan, even though the father killed him in a fit of anger). The rumor spread that Belski had attempted to also poison Feodor and murder all the boyars using former Oprichniks in order to place himself on the throne. The distrust of the crowds moved them to voice their opposition. Romanov and Mstislavski were decisive in their decision opposing the plan to restore the Oprichnin with Belski again as commander.

Inside the Kremlin the Shuisky princes were accused of spreading the rumor to foment revolt among the Moscow residents, while the Ryazan princes, the Lyapunov and Kikin families, were informing the mob that they were ready to deliver the new tsar from the wiles of the monster Belski. A cry of revolt echoed from one end of Moscow to the other and 20,000 armed residents, rabble, citizens, and Boyar servants rushed to the Kremlin, where the gates were barely closed in time to stop their entrance. Royal guards mounted the walls of the Kremlin, while the mob appropriated more artillery and cannons from the guard-posts of the city and directed them toward the Florovski Gate of the Kremlin. To quell the confusion, Tsar Feodor asked Pr. Ivan Mstislavski, Nikita Romanov, and officials Andrei and Vasili Shelkalov to show themselves to the mob from the Kremlin walls and ask them the reason for the revolt and their demands. "Belski," replied the crowd, "Hand the criminal over to us. His intent is to uproot the royal family and all the Boyar families." A thousand voices shouted in unison. "Belski!" The unfortunate nobleman, now regretting he did not join the royal retinue exiled to Uglich, was perplexed at the accusations, afraid of the malice of the people, and sought refuge in the bedchamber of Tsar Ivan. There he hid, shook and prayed for his safety. Godunov knew he was guilty, as did all the boyars. Afraid of bloodshed, the intermediaries entered into negotiations with the leaders of the revolt and were able to agree to the exile of the traitor and Bogdan Belski was quickly removed from Moscow to Nizhniy-Novgorod. Once hearing the agreement of the intermediaries for the exile of Belski, the crowd hollered, "Long live the tsar with his trusted noblemen," and they dispersed to their homes. In Nizhniy-Novgorod, Belski took the position of military governor.

Tsar Feodor, with his timidity and fear of authority, was frightened by the revolt and realized the possible necessity of severe measures for protection of the city and Kremlin from the vigilantes. But not having a good perspective of the matter or a firm will to enforce a decision, he sought for someone more than just a counselor or assistant. Feodor needed someone upon whose shoulders he could bestow the weight of the sovereignty, who had the fear of God to answer to Him and not to himself. Irina Feodorovna, the wife of Tsar Feodor, dominated her husband, although he loved her dearly. She was more than well aware of his flaws, both mental and physical, and attempted to compensate for them by having her brother Boris as the real power behind the throne. As a result, the person privately selected was the one closest to his wife's heart and who had been involved in state affairs of Moscovite Russia within the close confines of the palace as well as in the provinces: Boris Feodorovich Godunov.

Without any hint of guile and following her conscience, and yet very aware of the occasional ambitious intents and inclinations of her brother and his secret drive for power, Tsaritza Irina affirmed the covert and clandestine transfer of imperial authority from her husband the tsar to her brother. From the one unable to reign to the one that could, and who under the circumstances just could become the greatest ruler of Russia in its history. Godunov was 32 years old and a flower in full bloom, at the pinnacle of his physical and mental faculties, and at the prime of his life to inherit such a noble responsibility. Godunov was majestically appearing and handsome, with a stern facial expression — should he need it — and quick thinking, with a profound mind and depth in his conclusion on issues. Another aspect of his character was his eloquence, and more than most of the boyars he could be kind-hearted and benevolent should the occasion require it. He was regularly generous with state funds, provided that he receive loyalty or public adulation from the recipient, considering philanthropy not a goal but a means of attaining his goal. Godunov could also be flattering in his conversation with other dignitaries and covertly manipulative, all of which he learned over the years at the court of Tsar Ivan, his mentor.

The initial action of Godunov was the punishment of the Lyapunov brothers Zachari and Prokopi, the Kikin family, and other chief agitators of the Moscow rabble: they were exiled to distant cities and there incarcerated. The Duma and boyars and officials quickly divined who was responsible for such swift justice and were disturbed that Godunov already took this authority upon himself, not even waiting until after the coronation of Tsar Feodor. The people either kept silent or credited the justice to Tsar Feodor.

After the death of Tsar Ivan, Marfa, the daughter of Pr. Vladimir Andreevich of Staritzki, a cousin to the tsar, returned to Russia with her infant daughter. She was widowed from her husband, a Livonian Prince, and now decided it was safe to return, promising to conduct herself in a dignified manner appropriate for a person of royal descent.

Coronation of Tsar Feodor Ivanovich

At dawn of the day of Feodor Ivanovich's coronation, May 31, 1584, heavy rain pounded Moscow and flooded the city streets, as if a portent of future disaster. The superstition of the population subsided as the spring storm dissipated and the clouds dispersed and the sun shined in a clear sky. The number of people who gathered in Red Square for the occasion was innumerable for the era, so congested that the people had difficulty clearing a path for the tsar's confessor. The event began with ringing of church bells throughout Moscow and the tsar's confessor carrying the sacred royal regalia of Vladimir II Monomakh — the progenitor of the line of grand princes — from the palace to the Uspenski Cathedral (Cathedral of the Assumption of the Virgin Mary). He and his retinue of prelates carried a large traditional 8-pointed cross on a chain, the crown and shoulder mantle, while Godunov followed behind carrying the scepter. Feodor, ignoring the congestion, exited his palace with his retinue of boyars, priests, military commanders, and other officials and the commotion of the crowds ceased. The coronation was performed by Metr. Dionysi of Moscow.

The regalia worn by Tsar Feodor were brilliant due to the noon sun reflecting on the jewels embedded into his robe. The crowd was allowed to stream through the Kremlin to allow all attending to catch a glimpse of the sacred celebration as it begins, a glimpse of their father-tsar and the royal family. A few residents and peasants were also allowed inside Uspenski Cathedral as a sign that all Russians were participating in the coronation, and as a result deacons had to walk through the aisles telling the uncultured faction, "Pray and have respect."

Tsar Feodor and Metr. Dionysi sat near the west doors of the cathedral, and once the crowd silenced Feodor arose and spoke to the metropolitan,

> "The Sovereign, our father, the monarch Ivan Vasilyevich, has left his earthly reign and accepted the angelic form and departed to the kingdom of heaven. While me he blessed with the dominion of banners[2] of the state. He has commanded me in accord with ancient statutes to be anointed and crowned with the royal crown, diadem and holy mantle. His testament is known to the clergy, noblemen and populace, and so, according to the will of God and the blessing of my father, perform the sacred rite and I will become tsar and anointed."

The metropolitan held the cross over Feodor and replied,

> "Master, the beloved son of the church and our consolation, the elect of God and by God exalted to the throne. By the grace of the Holy Spirit we anoint and crown you, so you will be titled monarch of all Russia."

Dionysi hung the cross of Monomakh around the neck of Feodor, and placed the mantle on his shoulders and the crown on his head, while reciting a prayer for God to bless his rule. Dionysi then took Feodor by the right hand and led him to the customary seat of the tsar

---

2 Lit. the gonfalon, the traditional vertical-hanging two-piece banner

during services,[3] and then gave him the scepter, saying, "Observe the banners of Russia." Then the archdeacons standing on the ambo and the priests at the altar and choir began to sing of longevity to the newly-crowned king.

After the conclusion of the coronation hymn, Dionysi admonished Feodor with the obligations of a monarch: to uphold the law and government, to be submissive to prelates and the religion and supportive of monasteries, to be respectful toward noblemen, especially those of senior status and in the posterity of the royal lineage, to be considerate of his subjects, military and state officials. Dionysi continued,

> "We have kings in lieu of God, as God entrusted them with the fate of the human race. Preserve them from evil, deliver the land from disturbance, and fear the scythe of heaven. Just as gloom and darkness reign on the land without a sun, so is the soul of your people dark without education. Be a lover of wisdom and seek peace; be kind since kindness decorates the façade of the kings and is immortal. Do you want the consideration of heaven? Be considerate toward your subjects. Do not listen to evil slander, O king. May justice flourish during all your days and may the fatherland have rest, and God will exalt your royal right hand over all your enemies and your government will be peaceful and eternal generation after generation."

With tears flowing on their cheeks, the people shouted, "Live long Tsar Feodor Ivanovich and live longer."

Feodor, weighed down by the weight of the regalia and the crown of Monomakh and the mantle, and tediously holding the heavy scepter (made from whale bone) and by the length of the rite, became wearied and exhausted. To his right stood brother-in-law Boris Godunov, uncle Nikita Romanov, and his wife's uncle Dmitri Godunov, and other important figures. A table was set in front of the tsar's seat with the crowns of kings whom his father had defeated in various military campaigns. The eyewitness chroniclers could not compare the majesty and celebration to any other event in Russian history. The ambo and area where the clergy stood was covered in felt while the floor of the cathedral was covered with Persian rugs and English woolen cloth of bright colors. The garments of the officials, especially that of Godunov and Pr. Ivan Mikhailovich Glinski — great-uncle of Tsar Feodor — glistened

---

3 Parishioners stand during services at a Russian Orthodox Church, except for the tsar, who has a special chair.

with diamonds, telesia, and pearls of gigantic size. The foreign emissaries estimated the value of their garments in the millions.

The final rite of the coronation was Metr. Dionysi placing the chain of Monomakh, made of solid Arabian gold around the neck of Tsar Feodor, anointing him with holy oil and his participation in the holy Eucharist. Due to Tsar Feodor's exhaustion, he handed the scepter back to Godunov, and lifted the crown off his head and placed it back on the gold plate that was held by Nikita Romanov. The finality of the coronation was Tsar Feodor venerating the sepulchers of his ancestors[4] and praying that he inherit their royal benevolence.

Meanwhile, Irina Feodorovna, his wife, sat among the noblewomen wearing her own crown. As the royal couple left the cathedral coins were dispersed among the people outside, a sign of the charitable nature of the new tsar and tsaritza. They shouted to Tsaritza Irina, "Long live the queen," and they kissed the hand of Tsar Feodor. The royal couple were accompanied to the palace by mounted cavalry and the explosion of 170 cannons echoed in the Kremlin.

The initial acts of amnesty declared by Tsar Feodor — but not without the direct involvement of Godunov, as with all acts of Tsar Feodor — were purposed to reestablish stability in the society. Immediate was the release of the most important figures who had survived the exile imposed on them by Tsar Ivan his father: Pr. Dmitri Khorostinin, brothers Andrei and Vasili Ivanovich Shuisky, Nikita Trubetzkoy, Shestunov, two Kuryakin brothers, Feodor Sheremetev, and three Godunovs who were cousins of Boris — Ivan, Dmitri and Stepan — and Ivan Petrovich Shuisky. Their estates and patrimonies were also restored to them, some of them having been in exile or incarceration 20 years. Also released were prisoners-of-war from the campaigns of Tsar Ivan against Poland, Lithuania, Sweden, Kazan, Astrakhan, and Crimea.

But none of this was in comparison with the rewards Tsar Feodor showered upon his brother-in-law Boris Godunov, all that he possible could as autocrat, and by the manipulation of Godunov telling his brother-in-law that it was to the benefit of his reign to do so. Upon

---

4 The sepulchers are located inside the Arkhangelsk Cathedral (Cathedral of the Archangel Michael) in the Moscow Kremlin.

Godunov he bestowed the ancient title of Cavalry Master[5] (not having been bestowed upon anybody for 17 years now), and also the title of Regent of the Kingdoms of Kazan and Astrakhan. Such incomparable rank was accompanied by incomparable wealth as Tsar Feodor rewarded his brother-in-law with monetary gifts, a salary of 175,000 rubles a year. The finest land and estates in the Dvin Province along the Vag River in northern Russia, meadows and forests along the Moscow River, the income from state taxation of Moscow, Ryazan, Tver and northern provinces, as well as the taxation of his own Kazan and Astrakhan government regions, were all appropriated by Godunov. His income was supplemented by the family estates in Vyazem and Dorogobuzh. No other single Russian in its history received an income as did Boris Godunov and which totaled some 800,000–900,000 rubles in silver a year. (This was during an era when the average income of a Russian was less than a ruble a day.) In addition to land and money, Godunov could summon an army from the residents and serfs of his estates consisting of a hundred thousand soldiers. But Godunov was also very generous, his expenditures amounted to 100,000 rubles a year, contributing to monasteries, churches and the underprivileged, especially the victims of fire and famine that occurred in Russia.

Early Reign of Tsar Feodor

The initial days after the death of a tyrant are the most consoling for a nation; the conclusion of suffering enlivens the people's hopes and banishes their depression. But a cruel reign is often preparation for a weak one; the new king, afraid to be compared to his odious predecessor and wanting to condescend to the approval of his subjects, often inclines toward the other extreme and weakens the state. The dedicated subjects of Moscovite Russia were afraid of this, aware of the unusual meekness of the heir Feodor Ivanovich to the throne of Tsar Ivan IV the Terrible, his timidity, frail mind, inclination toward religious austerity, and his indifference toward royal grandeur and the majesty of the Russian monarchy. The reign of Tsar Ivan IV was not terrible just for a single class of people who suffered his wrath, nor for people in certain localities who were decimated by the Oprichnin, but the entire nation

---

5 Comparable to the US Congressional Medal of Honor.

suffered indirectly and which was made worse by the incessant wars with eastern Europe, Scandinavia, the Mongol tribes of Kazan, Astrakhan and the Crimea, and the Turkish Ottomans. The government of Russia was at a most unenviable condition at the death of Tsar Ivan IV. A person as Boris Feodorovich was an absolute necessity to the government under the circumstances of the era. The first legislation to be passed by Godunov over the government of Russia was to no more bestow a tax-exempt status to any person until the nation should recover economically.

The Duma was again in session, and Godunov called its regular session on Fridays. The tsar sat on his throne, the patriarch and clergy sat at a 12-chair table, while noblemen and officials would sit at another. One of the officials would announce the business of the day, opinions would be offered on the proposals and business and the matter would be resolved. A decree would be subsequently issued by the attending officials. The new government consisted of four primary departments: the Embassy (Posolski), the Distribution (Razradni), Internal Affairs (Pomestia), and the Kazanski for foreign affairs. The Palace Affairs (Dvortzovi) Department handled matters related to the royal family and the infrastructure of the Kremlin. Under Godunov the army was reorganized, now with the Oprichnin dissolved. Moscovite Russia could boast a standing army of 80,000 mounted cavalry and 12,000 royal guards, 5,000 of which were stationed in Moscow. With a summons of recruits it was possible for Russia to increase the size of its army to 250,000 in a few days.

During the reign of Tsar Feodor, Russian's boundaries increased considerably, advancing toward Karelia and Lapland in the northwest, and east to the Ural Mountains and Siberia, and south as far as Astrakhan, which was founded in 1589. Arkhangelsk was founded in 1584, Smolensk in 1596. Russia by 1598 had expanded to size of its present European portion, with the exception of Ukraine (the eastern half occupied by Crimean Mongols, and the western half by Cossacks) and Belarus (part of Lithuania), but including the western portion of Siberia, including Tobolsk, founded in 1587.

Even though Godunov trusted his brother-in-law Tsar Feodor, he still feared those who were envious of his rise to power and his enemies.

The best way to deal with them, Godunov felt, was to overwhelm them with his majesty, so that the thought of possible usurpation would not even enter their mind, and which would only be possible for some ambitious Boyar or hereditary prince. Malice was already fomenting secretly in the mind of disenchanted and envious state officials, clandestinely and silently, waiting for the opportunity to attack him. Godunov, to deal with them, routed his immediate drive toward matters that would benefit the society, so to gain the trust of the population and recognition of the nation and this would justify Tsar Feodor's decision to delegate such authority to him. The constituency of the Boyar Duma established by Tsar Ivan dissolved with the rise of Godunov as the power behind the throne. Nikita Romanov, Ivan Mstislavski, Vasili Ivanovich Shuisky became his advisors (Belski now exiled to Nizhniy-Novgorod), and no longer his counterparts, and they now were demoted to act at his whim. Godunov was able to gain the respect of the people to such an extent, that they felt only he could boldly steer the rudder of Moscovite Russia, working on behalf of his brother-in-law the Tsar, with a few boyars as counselors, but not having either rivals or friends. Superficially Godunov had reconciled with the honorable and tolerant Vasili Shuisky and with his younger brother, Dmitri. The latter married Godunov's sister-in-law, another daughter of Maluta Skuratov, and as a result Godunov honored him with a promotion to the rank of boyar. Godunov also made his cousins Dmitri, Ivan and Stephan Godunov boyars and members of the Duma.

While this was occurring, the government under Godunov was busy implementing a disciplined security force to provide safety for the population. Throughout all of Russia he removed corrupt judges, officials and rulers, and either training those that could be rehabilitated, or else replacing them and then threatening the new appointments with execution or exile to Siberia should they become corrupt also. Godunov doubled the salary of these men so they would not have to depend on bribes for survival. He reorganized the army and located regiments in the regions where their presence was needed for defense or local security. Godunov began at Kazan where war still raged along the Volga River between Russians and Cheremiss. Godunov utilized arbitration rather than force to quell the revolt, convincing them that the new tsar as the father of his country would provide amnesty for all the Cheremiss soldiers, provided they stop the violence. Cheremiss elders selected as representatives traveled to Moscow and pledged loyalty to Tsar Feodor. Forts were then constructed on both sides of the Volga River in various cities, which were then populated by Russians who were offered benefits to move there. By 1587 Godunov was able to install peace in the region, which they had not since Tsar Ivan IV's first campaign in 1551.

Next was Siberia, which was subdued by force using better trained regiments than under Tsar Ivan. By 1587, the native Nagoy Siberian tribes were defeated and the new capital of the region was installed at Tobolsk. Over the following years Godunov resettled Russian farmers from the Perm, Vyatka, Kargopol and Ural Provinces to develop the area. These vast regions of Siberia were the most important gains for Russian in its history. The native tribes were assigned large tracts of land (comparable to American Indian reservations) and taught to trade with the Russians.

Trade with England was opened by Godunov in 1587, at the expense of 2,000 pounds Sterling per year from the English treasury. The sea route was only available during the summer months with English ships arriving at Severo-Dvinsk, near Arkhangelsk in the White Sea. They would take ships to Yaroslavl via the Dvin River tributaries, and portage at Vologda to Yaroslavl, and then go by land or follow the Volga River and its tributaries to Moscow.

More important and more difficult a matter was peace with Lithuania. Russia had been at war with Poland-Lithuania several times during the reign of Tsar Ivan IV from 1558 to 1582 to gain access to a port on the Baltic Sea or Gulf of Finland in the region known as Livonia, now Estonia and Latvia. The perennial wars had drained both the armies of Russia and Lithuania. Stephen Batori, or Bathory, King of Lithuania and Poland, hoped to utilize the death of Tsar Ivan to intimidate Tsar Feodor into conceding more territory to Lithuania to keep peace, even though Tsar Ivan had signed a 10-year peace treaty on January 15, 1582 with Batori. According to the provisions of the treaty, Russia ceded all of Livonia to Lithuania. The only access to the Baltic for Russia was through the Neva River, which was permitted in a treaty with Sweden in 1583. As far as Batori was concerned, the treaty was a period of rest in order to train more troops for a subsequent invasion of Russia. Batori sent his delegate Lev Sapega to Moscow and demanded 120,000 gold ducats from Tsar Feodor for the release of Russian prisoners-of-war, and that he release all Lithuanian prisoners-of-war and compensate all Lithuanians living in Russia for their suffering during the wars. Tsar Feodor informed the delegate that he had already freed 900 prisoners-of-war consisting of Poles, Hungarians, and Germans on his coronation day, and that Batori should obligate in the same manner as a Christian act of charity. No conclusion was agreed at the meeting, except to prolong the conditions of the original treaty another 10 months.

A couple of years later, Godunov sent two delegates to Warsaw: Pr. Feodor Mikhailovich Troyekurov and nobleman Mikhail Beznin, to try to incline Batori to reconciliation. Hearing of events in Moscow, how Godunov was not shy to impose judgment on persons apprehended in criminal activities, and fearing the same should a foreign country invade Russia, Batori greeted the two delegates and returned them to Moscow with an extension of the peace treaty for another two years. Still having fresh memories of the 25 years of perennial war between Russia and Lithuania, Batori then turned to negotiations the following year to acquire more Russian territory. On December 12, 1586, Stephen Batori died, and no more was gained or lost between the two countries, except that more prisoners-of-war were freed on both sides.

Boris Godunov's Struggle for Power

Such states of affairs beneficial for the majesty and society of Russia proved the capability of the intellect and motivation of Godunov. However, many nobles still considered him an illegitimate usurper to the throne, remembering his Mongol descent, and they were ashamed of this humiliation of the Ivan Danilovich posterity. His sycophants listened to him coldly and his enemies with close attention, but they took his words lightly. Even though Godunov would put on a superficial display of humility, the noblemen knew his long term purpose and saw him as the son-in-law of Maluta Skuratov, a tyrant in preparation, with the legacy of a vicious henchman — although he tried his best to distance himself from this legacy. Godunov only increased their envy with his social accomplishments and economic and domestic success in re-building Russia after its devastation by the Oprichnin of Tsar Ivan IV. Godunov wanted peace with the Shuisky clan, the hereditary princes of Suzdal, and needed their support. But the Shuisky, Mstislavski and Lyapunov clans and others did not need Godunov and made their feelings known publicly.

Metr. Dionysi took upon himself the role of reconciler. He invited the opposition group to his cloister at the Chudovski Monastery inside the Kremlin and spoke on behalf of the fatherland and the religion. He touched their hearts and assured them — as it seemed to him — their necessity to work in unity, and Godunov with a display of humility gave his hand to Ivan Petrovich Shuisky. They swore to live in fraternal peace and have a sincere concern for the welfare of each other, and both to provide for the prosperity of Russia. Pr. Shuisky left the metropolitan's chamber with a smile on his face and walked across the square to the Granite Chamber to announce to an interested crowd that conciliation between the two families was concluded. It was some consolation for the populace to be assured that internal strife would not resurrect another reign of terror or a new agency of Oprichnin. Pr. Shuisky was the hero of Pskov, a highly respected military commander who successfully defended Pskov from its siege by Lithuanian troops during the Livonian wars under Tsar Ivan. The crowd listened to the dedicated nobleman in complete silence. After the assurance by Pr. Shuisky, two merchants stepped forward and said, "Pr. Ivan Petrovich, you reconcile using our heads; both we and you will perish due to Boris." By order of Godunov, these two merchants were arrested that night and exiled to some unrecorded place. Even though Godunov wore a façade of False friendship, they were still his enemies.

The ROC clergy over its history never strongly displayed a drive or ambition for secular power, always seeming to placate the will of the sovereign for the good of the nation. The ROC metropolitan's concentration was on rites and prayers, teaching the Christian religion and involvement in the conscience of society and the salvation of souls. On occasion they were present at Duma assemblies, invited for important state decisions: not part of legislating, but advising the tsars and boyars regarding the ecclesiastical statutes that dealt with the issue at hand,

and what would be best for the earthly needs of the Russian population. Prelate's suggestions always considered the personal capabilities and character of the tsar, the less during the reigns of Tsars Ivan III and Vasili IV, but more so during the reign of Tsar Ivan IV.

Feodor with his infantile mind and desire to excel in devotion rather than state affairs, discussed matters more with monks than with noblemen. Metr. Dionysi, an intelligent and sincere prelate developed a close relationship with Tsar Feodor as a result, and noticed the many concessions that the tsar wanted to make to the ROC and especially monasteries, and the greater involvement of himself — the metropolitan — in state affairs. But Godunov did not appropriate for himself such autocratic authority in order to share it with monks. He honored the ROC clergy with superficial occasional gratuities, would cautiously listen to the advice of the metropolitan, and discussed issues with him, but he acted independently, which vexed Dionysi. Godunov's will was inflexible, and this exacerbated the unfriendly disposition of Dionysi toward Godunov and the prelate's tight union with the Shuisky clan, who were hereditary princes.

Another conspiracy began to foment. Dionysi, knowing that Godunov's wealth and authority were the result of Tsar Feodor's marriage to his sister, felt that if the relationship between Tsar Feodor and his wife Irina was ruptured, this would also disassociate Tsar Feodor from Godunov and so his power base would collapse. As a result, fantasized Dionysi, the feeble-minded Tsar Feodor with his religious preoccupation would transfer the vacated authority to him — Dionysi. Since Tsar Feodor and his wife Irina were childless, justification could be made for the annulment of the marriage and her consignment to a convent as a nun. The precedent to justify the proceedings was the similar circumstance of Tsar Vasili III, who divorced his first wife Solomonia Yuryevna Saburova after 20 years of a childless marriage and consigned her to a convent for the balance of her life. Tsar Vasili, now about 45 years of age, married Elena Glinskaya, about 15. Their marriage produced two offspring, one of whom became Tsar Ivan IV, and the other passed away in infancy. Metr. Dionysi conspired with the Shuisky clan along with a few officials and noblemen to strike at the forehead of Tsar Feodor — his marriage — and so resolve in the name of the future of Moscovite

Russia two problems: severing Godunov from his power base, and a new marriage to produce an heir for the throne of Russia. No person in Russia — save for Godunov perhaps — wanted to see the termination of the royal posterity of Ivan Danilovich of Moscow. In order for the conspiracy to proceed smoothly, a bride was already selected: a sister of Pr. Feodor Ivanovich Mstislavski. The conspirators wrote a plan and vowed among themselves to execute it, even if it caused a rebellion among the people with a change in Tsar Feodor's marital status and the dissolution of Godunov's power base. For the boyars it would be the return of authority to the Duma rather than another despot as tsar, which they feared Godunov would evolve into, who still frightened them due to his earlier connections with Tsar Ivan's reign of terror. It would save Russia in the long run.

But as with earlier conspiracies against Godunov, subjects loyal to him and his spies relayed the conspiracy to him before it had a change to materialize. Again fearing imposing harsh punishment such as execution, least he be accused of reverting to the methods of his father-in-law Skuratov and the Oprichnin, Godunov acted with rare magnanimity. He confronted the metropolitan without anger or reprimand, and informed him that divorce was not an option to be considered, especially since the Tsar and Tsaritza were still relatively young and in good health. Godunov ignored discussing with Dionysi the existence of Tsarevich Dmitri, the youngest son of Tsar Ivan IV, who could still inherit the throne and continue the posterity should Tsar Feodor and wife Irina not have a family.

Deceived by Godunov's humility and condescension, Dionysi apologized and tried to excuse the other conspirators also from their involvement, claiming to be the sole conspirator, while the others were bystanders. The metropolitan also gave his word of honor to banish any further thought of the dissolution of the tsar's marriage. Godunov in return promised not to take retaliation on the others involved in the conspiracy, and forgive them all, but with one condition: that the intended bride take the vow of a nun and seclude herself at some convent out of the public's eye for the balance of her life. Godunov was aware that as long as the Mstislavski girl was free in society, she would be a threat to the royal marriage. However, the sister of Pr. Feodor Mstislavski later married Pr. Vasili Cherkassky, brother of Boris Cherkassky, who was brother-in-law to the Romanovs. (This marriage tied the three families together against Godunov during the rise of Dmitri Otrepyev.)

So as not to violate his promise of amnesty, Godunov sought for another method of imposing his vengeance, but not directly, so not to blemish his reputation. Godunov turned to a non-violent weapon of Tsar Ivan's: false and fabricated accusations of attempts to overthrow the tsar. A servant of the Shuisky clan was bribed and he appeared one day at the palace to inform Godunov of the plot. The Shuisky family was taken into custody, along with the Tatev, Kolichev, Nagoi and Bikasov families, and several noblemen and some Moscow merchants — all of whom that were part of the divorce conspiracy. A trial was conducted; the accused noblemen were interrogated while the Moscow merchants were tortured to acquire a confession. Even though none of the testimony collaborated with the accusations of the bribed servant, the conspirators were convicted. Pr. Ivan Petrovich Shuisky was exiled to Beloye Ozero, Pr. Andrei Ivanovich Shuisky — convicted as the chief conspirator — was exiled to Kargopol; Pr. Vasili Feodorovich Skopin-Shuisky was deprived of rank and property, but allowed to live in Moscow; Pr. Ivan Tatev was exiled to Astrakhan; Kruk Kolichev to Nizhniy-Novgorod, and Bikasov and others to Vologda, Siberia and other forsaken places. Feodor Nagoi, the Moscow merchants and six others were executed by decapitation in Red Square. This period beginning September 1588 and lasting for about a year was the first of two reigns of terror of Godunov (the second was in 1600–1602 after his recovery from illness). Scores of other nobles were also arrested and exiled to remote areas and their property confiscated. Ivan Mstislavski was exiled first to Solovetski Monastery in the White Sea, and then he was transferred to Kirillov Monastery near Beloye Ozero, where he was forced to be tonsured as a monk and take the new name Jonah. His son Feodor Ivanovich became head of the Boyar Duma in his stead.

Metr. Dionysi was not yet in custody, yet he was not going to be a timid spectator of such disgrace and malice toward honorable Russian princes and noblemen. He went directly to Tsar Feodor and boldly in his presence denounced Godunov as a slanderer and tyrant, and testified that they were suffering because of their good intention to deliver

Russia from the avarice and megalomania of Godunov. Accompanying Dionysi was Archbishop Varlaam of Krutitzk, who also reprimanded Tsar Feodor, threatening him with heavenly bolts of lightning and exposing the tsar's moral weakness and embarrassing blindness to the situation. However, their outburst only fated them next for disgrace. Godunov, hearing of the incident, had both of them arrested and defrocked of their ecclesiastical rank and exiled. Dionysi was incarcerated in a cell at the Khutinski Monastery, while Varlaam at the Antoniev Monastery, both in Novgorod. Arrangements were then made for Job, Archbishop of Rostov, to be ordained as metropolitan.

If this was not enough, by order of Godunov the two Shuisky Princes in exile, Andrei Ivanovich and Ivan Petrovich, were choked to death by henchmen at their respective places of exile. Having subjected the royal court to his authority, executed the two Shuisky princes, exiled Ivan Mstislavski, defrocked and incarcerated the metropolitan, installed a loyalist in the metropolitan's position, executed disloyal subjects in public, and filled the Duma with his relatives, Godunov expected no obstacle to appropriating the position of tsar of Russia at the death of Tsar Feodor. The survivor of the Shuisky family in exile, Vasili, spent two years in exile before gaining his freedom and returning. Godunov then restored to him the property that was confiscated.

Godunov, in his fear that the honorary prince and Mstislavski brother-in-law might use his title as a means to the throne, had the aged Semeon Bekbulatovich blinded and his title removed and then exiled to some remote place distant from Moscow.

Character of Tsar Feodor Ivanovich

When Tsar Feodor would become wearied by superficial secular grandeur and wanted to temporarily sever himself from the elegant feasts and entertainment, he would seek consolation in religion, and specifically the Russian Orthodox Church, and so would don the frock of a mendicant pilgrim and walk from monastery to monastery. He would travel to Troitse-Sergieva Monastery and other sacred shrines together with his wife, but always accompanied by a retinue of royal bodyguards. The arrangements were always made ahead of time by Godunov, so that the Tsar could gain the attention and respect of people as a holy ruler, to display himself as opposite the character of his father, Tsar Ivan IV the Terrible.

The daily routine of Tsar Feodor was recorded by a foreign visitor:

> Feodor normally rose at four o'clock in the morning and waited for his confessor in his bedroom, which was filled with icons and had candles burning day and night. The confessor would arrive with a cross, a newly composed blessing, holy water, and an icon of the saint to whom that day was dedicated on the ecclesiastical calendar. The sovereign would bow to the ground, pray aloud for at least 10 minutes, then go to Irina's bedroom — they slept in separate rooms — and attend Matins with her. Returning, they would sit on a large sofa in the great chamber, where they would greet guests and monks. At nine o'clock in the morning they attended liturgy, had lunch at 11, and then he would take a three-hour nap after lunch. He would again attend Vespers in the evening and in the interval before dinner he would spend with the Tsaritza, or play games with midgets[6] and watch their funny faces or listen to their songs. Occasionally, he would inspect the work of jewelers, goldsmiths, artists, or his tailor. At night, preparing for bed, he would again pray with his confessor and go to sleep with this recited blessing.
>
> Beyond this, every week he would visit a monastery in the vicinity of the capital, and on non-working days he would go on bear hunts. Occasionally, petitioners would approach Feodor at the entrance to the palace. Avoiding secular affairs, he would direct them to Boris.

Russian chroniclers of the era note the intense piety of Tsar Feodor, but they say little of his attraction to cruel types of amusements and bloody sports. He enjoyed watching fist-fights and especially bears fighting in a ring.

Inwardly rejoicing at this humiliating inactivity of Tsar Feodor, the subtle Godunov strove to exalt his sister in the eyes of the Russians. Often, the charity given to the underprivileged by Godunov would be in the name of Tsaritza Irina Feodorovna. He would ignore including Tsar Feodor as much as possible in his transactions, hoping to establish himself deeper in Russian affairs as a preparation for his future role.

---

6 Wealthy Russian aristocrats would hire midgets or dwarfs as playmates for their children.

War with Sweden

On December 12, 1586, Stephen Batori died, no doubt one of the greatest kings of 16th century Europe, and this opened the door for Godunov to increase his authority in leadership by expanding it to Eastern Europe. The indirect benefit was the annexation of lands that Tsar Ivan IV had fought for 25 years to acquire for Russia: Livonia and Baltic seaports, and even more of Poland and Lithuania. All of this was so needed by Russia for trade with Europe and to increase the economy of Russia, as well as its prestige and power base with the balance of Europe (the same reason for Tsar Peter's Narva Campaign and establishment of St. Petersburg). The personal gain for Godunov uniting the three great empires of Russia, Poland and Lithuania was worth the effort, and an emissary, Elizar Rzhevski, was immediately dispatched to Vilnius to introduce Tsar Feodor as a candidate. But the likely candidate to replace Batori was Sigismund III Vasa, son of King John III Vasa of Sweden.

Rzhevski returned with the news that all negotiations and elections for a new king were being held at Warsaw, Poland. But unlike the tsar of Russia, who was an autocrat, Poland-Lithuanian had a government closer to a constitutional-monarchy. For Godunov, this would be only a temporary obstacle. In his customary political arrogance, three emissaries on behalf of Tsar Feodor were dispatched to Warsaw: cousin Stepan Vasilyevich Godunov, Feodor Mikhailovich Troyekurov, and Vasili Schelkalov. They carried with them 48 copies of his proposal on the future government of the three-nation alliance. Essentially, Russia would absorb Livonia, Poland and Lithuania, arrange and conduct trade with the balance of Europe and the Far East, and protect them from any invasion by Crimean Mongols or Ottoman Turks. The proposal also excluded any inheritance of the throne by Tsar Feodor's offspring — should he have children — or by Tsarevich Dmitri Ivanovich.

Of course, it was easy for Godunov to inflate the ego of his brother-in-law Tsar Feodor regarding the acquisition of a throne over a three-state alliance, even though his authority would be temporarily reduced as a constitutional monarch — as if he actually had any authority anyway. The response from Polish nobility was the agreement of Russia's immediate concession to Unia — their subjection to Papal authority —

in lieu of Greek Orthodoxy, before any consideration of their proposal. The issue of national religion was a minor obstacle to Godunov, but the Polish nobility nonetheless declined the proposal, aware of the history of perennial warfare between Uniate Poland–Lithuania and Orthodox Russia, and it was not as if they were not aware that Godunov was the real power behind the throne of Russia and Tsar Feodor his puppet in the matter of unity and ascending the throne over the three-nation alliance. Before the Russian emissaries were able to return to Warsaw with another proposal, one more accommodating to the needs of the Polish-Lithuanian state and population, Sigismund was crowned on December 16, 1587.

The strife created between the two states as a result of the ascension of Sigismund eventually evolved into war with Sweden. A treaty of Tsar Ivan IV's with Sweden expired in 1586, and no response had been delivered by King John III Vasa. Godunov felt the necessity of Sweden returning to Russia provinces in the northwest, Karelia and Lapland, but then in 1589 Sweden invaded Karelia and occupied the region surrounding Lakes Ladoga and Onega. Tsar Feodor retaliated with a threat of war if the territory was not ceded back to Russia along with Estonia. For Godunov, the instigator in the matter, it was the opportunity for Russia to go to war.

Up to this time Godunov had displayed brilliance in handling on his own both domestic and foreign policy, also being careful of his actions and being reconciliatory whenever possible. Not being a person of military temperament, nor wanting the glory that accompanies military victory, Godunov nonetheless wanted to prove that being reconciliatory was not the same as being timid or cowardly, that on occasion bloodshed could not be circumvented. To fulfill this sacred debt — as he considered the war against Sweden to defend the honor of Russia — Godunov gathered an army of 300,000 soldiers and cavalry and 300 cannons (as the chronicler of the era records). As a display of royal strength to the Russian troops, Godunov summoned the passive Tsar Feodor to appear sitting on a military steed, which he accomplished reluctantly, and rode at the head of the regiment from Moscow to Novgorod, and his wife Irina on a horse next to him. The actual head of the military campaign was Feodor Mstislavski, while the rear was commanded by the valiant military hero Dmitri Khorostinin. Godunov and Feodor Nikitich Romanov considered themselves second-in-command. The campaign began at Novgorod on January 18, 1590 in three directions: towards Karelia, Livonia (Estonia) and Narva. The first victory was gained January 27, even in sub-freezing temperatures, as Khorostinin defeated the Swedish general Gustav Baner's army of 20,000. Narva was captured February 4, and Livonia was overrun by Russian troops by February 21 and Revel was taken, while the 3rd Division pressed on across southern Finland as far as Abo (today known as Turku). Sweden admitted defeat on February 25, and made concessions to conclude a peace treaty with Russia. They ceded to Russia the regions of Karelia and Narva and the portion of Livonia adjoining the Gulf of Finland; but not any of Finland or Lapland. Godunov claimed victory while Tsar Feodor rushed back to his wife at Novgorod, and together with her back to Moscow to celebrate the victory that his father could not attain in 25 years of wars against Scandinavia and eastern Europe.

ROC clergy met the royal entourage outside the capital, while Metr. Job in a pompous oration compared Tsar Feodor to Roman Emperor Constantine I the Great and to Grand Prince Vladimir, founder of the Kievan state. The metropolitan lauded the tsar in the name of the fatherland and church for the recovery of ancient Slavic lands back to Russia.

Eventually the treaty with Sweden led to a treaty with Poland-Lithuania. Tsar Feodor summoned clergy and noblemen to a council on January 1, 1591. A peace treaty was composed and sent to Warsaw, Poland, and was accepted by Sigismund for a term of 20 years. For a while Russia had rest from war on its eastern borders.

By this year 1591, Boris Godunov, in the eyes of Russia and adjoining nations, had reached the highest plateau of statesmanship, as the real power of Moscovite Russia, and he was at the pinnacle of his physical and intellectual capability. All Godunov sensed surrounding him were either silent servants or those lauding his achievements. Not only at the Kremlin palaces, but even at distant and remote parts of Russia and Siberia people publicly declared, "Boris Feodorovich Godunov is the ruler of the land; he is monarch and whatever he wants for Russia is accomplished, and we are impressed and glad over it." No other ruler in the history of Russia was sincerely lauded by both rich and poor, nobleman and serf, as was Godunov. But he was not humble in the least of his efforts, but drove forward to acquire for both himself and Russia greater prestige.

Establishment of the Russian Patriarchate

In 1586 Patr. Joakim V of Antioch arrived in Moscow seeking charity. During his visit, Tsar Feodor expressed to Patr. Joakim the desire to establish Moscow as a patriarchate. Joakim gave his word to offer a proposal on behalf of Tsar Feodor at the next council of patriarchs of the Greek Orthodox Church. Joakim returned to Antioch with some 8,000 gold ducats and many expensive gifts to obligate him to fulfill his promise.

Russia never sought such an appellation for its own supreme ecclesiastical prelate, not from Grand Prince Vladimir I the Great when Christianity was introduced into Russia in AD 988 to the present. Having been independent from Constantinople for over 50 years in their selection and ordination of a metropolitan, a different title would be irrelevant as far as his dignity or responsibilities were concerned. This attitude changed with the arrival of Patr. Joakim. Godunov saw the opportunity to create a Russian patriarchate and elevate Metr. Job, who would not deny the chance of gaining such a prestigious title. At the same time the ambitious Boris Godunov sensed the opportunity to confirm his own coronation by the sacrament of consecration by a patriarch and so officially route the dynasty of the Russian princes into his own. The benefit for the Greek patriarchs was indirect since every one of their sees was occupied by a foreign nation — the Ottoman Empire, and their infidel religion — Islam. The wealth of Russia could possibly be used to subsidize the destitution of their patriarchates, and they could perhaps even convince Russia to provide military intervention to defeat the Islam occupation.

In June 1588, Patr. Jeremiah of Constantinople arrived in Moscow, and to the great satisfaction of Godunov. The entire capital was overwhelmed, because Constantinople was considered primary among the four Greek Orthodox patriarchates (Rome was no longer recognized by the Greek patriarchates after AD 1054.) Accompanying him was Metr.

Jerofei of Monembasi and Archbishop Arseni of Esalon, both dioceses in Greece. When the ecclesiastical guests entered the Gold Chamber of the Kremlin palace, Tsar Feodor greeted them respectfully and sat them close to him. Graciously he accepted their gifts: an icon with several scenes of the passion of Christ, a few drops of the blood of Christ, a relic of the bones of Emperor Constantine I the Great (a saint in the Orthodox Church). Then Tsar Feodor asked Godunov to converse with the patriarch in private, and the two went into an adjoining room. Patr. Jeremiah condescendingly told his history. After 10 years as patriarch, he was betrayed by some dishonest Greeks on fabricated charges to the Sultan, and so he was exiled to the island of Rhodes. While exiled, and even though the Sultan promised not to intervene into ecclesiastical affairs, Sultan Mahomet II installed Theoleptus as patriarch. But after five years, the situation reversed, and Theoleptus was banished and he — Jeremiah — was returned to his see. During the five-year interval, as Jeremiah related, the famous Cathedral of Santa Sophia was converted into a mosque and the patriarchate became financially and spiritually destitute. Godunov knew that Jeremiah would play into his hands to gain financial solvency for his patriarchate, just as did Joakim a few years earlier. After further discussions and negotiations, Jeremiah agreed to ordain whomever Tsar Feodor would select as the first patriarch of Russia. The candidate was already selected, but for purposes of the sacred rite of selection, three candidates had to be proposed and one would be selected by ballot. The three were Metr. Job, Archbishop Varlaam of Rostov (later to be exiled), and Archbishop Alexander of Novgorod. Of course, the name on the ballot that was reported to Tsar Feodor was Job.

The date for confirming the selection was January 23, 1589. After Matins that morning, Metr. Job, wearing his stole, omophorium and vestments, performed Eucharist at the Uspenski Cathedral, many prelates and the tsar attending. At the conclusion of services, Job walked from the altar and to the ambo holding a candle in one hand and a letter of gratitude to the tsar and clergy in the other. One prelate addressed the crowd, "The Orthodox King, the Ecumenical Patriarch, and the Sacred Ecclesiastical Council exalt you to the See of Vladimir, Moscow and all Russia." Job replied, "I am a sinful slave, but if our Monarch and the Ecumenical Vicar Jeremiah and the Council assign to me such a majestic rank, I will accept it with gratitude." Job meekly bowed his head, turned to the clergy, to the people assembled and humbly recited the vow to preserve the flock entrusted to him by God.

January 26 was selected as the day of ordination. At the beginning of liturgy, Job stood before Jeremiah, who laid his hand on him, prayed and blessed him, and placed the patriarchal miter on his head; then both Job and Jeremiah completed liturgy. After liturgy, Tsar Feodor hung on Job a jewel-encrusted cross containing a piece of the cross of Christ, a velvet green mantle with long strips having pearls woven in them, and a white cowl with a cross embroidered on it. Tsar Feodor handed to Job the staff of the venerated saint Metr. Peter of Moscow and admonished him to call himself first among bishops, the father of fathers, patriarch of all the lands of the north, all by the will of God and will of the king. The newly-ordained Job then blessed Tsar Feodor and the gathered assembly. Leaving the cathedral, Job sat on a donkey and was led by two bishops and several state officials around the walls of the Kremlin, sprinkling holy water on them while holding a cross high. Along the way he recited prayers for the survival of the city. Later that day, both patriarchs were the tsar's guests at dinner.

To justify the entire event of Jeremiah approving and ordaining another patriarch without discussion with the other three Orthodox patriarchs, a charter was composed. The document explained that the first Rome fell due to their decline into the Appolonarian heresy, and the second Rome, Constantinople, was now occupied by the infidel Turks and descendants of Hagar, while the Third Rome was Moscow. According to this concept, the Papacy was the false shepherd whose vision was obscured by the spirit of sophism, and the new supreme prelate was the patriarch of Constantinople. The second after him was Alexandria, the third would be Moscow, the forth Antioch, and the fifth Jerusalem. Because the patriarchates of Antioch and Jerusalem were miniscule compared to the size of Russia, plus occupied by Islam and financially destitute as well, in the typical arrogance of Godunov he elevated his own institution of the Russian patriarchate over the two initial dioceses of ancient Christianity. A council of the Greek patriarchs later discarded Godunov's demand and placed Moscow at the end of the list of holy sees.

After the conclusion of the ordination, Patr. Job proceeded to install four metropolitans in Russia: in Novgorod, Kazan, Rostov and Krutitzk (a suburb of Moscow); and six archbishops: in Vologda, Suzdal, Nizhniy-Novgorod, Smolensk, Ryazan, and Tver; and seven bishops: in Pskov, Rhzev, Ustyug, Belozero, Kolomensk, Sever and Dmitrovsk. Patr. Jeremiah and his retinue remained in Russia through May 1589, visiting monasteries and churches as guests of the tsar. When the ecclesiastical prelates finally left Russia, they took with them 2,000 gold ducats and a copy of the patriarchal charter for the other patriarchs to approve.

Godunov had a perspicacious view of the future. Knowing that he could not always depend on the intervention of sister-tsaritza Irina into her husband-tsar's political affairs, and leery of the support of noblemen and officials, the obligation of newly-ordained Patr. Job and ROC clergy to him would definitely be of value. The installation of a tsar with the blessing of a native patriarch would be a first in the history of Russia and Godunov planned his future so this would fulfill in him.

Murder of Tsarevich Dmitri Ivanovich

If Godunov wanted nothing more, having all except for the crown worn by Tsar Feodor, he could have been content under the circumstances. Because of Tsar Feodor's poor and steadily declining health, he nonetheless might not inherit the throne because of the legitimate heir, Tsarevich Dmitri Ivanovich, who was being reared by his mother and relatives in an elegant and comfortable exile. The family retained resentment toward Godunov, whose decision it was to banish them from Moscow, from the public eye and state affairs, in order to acquire control of the Russia state from Tsar Feodor through sister Irina. Godunov had his own thoughts about the threat that the family in exiled posed, that maybe more than just resentment resided in the minds of the Nagoi family, and which possibly could erupt into hatred, malice and vengeance should Tsar Feodor pass away and the mother and uncle of Tsarevich Dmitri decide to act as regents on his behalf. Godunov contemplated. What would then occur to Irina? A forced vow as a nun and her permanent seclusion within the walls of some distant convent?

What would happen to him? A dungeon or the executioner's block? He envisioned himself in the same dark, damp and cold cell to which he had confined his rivals, or the public execution in Red Square where his traitors ended their life. To survive the possibility of any of this occurring to Godunov, Tsarevich Dmitri would need to be erased from existence permanently. Godunov considered the throne as not just a sacred, unassailable place of genuine independent authority, but a place of paradisiacal rest and safety that malice and envy could not reach. Such fantasies of the enticement of the supreme rule became more and more vivid to Godunov, and more and more agitated his emotions, until he was completely enveloped and obsessed by them. One contemporary chronicler recorded the following about Godunov:

> Even though he possessed a rare mind, Godunov still believed in the art of fortune-telling. He would invite them at the darkest hours of the night and ask them of his future. The sycophant wizards and astrologists would reply, "The crown awaits you," then they would fall silent as through frightened of the premonition for his future. The impatient Godunov would order them to relate the rest. He heard from them that he would only reign seven years. In lively joy he hugged the seer and shouted, "Even if only seven days, but only to wear the crown."

So did Godunov unveil his soul to the imaginary prophets of superstition, and he did not hide from himself the deepest thoughts of his soul, knowing what he wanted. Awaiting the death of the childless king, depending on the will of his sister the tsaritza, having filled the Duma, court and state departments with his friends and relatives, not doubting in the loyalty of the supreme prelate of the Russian Orthodox Church, and likewise relying on the brilliance of his own rule, Godunov did not fear the event unheard of in the fatherland since the time of Rurik: an empty throne and discontinuation of the royal line, to be followed by strife that will accompany the installation of a new dynasty. Godunov was convinced that the scepter, having fallen from the hand of the last king of the lineage of Ivan Danilovich, would be entrusted to the person who had for so long reigned without the appellation of tsar. The avaricious megalomaniac saw only one item standing between and the throne, a defenseless child, and viewed him as would a hungry beast at defenseless prey. As far as Godunov was concerned, the death of Tsarevich Dmitri was an absolute necessity.

To determine a method of fulfilling his intention, Godunov thought that declaring the Tsarevich to be illegitimate would be the least detriment to himself and others, since Dmitri was the son of the 6th or 7th wife of Tsar Ivan IV. Godunov began to advertise the illegitimacy of Tsarevich Dmitri and forbid any prayers on the child's behalf or to recite his name during liturgy. Later Godunov realized that the marriage was consecrated and tolerated by the ROC and that this offspring was still considered legitimate, even though the ecclesiastical statutes only permit four marriages. The next step was slander released by Godunov's confederates, that Dmitri was predisposed to violence and malice, inheriting the trait from his father, although only nine years old. The gossip spread throughout Moscow that young Dmitri enjoyed torturing and killing pets and was infatuated when he watched the slaughter of larger animals. Such rumors were supposed to engender hate toward Dmitri among the people. Stories were circulated that young Dmitri along with playmates created a line of snowmen during the previous winter, 20 of them, and then Dmitri named each one of them after some high ranking official in the government including naming one Boris Godunov. Dmitri then took a saber — one made from a stick — and began to hew them apart. When he reached the snowman named after Godunov, Dmitri decapitated him and then severed off the hands and feet, while saying loudly, "So will I do when I ascend the throne." To defuse the ludicrous rumors, people who knew the royal family said that the child showed an intellect and character that was above average, and he was already displaying character traits of leadership, but this was hardly spoken due to fear of reprisal from Godunov.

The initial attempt to kill Tsarevich Dmitri was by poison. The nursemaid of the tsarevich, Vasilisa Volokhova, and her son Osip accepted a bribe from Godunov and became his instruments. However the poison that was fed him did not harm him, whether he ate it or drank it. No doubt some conscience remained in the soul of Volokhova and so she probably diluted the poison. The failure vexed Godunov and which drove him to conspire the ultimate crime. His choice of thugs was two officials: Vladimir Zagryazhski and Nikifor Chepchugov, who were earlier part of Tsar Ivan's group of Oprichnin henchmen and in dept to Godunov, but they declined to execute his proposal. Although they were willing to die for Godunov, a proposition to murder a child was repulsive, especially from the royal family. They promised to keep silent, but nonetheless they were regularly harassed through the end of Godunov's life for refusing his order.

A palace insider and friend of Godunov, hoping to further his career, Andrei Kleshnin, found someone reliable who would execute Godunov's order: the official Mikhail Bityagovski, who already had a reputation as a henchman with a temperament and physique to match. Godunov bribed him with gold and promised more, and offered him security and protection should he be apprehended. Bityagovski gave his word of honor to Godunov and went to Uglich under the guise of attending to state and economic matters dealing with the widow-tsaritsa Marina Nagoi. Accompanying Bityagovski were two accomplices: his son Danilo and nephew Nikita Kachalov, who likewise had reputations as henchmen. Osip Volokhov, son of the nursemaid, was already at Uglich and agreed to help in the murder. They were to keep one eye on the Tsarevich and not allow the first opportunity to slip. They figured success would be easy, since from morning to evening they would be at the home of mother Marina, while she would be involved in domestic chores, overseeing the servants and cooking. They failed to realize that the nursemaid and tsarevich were always in the sight of the mother, so she would never lose track of him, not for even a moment, and she did not part from him, except to attend liturgy at church. Marina did not trust the nursemaid Volokhova, or the cook Irina Zhdanova. Time passed, the hired killers could not find an opportunity when the child was alone, and decided to carry out the murder in the open.

On May 15, 1591, at six o'clock in the evening, the mother returned from church with her son and was preparing for dinner. Her brothers were not at home, and the cooks were setting the dinner table. The nursemaid Volokhova called Dmitri to go outside with her for a walk while dinner was being prepared. Marina, who had been thinking of going with them, decided not to at the last moment or maybe it slipped her mind. The cook tried to hold back the child, but the nursemaid grabbed him and led him out of the room through the vestibule and to the balcony. Suddenly Osip Volokhov, Danilo Bityagovski and Kachalov appeared. Osip, holding a hidden knife, took Dmitri by the hand and said, "Master, you have a new necklace."

The child, with an innocent smile, raised his head and replied, "No, it is old." Osip Volokhov pulled out the knife and partially slit the child's neck, but then dropped the knife from the shock of his act and ran. Dmitri fell and the nursemaid fell upon him to shield him and began to scream. Danilo and Kachalov wrestled the child away from the nursemaid and severely beat her. They grabbed the boy and plunged their knives into his torso several times and slit his neck through to the neck bone and then threw him down the steps of the balcony. Mother Marina heard the scream of the nursemaid, ran out the door onto the balcony, and saw the dead child on the ground and the nursemaid lying on the balcony floor. The mother cried in despair at the sight. The cook went outside and pointed at the nursemaid as being complicit in the act and at the killers as they were running through the yard to the gate.

The sexton of the diocesan cathedral, who witnessed the incident from a distance — according to one account — rang an alarm bell and the streets were filled with people. Agitated, perplexed, they ran at the sound of the bell looking for smoke, a fire, wondering what was burning. The crowd burst into the estate confinement and saw the dead child lying on the ground. Both mother and nursemaid had fainted from shock and were lying on the ground alongside him. Once revived, they told them the names of the criminals. The people rushing into the estate stopped the murderers from leaving through the main gate. Hearing the alarm bell and frightened, and seeing the approaching crowd, the three murderers lost their bearings, and not knowing where to hide, they ran into an adjoining shed. Mikhail Bityagovski, hearing the alarm bell, ran to the cathedral and threw his body over the bell to muffle the sound and stop the sexton. He then ran to the body of the dead child and tried to dissipate the perplexed crowd, telling them that the boy had killed himself accidentally by falling on a knife during an epileptic seizure. (This was the excuse fabricated beforehand by Godunov to explain the death.) Within minutes the entire city was aware of the unexplainable incident.

The crowd hollered, "Murderers!" Getting angrier they picked up rocks and threw them at Mikhail. He tried to run into the quarters of one of the servants, Danil Tretyakov, whom he felt would protect him. The crowd went out of control and turned into vigilantes: they brutally murdered both Mikhail Bityagovski and Danil with their hands and feet. The crowd ran to the shed and there apprehended son Danilo and Kachalov and killed them in a frenzy. Osip Volokhov ran into a house, but the mob followed him and drug him to the church where the body of Tsarevich Dmitri had been taken, and there the unrestrained vigilantes killed him in the presence of the mother. Along with them, three others who were suspected of being part of the plot were killed by the mob, along with a retarded cleaning woman who lived at the Bityagovksi residence. The nursemaid Vasilisa survived, and only because the criminals kept repeating that the real culprit in the crime was Godunov and that they were just following orders.

After the upheaval and anger subsided, city officials composed a report for Tsar Feodor and dispatched couriers on horseback to Moscow. But Godunov already made arrangements and he had loyal officials stationed at a check point on the road from Uglich. Every person that traveled the road was retained, questioned and searched. The officials apprehended the couriers when they arrived at the check point and personally brought them to Godunov. The report was confiscated and a new report was dictated by Godunov, stating that the child had cut himself with a knife during an epileptic seizure, and that the Nagoi family was responsible for the death by neglecting the child and allowing him to play with such a sharp object. The revised report further stated that the Nagoi family blamed Bityagovski and the other officials in the death of the child and agitated the people to turn against them and brutally murder them.

With the report, Godunov went personally to Tsar Feodor, feigning sorrow and remorse at the incident. Together with the tsar, Godunov shed tears and loudly wailed over the death of the tsar's brother. After the emotional anguish passed, the tsar said, "Let the will of God be done."

Now what was Godunov to provide for the balance of Russia, who would not be as gullible as the tsar to accept such a fabrication, knowing that the tsarevich had no history of any health problems, much less epilepsy, and knowing the confessions of the accomplices as they were trying to save their own lives from the vigilante mob? Not wasting a moment, Godunov sent two popular statesmen to Uglich to perform an investigation. First was Andrei Kleshnin, a confederate of Godunov's in planning the plot, and no one was surprised at the selection. However to balance the scale, the second person selected was Pr. Vasili Ivanovich Shuisky, who earlier suffered at the hands of Godunov, but more respected among the people than the former choice.

On the evening of May 19, four days after the murder, Kleshnin, Shuisky, another official named Elizar Biluzgin, and Metr. Gelasi of Krutitzk, arrived in Uglich. They went straight to the Cathedral of the Holy Transfiguration (Preobrazhenski), where they viewed the butchered body of Tsarevich Dmitri and the knife that was lying alongside the body, which Volokhov had dropped before fleeing. The unfortunate mother, relatives and local residents wailed bitterly. Shuisky approached the coffin with a display of regret to view the body closely and see the wounds if possible. But Kleshnin, once he saw the angelic face of the child and bloodstained clothing, displayed shock. He become torpid and stood motionless, and tears began to flow down his cheeks, and he was not able to utter a sound as he viewed the consequences of his complicity. The laceration on Dmitri's neck was deep, the throat cut through with a strong hand, and very apparent not by a fall onto a knife or by the child's own hand. It was obvious homicide. In order to proceed with the funeral — postponed for the sake of the investigation — the accompanying metropolitan performed a requiem with those attending.

Pr. Shuisky began the investigation. He gathered clergy and local residents and asked them, "How did Dmitri stab himself while the Nagoi family was neglecting him?" All in unison, the monks, priests, men, women, old people and young, replied, "The Tsarevich was murdered by your own servants, Mikhailo Bityagovski and his confederates, by order of Boris Godunov." Shuisky did not want to hear any more and released them. He then interrogated the uncle Mikhail Nagoi, asking him, "How did Dmitri die? What infirmity did he have? Why did he — Mikhail — order the mob killing of Danilo and Mikhail Bityagovski,

Nikita Kachalov, Danil Tretyakov, Osip Volokhov, some local residents and the servants of Volokhov and Bityagovski? Why did he on Tuesday order knives and swords to be placed on the bodies of the deceased?"

Mikhail Nagoi replied that the child Dmitri was carved apart by Osip Volokhov, Nikita Kachalov and Danilo Bityagovski, and that the mob killed them on their own, without his order to do so. Shuisky then decided to question the suspects and witnesses in private and not peacefully, but with threats, and summoning only those he expected to comply with the investigation. Now the fabrications began for the witnesses to protect themselves. Rusin Rakov testified that Mikhail Nagoi ordered a man named Timofei to butcher a chicken and the blood was smeared on knives, which were placed on the bodies of the three suspects. The other Nagoi brothers, Grigori and Andrei, to protect themselves, knowing what their fate would be if their testimony did not acquit Godunov, likewise told the interrogators what they wanted to hear: that Dmitri fell on the knife during an epileptic seizure; that it was only an unfounded rumor that was spread by some unknown someone that the boy was murdered; and that the murder of the suspects was ordered by their brother Mikhail Nagoi, as vendetta toward Shuisky. Cook Irina and chambermaid Marya Samoilova, testified in the same manner, as did surprisingly, nursemaid Vasilisa Volokhova, perhaps to protect herself, saying that it was the mother Marina Nagoi who beat her up once she noticed the dead child, and that it was the mother who said the names of the culprits. One other eyewitness testified, a kitchen worker Semeika Yudin, whose testimony fell in line with the rest.

Regardless of the many inconsistencies of each of the witnesses' testimony, each version slightly different, the interrogators felt that they all agreed on the primary premise of a self-inflicted fatal wound during an epileptic seizure while the Nagoi family was negligent in their responsibility of caring for the child, and due to their spite toward Godunov the blame was placed on these others whom they brutally murdered. Shuisky recorded what he wanted to hear, and finally with Kleshnin and Biluzgin, composed the following report to the tsar, based as if on the reliable testimony of city officials, the nursemaid Vasilisa Volokhova, the cook Irina, the chambermaid Marya Samoilova, the butler, some residents of the royal estate, the two brothers of Marina

Nagoi: Grigori and Andrei Alexandrovich; and the tsaritza's attorney-at-law, along with a few local residents and clergy.

> Dmitri, on Wednesday May 12, suffered an epileptic seizure. On Friday he became better and walked to liturgy with the tsaritza and played outdoors. On Saturday, likewise after liturgy, he went outdoors with the nursemaid, cook, chambermaid and some local youngsters. He began to play with them holding a knife, and then suffered another seizure and stabbed himself in the throat with the knife and fell on it. He trashed violently on the ground and then died. Since he was afflicted with this illness earlier, he once even stabbed his mother and on another occasion bit the hand of Andrei Nagoi's daughter. Once the tsaritza discovered what occurred she ran outside and began to beat the nursemaid, and said that it was Volokhov, Kachalov and Danilo Bityagovski who stabbed him. But none of them were there at the time. The tsaritza and her drunk brother, Mikhail Nagoi, ordered them to be killed and also the official [Mikhail] Bityagovski, with no justification. The reason these men were blamed is that the official [Bityagovski] would not satisfy the greed of the Nagoi family and did not give them any more allowance than permitted by state orders. Hearing that state officials were to arrive at Uglich, Mikhail Nagoi ordered some knives and an iron rod, which he soaked in blood and laid on the body of the deceased, to attribute the murder to them.

This absurd report was affirmed by Archimandrite Feodorit of Voskresenski (Resurrection) Monastery, two monks, and the confessor of the Nagoi family, and obviously due to their cowardice and fear of reprisal. The only refutation on record was the testimony of Mikhail Nagoi, brother of the mother-tsaritza, although the notes taken by Shuisky portrayed him as the primary slanderer and rather than complying in the investigation he was obstinate in his testimony that Dmitri died at the hands of criminals.

Returning to Moscow on June 2, Shuisky presented his report to Tsar Feodor, who in turn sent him to Patr. Job and other prelates to read the report to them at an assembly of boyars. After hearing the report, Metr. Gelasi of Krutitzk decided to authenticate the fallacious report with a fabricated conversation with the mother. He arose and said to Patr. Job and the assembly, "I announce to the Sacred Council that the widow-tsaritza, on the day of my departure from Uglich, invited me to speak with her in private. She tearfully pleaded that the tsar would assuage his anger on those who killed the official Bityagovski and his friends, and that she acknowledges the crime done against them. She pleaded with me contritely so our sovereign would not execute capital punishment on her ill-fated relatives."

After fabricating this plea of widow-tsaritza Marina, Gelasi then presented another report to Patr. Job from the Uglich city manager, who wrote that Tsarevich Dmitri's death resulted from an epileptic seizure, while Mikhail Nagoi, in a drunken condition ordered the crowd to kill the innocent Bityagovski. After the reports and testimony were finished, the Sacred Council composed a summary and their conclusion of the event and presented it to Tsar Feodor:

> May the will of the Sovereign be done. We are assured without doubt that the life of the Tsarevich was terminated by the will of God; that Mikhail Nagoi is guilty in this horrible incident of death and that he acted due to motivation of personal malice and also had acquired advice from evil sorcerers: Andrei Mochalov and other Uglich residents, and they should suffer capital punishment for their treachery and crime. However this matter is of this world, and God and the Sovereign know the situation. Mercy and disgrace are held in the hands of the monarch, but we must pray together on behalf of the tsar and tsaritza unto the All-High for the safety and prosperity of the nation.

Tsar Feodor ordered the boyars to fulfill the recommended punishment and execute the guilty. The Nagoi brothers Mikhail and Andrei, cook Irina Zhdanova and her husband, and the so-called sorcerer Andrei Mochalov, were brought to Moscow in chains. They were questioned and then tortured, especially Mikhail Nagoi, but the torturers were not able to squeeze a confession out of him that Tsarevich Dmitri had killed himself. Finally the group was sent to some distant city and were there incarcerated. The widow-tsaritza Marina Nagoi was force to take the veil as a nun against her will and she was relocated to the Convent of Nikolai-Viksinski[7] at Cherepovetz, near Beloye Ozero. The bodies of those killed by the mob at Uglich, which were thrown into a pit outside of town and covered, were exhumed and brought to a church, where a requiem was performed, and a new funeral was held, burying them as martyrs in great honor. The residents of Uglich who were accused by state officials as being part of the mob were executed, about 200 men and women. Other residents who were suspected of being accomplices had their tongues excised or were incarcerated at a

---

7 Today under the water of the Rybinskoe Reservoir.

local prison. Even the innocent fled the town once they noticed a purge beginning. The majority of the city was exiled to Siberia, to the city Pelim, about 200 miles northwest of Tobolsk along the Tavda River. The end result was that the ancient and thriving city Uglich, near Yaroslavl on the Volga River, a bustling community of 30,000 residents and boasting of 150 churches, was reduced to a ghost town. By the time Godunov completed his wrath on the city for the death of the murderers and their accomplices, the city was desolate.

With the same zeal did Godunov reward the families of the criminals. The nursemaid Volokhova received a large estate of quality land, as did the wife and daughters of Mikhail Bityagovski. More gifts were distributed among the boyars who composed the council that approved the final version of events. Only Kleshnin refused the honors. His complicity and guilt overwhelmed him and psychologically devastated him. He became an ascetic monk shortly after the investigation, isolated himself from society, and declined in health until his death two years later.

But the populace was not to be fooled by either the investigation of Shuisky, or the verdict of prelates, or the conclusion of the Boyar assembly. The echoes of the population's refusal to acknowledge the official report resounded in the tsar's court and churches. Godunov's spies heard people whispering under their breath about the tragic and horrible murder, the secret of the actual guilty party, the pitiful blindness of the tsar to the entire matter, and the shameful feign and cowardice of nobles and clergy. Godunov's spies noticed the people were disenchanted and melancholy.

Russian Tragedies and Godunov's Maneuvers

Godunov, agitated by the rumors, now devised a manner of consoling the people as a result of a planned tragedy that affected the capital. On the eve of Pentecost 1591, while the tsar was on a pilgrimage to the Troitse-Sergieva Monastery with other officials, a fire broke out in Moscow at the Kolimazhni courtyard, and within a few hours had consumed the buildings of Arbatskaya, Nikitskaya, Tverskaya and Petrovskaya Streets, the White Quarter (Beli-Gorod, location of the low-income residents and the shopping area), and the outskirts of Streletski and Zaneglin. Homes, shops, churches and people were consumed by the flames. But the Kremlin and Eastern Quarter (Kitai-Gorod), where the officials, noblemen and princes had their residences, and the commercial center of Moscow, survived. Tens of thousands were now without shelter and possessions, and moaning and wailing was heard from every pile of ashes. When Tsar Feodor returned the day after Pentecost, the people ran in crowds to him along the Troitzi Road wanting charity and assistance, but Godunov would not allow them near the tsar. He stood in front of them with a display of compassion and concern, listened to them, gave them promises, and assured them that he would help them to the extent he could.

Under Godunov's orders, entire streets of homes were rebuilt, including large buildings, money was distributed, and favors and petitions were granted. He showed immeasurable generosity to such an extent that Moscow residents, now consoled and overwhelmed by his kindness and concern, began to praise Godunov.

Or was it just coincidental that Godunov utilized the misfortune of Moscow to acquire the gratitude of the people, and was he secretly guilty of starting the fire to route people's attention away from the scandal surrounding Tsarevich Dmitri and the devastation of Uglich, as the chroniclers of the era surmised and as some of his contemporaries felt? Some chroniclers relate that criminals started the fire, Godunov somehow involved, since the fire extended to the area of Moscow of wood structures that were easily destroyed, but not in the sections of wealth and commerce. Godunov routed the suspicions of the people to his enemies. Afanasi Nagoi and his brothers were taken into custody by Godunov's henchmen, who questioned them and convicted them of arson. The men were not executed, and the matter of blame for the incident was never concluded.

A severe and unexpected calamity then struck central Russia: an invasion of Crimean Mongols in the early spring 1591, tribes that composed the Khanate of Crimea under Khan Kazi-Girei. This invasion was likewise utilized by Godunov to his advantage to route people's attention from the Tsarevich Dmitri murder and devastation of Uglich.

It was not until April that the Duma dispatched military leaders and regiments to the south. In May, no Mongol army was noticed along the northern Don River, but on June 26, a scout arrived in Moscow relating that some 150,000 Mongols were approaching Tula, about 120 miles south of Moscow. Godunov then took charge. He immediately dispatched orders to the commanders of the forts in the Russian steppes for them and their regiments to hurry to Serpukhov, 50 miles south of Moscow on the Oka River, and join the army of Pr. Mstislavski. They would engage the enemy in the field outside the city. Unfortunately, the majority of Russian troops were in Pskov and Novgorod, protecting Russia from any invasion by Sweden or Poland-Lithuania, and not enough time was available to travel to reach Serpukhov by the time the Mongols were expected to arrive, and these troops were not at all concerned about the Mongol invasion.

Moscow was notified of the siege of Tula, and by the next day, June 27, the Mongol regiments had overrun Tula and were advancing northward. Godunov and his military commanders realized the impossibility of assembling all the regiments at Serpukhov before the arrival of the Mongols, and changed their plans. Godunov ordered Mstislavski to Moscow and a retreat of all the troops. They felt that a defense would be more successful with the available troops surrounding Moscow than in the open plains. On June 29, the Russian army vacated Serpukhov, and returned to Moscow on July 1. The regiments were stationed along the Moscow River near the village Kolomensk, while inside the city monasteries were converted into forts. On July 2, Tsar Feodor inspected the troops and encouraged them. On July 3, the Mongols crossed the Oka River, and were spending the night at Lopasha. The first engagement was under the command of Pr. Vladimir Bakhteyarov with 250,000 Russian troops. They defeated the Mongol's initial attack and the enemy retreated.

The regiments reorganized for a massive battle with the arrival of Godunov to the front in full military dress. Tsar Feodor entrusted the Russian army to Godunov's command and returned to the Kremlin, while Godunov spent the entire night, arranging and encouraging the troops. The battle was fought July 4, with 150,000 Mongols and 250,000 Russians on the field, but the battle was not conclusive. A few Russian soldiers that were captured informed the Khan that reinforcements had arrived from Pskov and Novgorod to fortify the ranks. The

Khan misinterpreted the information as meaning that Swedish troops were arriving. Not wanting to further engage the Russians after many dead that day and both sides still strong, the Khan ordered a retreat. One hour before sunrise on July 5, the Mongols were leaving.

On July 10, Ivan Nikitich Yuryev, the brother of Feodor Nikitich Romanov, arrived at the battle site and on behalf of Tsar Feodor awarded gold metals to both Mstislavski and Godunov. The victory, of course, was attributed to Godunov's leadership. Leaving a small guard at the battle site, Godunov and the others returned to Moscow. There Tsar Feodor gifted to Godunov for the victory a traditional Russian fur coat with gold buttons valued at 5,000 gold ducats, a gold chain, a gold cup confiscated from the Mongol Khan Mamei after the battle of Kulikova, three cities in Vyazhki province, and the renown title of Servant of the Tsar, which only three others held so far in Russian history. Tsar Feodor then held a gallant banquet in honor of Godunov, the hero of Serpukhov, all of which was arranged by Godunov ahead of time.

This latest triumph of Godunov was supplemented with arrests, tortures and executions. Rumors circulated in one province that Godunov somehow enticed the Khan to invade Russia and surge toward Moscow in order to distract the preoccupation of the people with the death of Tsarevich Dmitri and its consequences. Godunov dispatched spies and a clandestine wave of terror began. The one region where people were gossiping was Aleksin, north of Tula on the Oka River, and because the Mongol army passed through there on the way to Serpukhov and on their retreat. If the suffering already incurred was not enough, Godunov's loyal henchmen arrested people arbitrarily, questioned and tortured them, until they received the expected confession. The victims died from the torture imposed, or were executed, or had their tongue excised. Some cities in northern Ukraine were depopulated just as was Uglich, due to the suspicion that the spies had about the loyalty of the residents. Godunov was able to impress upon the people respect for him, whether due to his accomplishments on behalf of Russia and charity toward people, or else out of fear for their own safety.

Godunov's Administration over Russia

The royal couple had been married some 10 years now and the marriage was still childless, except that now good news was announced from the Kremlin palace: Tsaritza Irina was pregnant. In the entirety of Moscovite Russia, only Godunov was not pleased with the announcement. Nonetheless, he forced from his lips words of complement and a congratulation, while psychologically in anguish after all his effort in the murder of Tsarevich Dmitri. Now Godunov had another heir to the throne to deal with, even if it was his nephew or niece.

May 29, 1592, Tsaritza Irina gave birth to a beautiful baby girl. On June 14, the child was baptized at Chudovski Monastery inside the Kremlin, and was named Fedosia Feodorovna. At no time in history was Moscow this joyous over the birth of a heiress. Tsar Feodor acted in the same manner as if a male successor to the throne was born and issued acts of amnesty, releasing criminals and political prisoners from jails. A series of royal grants were issued by Tsar Feodor in honor of the event: criminals were released from prisons, those sentenced to death had their punishments commuted, those whose property was confiscated had it returned, jails were opened and monetary gifts were provided to monasteries. People rejoiced, but there were also some that gossiped saying that the tsaritza actually gave birth to a son, but Godunov exchanged the child for girl born at the same time to some destitute woman. Others questioned a female inheriting the throne, but purposefully would permit it to continue the royal lineage.

Once she turned a year old, court officials began investigating a method for Fedosia to acquire the title of tsaritza at the death of her father, Tsar Feodor, regardless of her marital status, and so at least indirectly salvage the succession of Ivan Danilovich and the royal posterity. Official Andrei Shelkov even had a secret discussion with an Austrian delegate in Moscow at the time to present a proposal to the Emperor of Austria-Hungary. Shelkov requested an Austrian prince between 14 and 18 years of age to be sent to Moscow. He would learn Russian and the religion and culture of Russia and eventually marry the tsarevna and ascend the throne.

Godunov could have sighed with relief at the birth of Fedosia, knowing that at the death of the tsar all of Tsar Ivan IV's court favorites that he installed would lose their positions, and with a niece as tsaritza Godunov would continue to administer the government in her name as regent, just as in the name of Tsar Feodor. Nonetheless, it grieved Godunov that he would still not sit on the throne itself.

The child Fedosia was born weak and she remained frail, failing to grow and physically develop as a normal child. She passed away a few months short of her second birthday and was buried at the Vosnesenski Cathedral inside Novo-Devichi Convent. All Russia wept with Tsar Feodor and Tsaritza Irina, and Godunov also forced a few tears at the misfortune of the royal couple. Others suspected he was involved with her death.

A second channel that Godunov contemplated to remain as the power behind the throne was the adoption of his daughter Ksenia by the royal couple. Shelkov proposed that wedding arrangements be made in advance with Maximilian, the future Duke of Bavaria, who was now 20 years of age. Ksenia Borisovna was now 15 years old. However, the fantasy never proceeded beyond the initial conversations.

The decrees issued by the tsar during this era were executed, "In the name of Tsar Feodor Ivanovich, Tsaritza Irina Feodorovna and the tsar's bother-in-law Boris Feodorovich." This was unheard of in earlier years, and was never repeated in the future. The official title of Godunov in 1595 was "Tsar's brother-in-law and ruler, Servant of the Tsar and Cavalry Master, Palace Commander and Sovereign of the Great Kingdoms of Kazan and Astrakhan." Godunov became more self-confident in the years of Tsar Feodor's declining health, no longer intimidated or threatened by the hereditary noblemen and princes. In 1597, the younger brothers of Pr. Vasili Ivanovich Shuisky were promoted as boyars: Alexander and Ivan, as well as Ivan Golitsyn in 1592, Andrei Kuriakin in 1598 and Boris Cherkassky in 1592. Feudal Pr. Ivan Mikhailovich Vorotinsky, who was also brother-in-law to Vasili Shuisky, returned to service in 1594 as military commander of Kazan. Godunov continued to acquire the favor of the peasants by distributing land to them confiscated by Tsar Ivan IV during the terror of the Oprichnin. Although most of the land was returned to their rightful owners during the early years of Tsar Feodor's reign, Godunov later divided into parcels the remaining confiscated estates of the opulent landowners and hereditary princes and distributed them to peasants. Travels of Godunov through the countryside and provinces were always accompanied by feasting and dinners and distribution of charity. The measures of Godunov to secure the loyalty of Russia's residents, both rich and poor, royalty and peasantry, reached its goal to stabilize Russia economically and secure peace. Some officials, such as Avraami Palitzen, confronted and chastised Godunov for using superficial generosity as a pretence for power and loyalty. Such critics were quickly incarcerated.

Foreigners who visited Russia and saw the effects of Godunov's administration recorded favorable comments, such as the Swede Peter Petrei. He recorded, "Boris was acute, intelligent and a considerate nobleman, but extremely shrewd, roguish and deceptive." The scandals surrounding the death of Tsarevich Dmitri were largely forgotten by the population at the end of Tsar Feodor's life, now that five years had passed.

Regardless of all the benefits that the nation received as a result of Godunov's administration, the one major legislation to his disservice and which would play a large role in the peasantry turning against him and joining Otrepyev was the abolition of Yuryev Day. The provisions of this law codified the relationship between landowner and serf, how the feudal system tied the serf to the land, including emancipation. The first Russian nomocanon of 1497 established the judicial validity of emancipation of serfs during the week before and after Yuryev Day, November 26. During these two weeks, a serf had the choice of leaving the estate he was bonded to and gaining his liberty, but at the cost of 1 ruble. However all his property had to remain with the landowner. It was a choice that few made, but the law on the books still allowed the serf liberation from feudalism.

The law was to the benefit of the serf, and the abolition of the law was a victory for landowners, noblemen, princes, and most of Russian aristocracy. Even though this law to abolish the provisions of Yuryev Day was legislated in the name of Tsar Feodor in 1597, it was the work of Godunov, likewise to his own benefit, since by this time he was the largest single landowner and serf-owner in Russia.

4. The Era of Tsar Boris Feodorovich Godunov

Death of Tsar Feodor Ivanovich

Tsar Feodor died January 7, 1598, at 1 o'clock in the morning, and the male posterity of Grand Prince Ivan Danilovich Kalita of Moscow did also. Apart from Ivan, Feodor and Dmitri, Tsar Ivan IV's four other children seldom mentioned, two girls and two boys, died in infancy.

To secure his dynasty, Tsar Ivan IV had murdered his cousin Vladimir Andreevich of Staritzin, the only other direct male descendant of Ivan Danilovich known to be alive, as well as his wife and 9-year-old daughter. The other daughter of Vladimir Andreevich, Marfa, survived by living in Livonia with her husband. By now a widow, she had returned to Russia and was still alive, but Godunov to secure his own right to the throne had her committed to a convent as a nun along with her infant daughter. The daughter passed away shortly after her arrival, and Marfa later died at the convent.

Not having any offspring, and failing to take the matter of a successor seriously, in accordance with his nature, Tsar Feodor passed away without a documented testament. Patr. Job and noblemen present at his bedside asked him, "To whom do you bequeath the reign, to us orphans or have you related this to the tsaritza?"

In a quiet voice Tsar Feodor replied, "God's will be done in the realm and with you. What pleases Him will be done. God has willed already how my tsaritza will live, which is also agreeable to me." Feodor was referring to the previous wives of his father Tsar Ivan IV who became nuns, although involuntarily, but Patr. Job reinterpreted this to mean that Tsaritza Irina would assume the throne of Russia, and so immediately after the death of Tsar Feodor the clergy, noblemen and palace officials swore loyalty to Irina as her husband's successor. However the tsaritza refused the throne and unveiled her desire to take the vow as a nun. Patr. Job and noblemen pleaded with her to remain as their Royal Highness, but she was adamant regarding her decision and stated that her brother Boris Godunov should govern, just as he had already done during the reign of her husband. Some historical accounts state that Patr. Job attempted to persuade Tsar Feodor, while on his death-bed, to bequeath the throne to Godunov but he declined, mentioning instead his cousin Feodor Nikitich Romanov.

Due to Tsar Feodor's serious ill-health for several months, preparations for his funeral had long been made by Godunov. He was buried the following day, January 8, and placed alongside his father Tsar Ivan IV in the Arkhangelsk Cathedral in the Kremlin, he was 40 years of age. Later that day, Tsaritza Irina left the palace for Novo-Devichi Convent, where she took the vow as a nun and the new name Alexandra. Prior to leaving the Kremlin palace Irina gathered a circle of lower-level police and military officials, promising them rewards if they would rouse the residents of Moscow to advocate her brother's ascension to the throne. The same day, Tsaritza Irina/nun Alexandra issued a decree from Novo-Devichi Convent for a full and universal amnesty, to immediately release all prisoners and inmates from all jails in Russia. As with all other decrees, this was the pre-meditated work of Godunov.

Hearing of the tsaritza's vow and departure prelates, officials and the Boyar Duma assembled at the Kremlin on January 9, where Vasili Shelkov presented to them the possible results of anarchy and requested them to swear allegiance to the Boyar Duma, feeling this would secure stability without a supreme ruler. All assembled refused his suggestion, stating that they had already sworn allegiance to Tsaritza Irina, and even if she was a nun they considered her the valid sovereign.

After more discussion and having to accept the fact that the tsaritza was isolated from society and refused the throne and to avoid anarchy, the assembly announced, "Then let her bother reign. Long live Boris Feodorovich. He will be successor to our mother, Tsaritza Irina." The entire assembly streamed out of the Kremlin Palace, out of Moscow and across the Moscow River, the short walking distance to the Novo-Devichi Convent. There Patr. Job admonished Tsaritza Irina in the name of the fatherland to bless her brother as Sovereign, to fulfill both the will of God and the will of the people. Job turned to Godunov and offered him the crown, but he turned down the offer, not having the support he needed among the hereditary princes. Job and the boyars decided to wait and then assemble a Boyar Duma after the requiem for Tsar Feodor to be held 40 days after his death. In this manner, prelates and noblemen from all Russia could arrive in Moscow for the event of an official selection. Godunov wanted all of Russia involved and not just Moscow.

Tsaritza Irina made the right last call to withdraw from both society and politics when she became a widow, to live the balance of her life in quite solitude and contemplation. Perhaps her brother Boris was also involved in this decision, to vacate her presence for him to take total control and also because of her illness. Unknown to others she suffered with tuberculosis. As an orphan, raised by an ambitious uncle, her life was a pattern of circumstances to the political aspirations of others, including father-in-law Tsar Ivan IV needing a submissive and supportive wife for his under-developed son. She had risen as in a fairy-tale: from being an orphan cared for by an uncle, to queen of Russia, and in her case the second most powerful person in Russia for 13 years, next only to her brother Boris, the power behind the throne.

Irina Feodorovna restricted herself to the Novo-Devichi Convent; she had no public or social appearances after the rise of her brother to the throne of Russia. On October 26, 1603, Irina Feodorovna passed away in her cloister at Novo-Devichi Convent, probably from tuberculosis. Six years she lived isolated in her cloister as a voluntarily self-imposed exile from the world and attended only church, but never leaving the premises or showing herself to Russian society. She was buried next to Maria Ivanovna, a sister of her husband Feodor who had passed away in infancy.

Godunov's Effort to become Tsar

Unable to immediately acquire loyalty as the new tsar, Godunov sensed the conflicts and struggle for power in the Boyar Duma and on January 17, went to live at the Novo-Devichi Convent with his sister. While he lived at the convent, the Boyar Duma ruled Russia in the name of Tsaritza Irina. It was obvious that his ascension depended on the support of his sister, the widow-tsaritza and still semi-legitimate queen, as well as Patr. Job, and winning the confidence of the Boyar Duma and the hereditary princes. The kindness and generosity of Godunov to all of Russia was to his benefit and Godunov felt assured that the Duma would incline in his direction, even the hereditary aristocracy. Godunov was right in his suppositions, calculating every move and planning the future carefully.

As a whole, the boyars feared Godunov because of his early career as an Oprichnik and officer in the palace of Tsar Ivan the Terrible. Godunov's ambition to ascend the Russian throne dismayed them. The Suzdal princes and the posterity of Grand Prince Andrei Yaroslavich — the Shuisky, Sitzki, Vorotinsky, Rostovski and Telyatenski clans — and others decided not to intervene with their hereditary right as second in line next to the Moscow princes to the throne of Russia, not having the popular support as did Godunov. The feelings of these families were slighted and they were disappointed with the elevation of someone they considered having an ignoble posterity and Mongol blood as well as having ties to the Oprichnin terrors of Tsar Ivan. Other families took offense at Godunov's ascension to the throne of Russia, calling him a usurper. Such were the Lithuanian princely families: Mstislavski, Golitsyn and Trubetskoy. As a result, the Boyar Duma turned not to Boris Godunov but to Feodor Nikitich Romanov (later named Filaret), son of the late nobleman Nikita Romanov Yuryev-Zakharin and first-cousin of Tsar Feodor, as he most plausible contender to the throne. He was middle aged but still was considered handsome, dashing, kind and very popular and was well-liked by the people and of noble character. The influence and authority that his late father possessed in the

Boyar Duma played in his favor. The unsubstantiated account of Tsar Feodor on his death-bed referring to his cousin as his successor was in their favor. The aristocracy of Russian boyars and princes who refused to recognize Godunov's right to the throne could not themselves conclude on nominating Feodor Romanov. The family was still little experienced in government as large a country as Russia, their capabilities being restrained to their provincial estates, and the Suzdal and Lithuanian princes were not about to relinquish their right to the Romanovs either. (The future tsar Mikhail Romanov was only about three years of age at this time.) Yet these aristocratic families rejected the pretensions of the patriarch to guide the matter of selecting a new tsar, feeling it should be handled by the Duma and not by the clergy.

On February 17, 1598, over 500 prelates, noblemen, and court and state officials gathered for a popular assembly at the Kremlin, the largest legislative assembly of its kind so far in Russian history. Their purpose: to select a new sovereign. Patr. Job, having an obligation to Godunov for installing him as patriarch, gave a speech to route the assembly to nominating Godunov.

> "Russia, grieving without a king, impatiently awaits one from the wisdom of the council. You, prelates, archimandrites, monks; you, boyars, noblemen, state officials, hereditary princes, and all ranks of our capital city Moscow an all the land of Russia, disclose to us your thoughts and give us counsel, whom our next sovereign will be. We, who witnessed the [final] scene of Tsar and Grand Prince Feodor Ivanovich, feel that no one other than Boris Feodorovich should be sought as sovereign."

The entire assembly exclaimed in unison, "Our counsel and desire is the same: we must immediately petition Boris Feodorovich to be monarch and not seek another sovereign for Russia other than him." The excitement erupted into celebration and nothing was to be heard in the building except for the name Boris. The laud of Godunov did not cease during the assembly, as one nobleman addressed to the audience:

> "Our empress Irina Feodorovna and her illustrious brother from childhood matured in the chambers of our great tsar Ivan Vasilyevich and ate at his table. When the tsar felt Irina worthy of being his daughter-in-law, Boris Feodorovich lived with them continually, learning the wisdom that pertains to government rule. Once recognizing the malady of his son, the tsar came to us [boyars] and kindly said, 'Boris, I strive on your behalf as I do for my own son and for my daughter-in-law.' Then he raised three fingers of

his right hand and muttered, 'Behold Feodor, Irina and Boris. You are not my servant, but my son.' During the final moments of his life, reserved for confession, [Tsar] Ivan held Boris Feodorovich next to him as he laid in bed, saying to him, 'To you I disclose my heart. To you I assign my son and daughter[8] and the entire government. Preserve it, or you will answer to God.' Remembering these unforgettable words, Boris Feodorovich cared for the young tsar as the apple of his eye and for our great country."

Other boyars likewise lauded the feats of Godunov, how he stabilized Russia after the Oprichnin and Tsar Ivan's reign of terror, his defeat of the Swedes and the Crimean Mongols, restraining Lithuania from further incursion into Russia, expanding Russia into Siberia, increasing the number of its foreign subjects, magnifying Russia in the eyes of European nations and rulers, bringing peace internally and especially the Kazan region, organizing a regular army, establishing honor in the judicial system, uprooting corruption in provincial governments, and assisting the underprivileged. Patr. Job also appended his speech with the manner Tsar Feodor bequeathed Russia's throne to Godunov, and which was from ancient times predestined by heaven itself. Again voices echoed in the assembly hall, "Long live our sovereign Boris Godunov." Patr. Job again addressed the assembly, "The voice of the people is the voice of God; we will do what is pleasing to the On-high."

By sunrise the following day, February 18, the Uspenski Cathedral in the Kremlin was filled with people praying to God, beseeching him to soften the heart of Godunov so that he accepts the crown, and services were likewise held the mornings of the next two days. On the afternoon of February 20, Patr. Job, prelates and noblemen informed Godunov that he was selected as tsar not just by Moscow, but by all of Russia. Godunov again in a theatrical display of humility refused the throne. On February 21, again services were held in all the Moscow churches, asking God to motivate Godunov to accept the crown. The services lasted through the night.

Arrangements were made by Patr. Job for a great procession of all parishioners for the morning of February 22. At sunrise, the bells of all the churches of Moscow began to ring and the doors of all churches and resident's homes opened. Prelates and a singing choir streamed from

---

8 According to tradition, parents referred to daughter-in-laws as their daughters.

the Kremlin to meet a large crowd at Red Square. Patr. Job held the icon of the Theotokos of Vladimir and another prelate held the icon of the Theotokos of Donskoi as representing Holy Russia. Behind the prelates was a procession of other clergy, state officials, noblemen and residents, including women, children, local rabble and derelicts. The procession streamed to the Novo-Devichi Monastery where the icon of the Theotokos of Smolensk was brought out and followed by Godunov.

As the procession entered the convent, Godunov met Patr. Job and fell on his knees in front of the icon of the Theotokos of Vladimir, Godunov burst into tears and cried aloud, "O Mother of God, what is the reason for this endeavor? Protect, protect me in the shade of your shelter." Job then spoke, "My beloved son, do not allow sorrow to overwhelm you, but believe in providence. This endeavor was accomplished by the Theotokos to display her love towards you, humble yourself before her."

Patr. Job with Godunov and a few officials and prelates and the choir entered a church and there liturgy was performed. Then Job and Godunov went to the cloister of Tsaritza Irina with a couple of select officials as witnesses. In her cloister Job bowed to the floor in front of Godunov. At that moment an official gave a sign to the officials outside for the entire gathering to likewise fall on their knees. The crowd began to shout, "Be our father, Boris Feodorovich." Any person that did not show sufficient emotion was told by an ecclesiastical official to place saliva on his cheeks to emulate tears. In the cloister of the tsaritza-nun, Godunov accepted the offer of Patr. Job and the transfer of royal authority from his sister and in a public display of superficial humility stated, "May your holy will be done, Lord. Direct me on the correct path and do not enter into judgment with your servant. I subject myself to You, fulfilling the desire of the nation."

Rumors spread that Godunov poisoned Tsar Feodor to ascend the throne, and these rumors were active in the background of Godunov to his death. The rumor caused agitation among the residents of Moscow and Godunov's move to the security of a convent may have been the result of an attempt or threat on his life. The Duma took over the government, ruling by law and tradition. The members felt that in the absence of a monarch, it had to the sole responsibility to rule Russia and select a successor. The populace rejected the claims of the Duma and still favored Tsaritza Irina as legitimate sovereign or Godunov, who had gained their confidence.

The Royal Guards — Streltzi — backed Godunov, because he had organized them into a standing army with adequate pay. The government departments, organized by Godunov and packed with his relatives and loyalists, likewise supported Godunov. By February 25, it was apparent that the Boyar Duma could not acquire the support of Moscow's populace with Godunov's supporters surfacing both in the palace and in the streets. Patr. Job was also planning for a procession the next day to Novo-Devichi Convent to retrieve Godunov, figuring his support was now adequate for him to make this move.

On February 26, Godunov entered Moscow from the Novo-Devichi Convent. His supporters did not spare any expense in the celebration of his return to ascend the throne as Russia's next tsar. The streets, walls, and rooftops were congested, girls holding the traditional bread and salt met him as he entered, others gifted him goblets of gold and silver, still others presented furs and jewelry. Godunov gratefully thanked them but refused to accept any of it, except the traditional bread and salt. He told them that Russia's treasuries were already full and that these gifts were best in their own homes. As in earlier years, Godunov was professional at displaying humility and gaining the affection of the people.

Patr. Job met Godunov as he arrived at the Kremlin gates and the procession entered the Uspenski Cathedral. Liturgy was performed and Patr. Job blessed Godunov a second time as Russia's new tsar with wife Maria Grigorievna, son Feodor and daughter Ksenia at his sides. After liturgy Patr. Job raised his hands and said, "We glorify you Lord, for You have not disdained our petition, but heard the wail and plea of Christians, turning their sorrow into joy and gifting us a king, whom we asked for of You day and night with tears." From the Uspenski Cathedral the Godunov family and prelates proceeded to the Arkhangelsk Cathedral, where Godunov fell prostrate at the sepulchers of Tsars Ivan IV and Feodor, as well as venerating the sepulchers of ancient grand princes of Russia: Ivan Danilovich, Alexander Yaroslavich Nevsky, and

Tsar Ivan III. Godunov then went privately to Patr. Job's cloister at Chudovski Monastery, where they met to plan future strategy.

Godunov then announced that he could not leave sister Irina in her sorrow and would have to postpone coronation until after Easter. Godunov said the same in a letter to the Boyar Duma, but informed them that he was taking over administration of the government. He returned to Novo-Devichi Convent. Meanwhile, lower-level state servants were zealously swearing fidelity to Godunov as tsar. None of these events had any effect on state matters as Godunov administered the government, part of the time at his cloister at the convent and the rest at the Duma. People were amazed by his indefatigable endurance, working day and night, while using his grieving sister as the reason for his residence at the convent.

Patr. Job on March 9 held another special liturgy for God to subdue the heart of Godunov for him to take the throne. At the same event, the patriarch instituted February 22 as a holiday to commemorate the day that Godunov accepted the offer to become tsar. The patriarch then proposed that the Estates (Zemski) Duma, which was separate from the Boyar Duma, vow allegiance to Godunov as tsar. The members agreed and announced, "We give our promise to lay down our lives and heads for the tsar, tsaritza and their children." Patr. Job then announced a day for Godunov's next return to Moscow, April 30.

This day belongs to the most celebrated events of all Russian history, but not to the excess of the triumphal entry of Godunov on February 26. At one hour after sunrise, the patriarch and a large retinue of clergy, officials and residents waited at the stone bridge over the Moscow River, near the Church of St. Nikolai Zaraiski. Godunov and his family were in an elegant carriage arriving from the convent. Reaching the bridge, they exited the carriage, he and wife Maria, who was most beautifully dressed, 9-year old Feodor and 16-year old Ksenia, whom eye-witnesses described as angelic beauty. The crowd roared, "You are our sovereign, we are your subjects." The gifts offered them were refused again, except for the traditional bread and salt. During the short walk to the Kremlin, the family walked behind the clergy who carried icons and traditional Russian two-banner vertical flags. At the Uspenski Cathedral Patr. Job hung on Godunov the jewel-embedded cross of Metr. Peter, and again blessed him for the throne. After liturgy Godunov, holding son Feodor by one hand and daughter Ksenia by the other, visited all the churches of the Kremlin, accompanied by prelates and noblemen, and hearing cries of celebration and encouragement from the crowds. The Godunov family moved back into the Kremlin palace, now as the recognized absolute sovereign of Russia, even though the crown was not yet on his head.

During March while at his convent cloister Godunov dispatched a message to the Khan of Crimea with a letter of friendship. But then, on April 1, Godunov was informed that a Mongol warrior was taken captive by some Cossacks in an altercation with a gang of Crimean Mongol raiders. The warrior was interrogated and he disclosed to them the intention of Khan Kasi-Girei to advance toward Moscow with his Horde and 7,000 Turkish Ottoman warriors. Godunov had no doubt in the validity of such unsubstantiated and sensational news and decided not to waste time, but to immediately mobilize his army and move it to the Oka River, the same area where the Russians defeated the Crimean Mongols just a few years earlier. The entire nation rallied around Godunov's request for troops. The main camp would be located at Serpukhov, a left flank at Kashir, the right flank at Aleksin, with more regiments at Kaluga and Kolomna.

More news was received April 20, Don Cossacks captured some Crimean Mongols at Belgorod in Ukraine, who informed them of a massive mobilization or deployment of Crimean Mongols by the Khan and that they were already noticed pursuing Cossacks. Godunov then commanded all to prepare and the military procession departed Moscow May 2, a total of 500,000 to assemble at the designated areas. Along with Godunov were the princes Mstislavski and Shuisky, and Romanov and Belski noblemen, and Godunov's own family, all installed as military leaders of his royal campaign against the Islamic invaders.

On May 10, at the village Kuzminski, two captives were brought to Godunov, a Lithuanian and a Cherkassian, who said they escaped from captivity in the Crimea. They likewise confirmed the report that the Khan and Horde were already progressing toward Moscow. The 500,000 troops gathered in the camps along and south of the Oka River and they waited. Godunov sent spies to Russian cities further south to inform them of his readiness for defense and attack. An entire city of white tents rose in the fields and meadows of the Oka River, and they waited for the enemy to appear. For six weeks they waited with a military mobilization unheard of in Russian history. After no appearance of an enemy princes and soldiers began to doubt in the campaign, and rumors began to circulate that the reports were being fabricated by Godunov in order to artificially war against a non-existent enemy. Instead of hordes of enemy warriors, a peace delegation of Khan Kasi-Girei arrived at the main camp on June 18, accompanied by some Russian soldiers. Immediately Godunov rewarded the soldiers. First they were unable to speak due to amazement and perplexity at the size of the camp and number of warriors, then they related the message that Khan Kasi-Girei wanted eternal peace with Russia, renewing the treaty of a few years earlier. The delegates dined at the Russian camp and returned with Godunov's acceptance of the treaty. Slowly the camp disbanded and officials and soldiers returned to their homes.

In Moscow on July 2, the celebration that greeted Godunov on his return was only comparable to the one held when Tsar Ivan IV returned from the defeat of Kazan in 1552. Patr. Job led the celebration with a speech of gratitude. All the houses of Moscow were covered with leaves and flowers.

Godunov postponed his coronation to September 1, 1598, New Years Day according to the ROC calendar of the era, a day to be indelibly etched in the memory of every resident of Russia. Coincidentally, the patriarch of Constantinople — probably Mathew II — was visiting Moscow at the time, and on the day of coronation Godunov accepted the royal regalia of Vladimir II Monomakh from the hands of the patriarch. After liturgy Godunov spoke, "Father, great patriarch Job. God is my witness, that in my kingdom there will be no orphans, no destitute," and shaking his royal garments added, "I will give my last shirt to my people." No other coronation in Russia's history had such an effect on the imagination and feelings of people. As Godunov left the cathedral Pr. Mstislavski scattered gold coins to the crowd. Godunov in his crown and holding the orb and scepter went to the Kremlin palace to take his place on the throne to legislate decrees to commemorate the occasion: he distributed charity, and granted amnesty and privileges. His loyal supporters — as well as the not-so-loyal — received promotions in the government, while all other state employees received a double salary for that year; foreign merchants received two years free trade without duty, while farmers on state land and Siberia were free from state taxation for a year. Criminals fated for capital punishment had their sentences commuted and freedom gained if they would move to Siberia to colonize new land. All went well for Boris Feodorovich Godunov as the most efficient and effective king that ever ruled Russia until the appearance of Otrepyev six years later. For many in Russia, Godunov on his throne remained the same type of ambitious and power-driven person that he was while during the reign of Tsar Feodor. Yet other people were impressed at his efforts to uproot violence, theft, bootlegging and other crimes and vices from Russian society.

If Boris Feodorovich Godunov was born an heir to the throne of Russia, his name would have excelled them all, past and future. But he was born a subject of the state with a dubious genealogy and with an unrestrained passion for control that was molded into him as an orphan struggling for survival and as a member of the Oprichnin. His efforts restored the nation economically and socially after the brutal reign of Tsar Ivan IV the Terrible, taking over the reins from his brother-in-law Tsar Feodor. But Godunov to his own detriment was not able to defeat temptation whenever malice could be utilized to his advantage. Tsar Boris Godunov's despotic authority and his inevitable capitulation to the manner his mentor Tsar Ivan IV controlled Russia would eventually erase from history the benefits that he provided for his country. Boris Godunov was the best and the worst Russian tsar.

In later years Patr. Job could not speak of the era of Godunov's selection and coronation without bitterness. The patriarch reminisced later in his life that during these months he became depressed and melancholic, and he endured slander, discredit, wailing and tears from the people. Job endured these confrontations contritely, knowing well that the entire installation of Godunov as tsar was a farce in light of Godunov's guilt in the murder of Tsarevich Dmitri and the devastation of Uglich, and in his own selection and ordination as patriarch. In later years, his past would resurrect and haunt him, leading him to confess to his culpability in the crimes against the Nagoi family and Uglich, and he would be shamefully defrocked and face possible execution.

The Engagement of Ksenia Borisovna

During the era of 1598–1604, new cities were created in Russian Siberia: Vertokhurya near Sverdlovsk in the Urals in 1598, Mangazei and Turinsk in 1600, and Tomsk in 1604. Free land was distributed to willing setters to develop and civilize the region. Wars were few, against the Crimean Mongol Khan in 1602, as he invaded the northern part of Ukraine, but the effects were minor. Likewise, altercations were at a minimum between Russia and Poland-Lithuania, with additional treaties concluded in 1601 and 1602.

The marriage of his daughter Ksenia was important to Godunov in terms of increasing his prestige. A beautiful lady, at the age of 20, in 1602, she was the envy of every father in Russia. Godunov sought a European prince in hopes of erasing his own Mongol descent from the memories of people. His first choice was Pr. Gustav of Livonia, but this attempt failed. Next was Count Johan, son of King John III and brother of Christian II, future King of Denmark, Norway and Sweden. An alliance of this type would open for Russia an opportunity to occupy Estonia, which was under the rule of Denmark at the time. A proposal was offered to the father and he was delighted at being in-law to the Tsar of Russia, since by now Godunov's reputation was at its pinnacle. On August 10, 1602, the prospective groom arrived at the port of Narva and was jubilantly greeted by Russian dignitaries. Expensive Russian furs were given as gifts and he was taken to Ivangorod (presently on the border with Estonia), a short distance inland, in a carriage that reflected gold and silver inlaid. There the count was more lavished with gifts and vacationed at the expense of Godunov for a while, and then he began the journey to Moscow at the rate of 20 miles a day, with festivities held every evening and at every city they passed through. By September 19, they were outside Moscow, but he had yet to see his bride.

A parade of both Russian and Danish officials and the residents of Moscow greeted the count on his entry into the city, and he was led to his quarters at one of the finest buildings in the Eastern Quarter. On September 28, the members of the Boyar Duma accompanied the count to the Kremlin Palace Gold Chamber where he met with the tsar dressed in royal regalia to impress and his son Feodor, now age 13. Seeing the count, Tsar Godunov and son rose and hugged him in the traditional Russian manner and set him alongside them. All those attending were captivated by the handsome young man, while Godunov saw another son for his family. They dined in the Granite Chamber, Godunov sitting on a solid gold chair at a solid silver table. After dinner, Godunov and son Feodor gifted the count jewel-embedded chains, while other officials brought even more gifts, but the count had yet to see Ksenia. Chroniclers relate that she was average height, plump and in good proportions as a typical Russian woman, but her skin was milk-white. Her hair was thick, black and long, and she possessed a face that was fresh with red cheeks. Ksenia had a meek character and was well educated, enjoying reading and singing. From a distance Ksenia and mother viewed the prospective groom.

The engagement and wedding were scheduled for early winter. To acquire further success of the prospective marriage, the Godunov family traveled to Troitse-Sergieva Monastery, where they stayed for nine days in prayer at the sepulcher of St. Sergei of Radonezh, so heaven would bless the union of Ksenia and Johan. Meanwhile the count was honored every evening with dinner at his new residence and daily received gifts of furs, linen, blankets, clothing, and silk and velvet cloth. The count began to study the Russian language and the Greek Orthodox faith to be part of the same culture and religion as his wife. Then, on October 16, on the journey home from Sergiev Monastery, word reached Godunov that Johan had become ill. His fever rose and his body became weak. Godunov admonished doctors to waste no time, promising them unheard-of rewards should the count recover from his illness. On October 19, son Feodor visited Johan, and on October 27, Godunov and Patr. Job visited him. The young count could not rise from his bed or speak, and by the following day, it was obvious Johan was close to death. Godunov was desperate, promising to God the release of 4,000 prisoners should Johan regain his health. At six o'clock that evening, Count Johan of Denmark passed away at the age of 20.[9]

---

9 The cause of his death is a matter of conjecture, and include appendicitis or obstruction of the alimentary canal or some disorder related to an unhealthy diet.

As consolation, Godunov opened the state treasury and distributed charity to orphans, widows and other under-privileged. The funeral was November 25, allowing time for family and other dignitaries to arrive from Denmark. The Godunov family rode in a carriage behind the coffin, tearfully crying during the entire procession and services, sorrowful more for the failure of the engagement between daughter Ksenia and a European prince. Visitors from Copenhagen attending the funeral took many gifts back with them, presented by Godunov as a consolation and his gratitude for their attendance.

But this incident did not inhibit Godunov in the least as far as his administration of the government was concerned, and he still planned for a European prince as a husband for his daughter. In early 1604, delegates were sent to Denmark and were able to contact Count Johann of Schleswig, who had a son Philip that Godunov wanted to arrange for Ksenia, but nothing further occurred due to events of greater importance that affected the country.

The Reign of Terror

The initial two years of Godunov's reign, according to chroniclers of the era, were the best of times for Russia since its inception with the rise of Kiev in the 10th century. Russia was at the pinnacle of its might, safety and prosperity with strong leadership, not only in their tsar, but in the Boyar and Estates Dumas. Godunov's goal was to reign without a single drop of blood to be shed for any reason, whether war or capital punishment, preferring peace to battle and exile to execution. The Russian Orthodox Church, now with a native patriarch, was expanding its number of prelates and clergy, building churches and monasteries wherever Russians were residing and especially Siberia. Godunov raised the status of Russia among the European and Asian nations without the need of victory in war or subjection. More than all, Russia loved its sovereign, and did its best to forget the scandal of Tsarevich Dmitri and the devastation of Uglich, or at least doubted Godunov's culpability in the matter. Yet was Godunov content having attained his goal, having risen from orphan-hood to the highest office and supreme authority and greatest personal wealth in the Russian state, even though he had to use coercion, deception, malice, torture and murder to attain his goal?

Yes, but only for a short while. Godunov knew his secret and as a result, after about two years of reign as an effective king, he began to isolate himself from the people. He no longer appeared in public at the traditional events or listened to the complaints of people on an individual basis or personally accepted and granted their petitions. Less and less did he appear in public and society. Godunov sensed that when people looked at him they were looking at the successor of Tsar Ivan's reign of terror, and suspicions of conspiracy materialized in his mind.

Godunov became ill in January 1598, no record states what the illness was, but conjecture is a bleeding ulcer. His health slowly deteriorated. Doctors were unable to help and Godunov regularly called on clergy to pray for him. By the end of 1599, Godunov would not travel outside of Moscow and was confined to Moscow for the most part. By autumn of 1600, many felt that Godunov was near to death, if not dead. To assure the people that he was still alive, Godunov was placed on a stretcher and brought out from the palace and shown to the public. At the end of 1600, a doctor Christofer Richtinger arrived in Moscow from London, and he was able to assist Godunov in his recovery (probably with antacid solutions).

The void in authority during Godunov's illness was filled by the Boyar Duma and especially Feodor Romanov and his brother-in-law Boris Cherkassky and members of their extended families. They also made arrangements to usurp authority from the Godunov family if the tsar should pass away. Young Feodor, age 10, hardly had a chance at ascending the throne should his father die. As a result, a second wave of clandestine terror occurred after Godunov's recovery, against those who conspired for the throne during his illness.

The initial important victim of his phobia was the cousin of his wife, Bogdan Belski, a nephew of Maluta Skuratov and formerly an important figure in the Oprichnin. Godunov never forgot Bodgan's attempt to usurp power in the days following Tsar Ivan's death and whom he had to exile. In 1600, Bogdan Belski was again exiled, and this time to the far north. Bogdan eventually repented of his collusion in the murder of Tsarevich Dmitri, which was one reason for his exile. Bogdan had confessed his role to a priest who relayed the confession to Patr. Job, and who in turn to Godunov. Bogdan was tied to a pole and his beard was pulled out one hair at a time. Not only was the torture painful, but now he also had to face the embarrassment of a Russian without a beard. He was then imprisoned, and not released until mid-1605 by Godunov's son.

Next was the remainder of the Romanov clan, the nephews of Tsar Ivan's first wife Anastasia Romanova. In June 1601, Feodor Nikitich was forced to be tonsured as a monk, receiving the new name Filaret (the future patriarch), and was exiled to Seiski Antoniev Monastery in the far north-east. His wife Ksenia Ivanovna was forced to take a vow as a nun with the new name Marfa and was exiled to a convent near Lake Onega. Ksenia's mother, the noblewoman Shestova, was exiled to the Nikolski Devichi Convent in Chebosar, near Kazan. Sister Alexandrovna Nikitovna was exiled to a small town along the White Sea; brother Mikhail Nikitich to Perm in the Urals; Vasili Nikitich to Yarensk in the far north; brother Alexandr was incarcerated locally. Their brother-in-law Boris Cherkassky with wife and nephew Mikhail Feodorovich Romanov (the future tsar), age six, were exiled to Beloye Ozero, while Ivan the son of Boris Cherkassky to Malmizh in the far north-east. Pr. Ivan Vasilyevich Sitzki was exiled to Kozhe-Ozero Monastery, while the balance of the extended Sitzki family, and the Shestunov, Karpovi and Repnin families were imprisoned in cities distant from Moscow. The estates and property of all the above families were confiscated and appropriated into the state treasury. If this was not enough for Godunov, he sent spies to observe their actions and to report to him if they would say anything about him. The spies also restricted public access to the inmates and exiles. Godunov then moved Vasili Nikitich Romanov to Pelim to be in the same cell as his brother Ivan, who by this time had suffered a stroke and was incapable of moving either his arms or legs, for them to suffer together. Vasili passed away from illness in his prison cell on February 15, 1602. Brothers Alexander and Mikhail Romanov died likewise shortly after. By order of Godunov, Pr. Ivan Sitzki and his wife were strangled to death in their monastery cloister. There were no public executions, Godunov holding to his promise, but his imaginary conspirators were exiled to torture of the elements in distant monasteries and prisons, and languished in the most cruel of conditions until they died in oblivion.

The clandestine terror spread underground: those threatened with torture disclosed the names of noblemen, monks, priests, officials and anyone they could think of to save themselves from the rack or incarceration or exile. Unlike Tsar Ivan, Godunov's tortures were all in private, but just as ruthless and inhumane. By 1604, Russia regretted its earlier loving attitude toward Godunov and subconsciously despised him. His loyal sycophants, spies and hatchet men continued to superficially support him, and also the upper-clergy due to the inescapable obligation of Patr. Job toward his benefactor. The name of Godunov and his wife and children were still lauded in church services, but to deaf parishioners who now recognized him as a covert tyrant. The memories of the murder of Tsarevich Dmitri and the fate of Uglich resurrected in their memories and in their minds they visualized the boy's blood — and the blood of the residents of Uglich — splattered on the royal purple of the sovereign. The people were silent, fearing the presence of spies or betrayal by a Godunov loyalist. They whispered to each other in private about his latest crimes and those of the past, and wondered what next was in store for Russia.

A vicious circle was conceived as a result of Godunov's phobia, and the following situation regularly occurred. Five or six servants or serfs of the estate of a nobleman would clandestinely gather together and conspire against him for personal gain or spite or vengeance. One would approach a Godunov loyalist or spy with a fabricated tale and the rest would testify against the nobleman and verify the account. The nobleman would be arrested and he and his entire family would be exiled to some distant city and his property would be confiscated. The traitors would be rewarded from the proceeds of the estate, while the balance was routed to the state treasury. The other servants of the nobleman who would refuse to testify against him would be arrested, beaten, have their tongues excised, or imprisoned. Those subjected to torture — and the rack was prevalent — died, while others were executed — decapitation a regular method. A cruel manner of death for the most insolent was being tied to a pole as a spit and burned over a fire until cremated. For personal reasons a clergyman would even betray another clergyman to remove him from the church, claiming a conspiracy against Godunov. Priests, monks, friars, sextons, and even the woman who baked the wafers for Eucharist were betrayed as accomplices of a conspiracy. Rabble and riff-raff hoping for monetary compensation offered their services to Godunov to betray someone he sought to eliminate.

Fear of a usurper of the descendents of Alexander Nevsky led Godunov to proscribe princes Mstislavski and Shuisky from marrying, lest their offspring be a threat to the son of Godunov for the throne of Russia.

Tsar Godunov exiled many of his political criminals to the Lithuanian part of Ukraine. Tsar Ivan IV did not hesitate to send criminals and felons there, offering them freedom if they would relocate and develop the area. The tsar also felt that because of their criminal background, they would be more inclined to defend themselves from invaders, and so provide an excellent border guard. Tsar Godunov followed the same procedure, but in his situation those exiled to these regions were the ones he ordered to be arrested as a result of his suspicions of conspiracy, and in the end these individuals ganged together and turned against him during the rise of Otrepyev.

The rise of the Cossacks also posed a threat to the authority of Godunov as tsar. Fugitives fled from central Russia to the south and joined the self-styled militias. Although dissatisfied with the reign of Godunov, they were still disorganized and could not unify into a solid front against Russia's army. Many that joined the Cossacks were crowds of serfs that were expelled from their estates by landowners during the famine. For their own survival and since food was scare many noblemen or landowners felt it to their best interests to rid their estates of serfs so they would not have to feed them, and then after the famine they would demand their return. Others were resettled at the borders to live with the offer of free land. As a result of this combination of displaced serfs, fugitives, rabble, criminals and Cossacks, the northern Ukraine was a steaming kettle of discontent. With the rise of Otrepyev, all of them would rally together and join his cause against Godunov.

The Great Famine

In the spring of 1601, Russia's farmlands were inundated with ten weeks of steady rain, and the entire planting and future harvest was ruined. The grain from the previous harvest was used to sow the fields after the flood subsided, but then an unusual frost descended on central Russia on August 15, destroying everything that had been replanted or that may have survived the rain. Now there was nothing to grow: no more seed remained and it was too late in the season to expect a crop with the cold already arriving the end of September. What food was stored from previous years was sold at 12 to 15 times its regular price.

Godunov, winning the confidence of the people as usual through charity, opened state food supplies in Moscow and other cities. He also ordered, under threat of punishment, the sale of old stored food at inflated prices. Money was also distributed in order for the destitute to buy food. Crowds from the provinces flooded the capital hoping for royal charity for their survival, but the efforts were meager relative to the size of the famine in late 1601. People ate grass and straw to fill their stomachs; horses were butchered, as well as cats and dogs, and carrion was eaten to survive the famine. People conducted themselves worse than vicious animals, refusing to share food with their spouse and children. They stole and then killed for a morsel of bread, and then cannibalism began to be practiced. Hotels became butcher shops: a guest would be trampled or strangled in the night, and be carved up for food and sold in the market place that day. Soldiers would apprehend the criminals, execute them, and cremate them publicly or drown them; but the cruelty and crime continued. People died in the streets, city squares, to the extent that the entirety of Moscow stank from the decay of putrid human corpses. Godunov ordered the burial of all the dead that could be found. Over the course of two years, from mid-1601 to mid-1603, 127,000 corpses were buried by state soldiers, not including those buried by family or those left without burial in the provinces or those cannibalized. One contemporary chronicler estimated that just in Moscow a half-million perished, while more in the provinces from both hunger and cold.

Carts of food brought from areas where a harvest was available were in convoys and heavily guarded by soldiers. It was not until the harvest of summer 1603 that Russia recovered from the famine. But it was only the poorer Russians who suffered the famine. Foreign guests, such as Godunov's prospective son-in-law, the Danish Count Johan, were isolated from the famine's effects and ate and drank at regular dinners in the Kremlin royal palace. The monasteries likewise had food stored for emergencies, which they kept hidden from the general population and so most of the clergy were able to survive. The monasteries and nobles were deaf to the cries of starving peasants and the demands of Godunov as they hid and horded stores of grain for themselves. As a result, people continued to harbor respite and resentment toward Godunov, now convinced that the famine and frost were God's wrath on Russia for the crimes of their sovereign. The prosperity of the reign of Tsar Feodor somehow could not materialize at this time in Tsar Godunov's reign. To compensate the serfs due to their suffering at the hands of their landowners Godunov issued an edict August 16, 1603, liberating all serfs who were deprived of sustenance by their landowners during the famine. Many of these took advantage of the opportunity and fled to the border areas along Lithuania: Chernigov and Severski in western Ukraine. They would later join Otrepyev against Godunov.

Repercussions from the abolition of the provisions of Yuryev Day in the law of 1597 began after the end of the famine, as many serfs had fled or died, and landowners imposed their authority and coercion to stop any further departure of serfs from their estates. Chroniclers relate that financial and moral corruption was widespread after recovery from the famine: immorality, bribery, avarice and a general lack of empathy for the suffering, including family and close associates, plagued Russia. The Russian people lost its respect for the clergy due to alcoholism and moral perversion rampant in the monasteries and the opulent life of the prelates at the expense of charity and contributions. A portent interpreted as a premonition of horrible events to next affect them after the famine was the comet of 1604, which was seen even on a clear day.

5. The Rise of False Dmitri I

Early Life of Otrepyev

False Dmitri I was Yuri Bogdanovich Otrepyev, the grandson of a boyar from Galitzia, Yakov Zamyatni Otrepyev, who had migrated to Moscow. One chronicler states that grandfather Yakov in his later years was a monk at the Kremlin Chudovski Monastery. False Dmitri's father was Bodgan Otrepyev, a royal guard in the palace of Tsar Feodor. During a street fight in Moscow, father Bogdan was killed by a drunk Lithuanian soldier stationed in the German quarter. Yuri was able to serve as a lower-level official in the Moscow offices and homes of the Romanovs and at Pr. Boris Cherkassky's, where he acquired a good education. As a result, Otrepyev was on the list of Tsar Godunov's suspicious characters. An uncle, Nikita Smirni Otrepyev, was an official in the court of Tsar Godunov. During the serious illness of Tsar Godunov, Otrepyev hoped for a promotion in the event that one of the Romanovs would ascend to the throne. Due to palace politics and the threat of his own welfare during the era of betrayals, and probably at the time of the arrest and exile of the Romanov clan, Otrepyev was tonsured as a monk by Bishop Trifon of Vyatka, becoming monk Grigori. It was a manner of escaping becoming another victim of Godunov's suspicions.

His tonsure began an era of treks across Russia as a mendicant monk, residing in Suzdal at the Monastery of Spasso-Evfimiev, then appearing at the Monastery of St John the Baptist in Galitzia, and at the Boris and Gleb Monastery in Murom, and then back in Moscow, now at the Chudovski Monastery, at his grandfather's old cloister.

Patr. Job took notice of monk Grigori and ordained him as a deacon to take advantage of his education to copy ecclesiastical literature. Often Grigori accompanied Job to the palace, where again he was exposed to palace intrigues and secrets and gossip and Tsar Godunov's suspicions, and no doubt much dealing with the murder of Tsarevich Dmitri. On several occasions, monk Grigori told other monks at Chudovski, "Do you know that I will be king in Russia?" Some laughed, others developed contempt for him. His comments reached the ears of Metr. Jonah of Rostov who relayed them to Patr. Job and Tsar Godunov. Job discarded the rumors as superfluous, while Godunov suspected monk Grigori as a contender. The tsar ordered a palace official named Smirnov Vasilyev to take monk Grigori into custody and have him exiled to Solovetski Monastery in the White Sea or to Bel-Ozersk Monastery for permanent penitence, accusing him of heresy. Vasilyev then entrusted the matter to another official named Semeik Efimyev, who happened to be a close associate of monk Grigori from their earlier years in the palace before Otrepyev became a monk, or a brother-in-law according to another account. In February 1602 (the only reliable date of Otrepyev's early history) and after a year at Chudovski, monk Grigori took the advice of Semeik to flee Moscow, taking with him Varlaam, a monk from Borovski Monastery and monk Misail Povagin. The three vagrant mendicants traveled first to Novgorod Spasski Monastery. After a short stay another monk Pimen joined them and they journeyed to the Kiev Pecher Monastery.

A timeline can be determined at this point: Yuri Otrepyev accepting tonsure as monk Grigori in late 1600, about the time of Godunov's vengeance toward the Romanov's after his recovery from illness, and then moving into Chudovski after a few months as a mendicant monk. Otrepyev was about 30 or 32 years of age in 1602, some 10 years older than Tsarevich Dmitri would have been.

After their departure from Novgorod, the monastery archimandrite found a note in the cloister with the words, "I am Tsarevich Dmitri, son of Ivan, and I will not forget your hospitality when I sit on my father's throne." Nothing was said of this until Otrepyev began his invasion.

In Kiev, monks Grigori, Varlaam and Misail resided at Pecher, Nikolski and Derman Monasteries, but only a few weeks at each place. Here he would relate rumors of Tsarevich Dmitri's escape from murder and his refuge from Tsar Godunov in Lithuania. During monk Grigori's stay at monasteries, he would fulfill his role as a deacon during liturgy, but ignored the rules of abstinence and prudence. He would boast of freedom of thought, loved to debate the law of God with members of other religions, and even associated with Anabaptists in western Ukraine where he stayed some considerable amount of time. The three then traveled to Ostrog in Lithuania where monk Grigori separated from his companions and routed his life in a different direction. There he removed his monk's frock and identified himself as Grigori Otrepyev, a layman. He joined one of the many Cossack bands of raiders, this one with Gerasim Evangelik at the head, and learned horsemanship and how to fight using a sword. As a Zaporozhski Cossack raider, Otrepyev learned how to protect himself in the face of danger and acquired experience in raiding towns and living in the wild. The next time chroniclers relate his location is at a school at the peaceful city Gaschi in Lithuanian Volyn, learning to read and write Polish and Latin. Completing his education sometime in late 1603, Otrepyev move to the city Bragin, in Poland, and joined the service of Pr. Adam Vishnevetzki (Wisniowiecki), son-in-law of Yuri Mnishek (Jerzy Mniszech) and a prominent and wealthy nobleman and landowner and part of the Polish State Duma.

Having gained the attention and consideration of his employer Pr. Vishnevetzki, Otrepyev feigned illness and requested the presence of a Catholic priest for confession. Otrepyev told him, "I am dying. Deliver my body to the ground in honor, just as the offspring of kings are buried. I will not unveil my secret to you until I reach the grave. When I close my eyes forever you will find under my bed a letter that will tell you all, but do not relate it to others. God has destined me to die in misfortune."

At this moment monk Grigori Otrepyev evolved into a False Dmitri.

The priest was a Jesuit and immediately informed Pr. Vishnevetzki of the confession and secret, and the prince hurried to Otrepyev's bedside. The prince had the bed searched and found the letter — written and placed there earlier — and read it. The letter stated that his new servant was Tsarevich Dmitri Ivanovich, saved from death by a competent doctor. The criminals that were dispatched to Uglich had killed another boy, a son of a local priest, in place of him when his murder failed. Noblemen and the official Schelkalov had hid him and accompanied him to Lithuania as Tsar Ivan had told them to do if the boy's life was in danger. As proof, Otrepyev had in his possession a gold and jewel-encrusted cross that he claimed was given to him by his god-father Pr. Ivan Mstislavski. He was wearing the cross under his clothes, which he showed to Pr. Vishnevetzki and the Jesuit priest.

The Polish prince was in ecstasy, and called in the best of doctors to help Otrepyev recover from his feigned illness. In just a short time, Vishnevetzki granted Otrepyev an elegant residence at his estate, servants, new clothing, and he did not hesitate to advertise to all of Poland the miraculous deliverance of Tsarevich Dmitri Ivanovich. Two other important figures in Polish nobility, Konstantine, the brother of Adam Vishnevetzki, and Yuri Mnishek, Adam's father-in-law and military commander of central Poland and a prominent Polish statesman, took special consideration in the fate of such a famous Russian refugee, apparently accepting all the evidence at face value. Two witnesses testified to the validity of Otrepyev's claims. One was Petrovski, a fugitive thief who was a servant of Lev Sapega and living at the time at the Vishnevetzki estate. He claimed that Otrepyev possessed certain distinguishing physical traits of Tsarevich Dmitri, which were heretofore unknown to anyone: warts on his face and one arm shorter than the other (although this was fabricated and not the case with Tsarevich Dmitri). The second was a serf of Mnishek's estate who had been a captive in Russia during the reign of Tsar Ivan and may have seen the child at the age of two or three in Uglich. Vishnevetzki reported all the above to King Sigismund, verifying Otrepyev's claim that he was heir to the throne of his brother Tsar Feodor Ivanovich.

The king replied, expressing his desire to visit Otrepyev in person, having doubts since so many pretenders had been resurrected over the years since the murder. Papal Nuncio to Poland Claudio Rangoni and zealous Jesuits convinced Sigismund of the valuable and significant results for Poland should this really be Tsarevich Dmitri. What could not have been better for either Rome or Poland? Both had everything to gain and nothing to lose, whether their claims was valid or not. This is the reason why the Polish King and Papal nuncio easily accepted the validity of his claim and the testimony of the witnesses. They were not thinking in terms of the truth of the matter — was he or was he not — but of Otrepyev's use to them to defeat Russia militarily and ecclesiastically. The fantasy of such a feat captivated their minds.

Otrepyev agreed to his conversion to Roman Catholicism, meaning Unia or Eastern Rite Catholicism, and promised the same for Russia should he ascend the throne. Rangoni visited Otrepyev and on April 17, 1604, Otrepyev converted to Roman Catholicism. Rangoni then urged Otrepyev to travel to Krakow; he consented and together with Vishnevetzki and Mnishek went to visit King Sigismund in spring of 1604. The king met Otrepyev at the palace along with many officials and princes of Poland. After taking a close look at Otrepyev Sigismund exclaimed that he did resemble his father Tsar Ivan IV and that all testimony confirmed that he was Tsarevich Dmitri. During the course of the conversation Otrepyev requested some monetary assistance for his future, since for all practical purposes he was destitute. Sigismund offered Otrepyev 40,000 gold ducats a year to cover his expenses.

The conversation lasted a while longer and then Rangoni took Otrepyev to the residence of Mnishek, who urged Otrepyev to act quickly with an invasion of Russia to appropriate the throne from Godunov. While visiting, Otrepyev was captivated by Mnishek's older daughter Marina (the younger was married to Konstantine Vishnevetzki). It was love at first sight (at least, according to Alexander Pushkin's novel). The idea of his son-in-law being tsar of Russia and having the country at his feet exhilarated Mnishek; this was a business venture that was worth the investment. A contract was signed May 25, 1604, Otrepyev promising to marry Marina and promising to deliver to his future father-in-law one million gold ducats plus expenses from the Moscow state treasury. Otrepyev would also present to his wife the provinces of Novgorod and Pskov as her dowry. On June 12, 1604, the contract was emended, adding a provision for Otrepyev to deliver to Mnishek the provinces of Smolensk and Severski (northwest Ukraine) also. All of this was contingent upon Mnishek, as military commander of Poland, subsidizing an invasion of Russia and providing Polish troops. For Poland, it was worth the gamble.

Marina Mnishek was not considered pretty or attractive. Artists trying to paint her portrait worked tediously to improve her looks without making her look like someone else. She had thin lips, an exceptionally long nose, narrow face, and thin black hair, a feeble physique and small body. She did have — like her father — a dominating personality with a tomboy inclination. Even wearing the finest of royal wardrobes, she had little femininity to display.

Who Actually Was False Dmitri I

Yuri Otrepyev would not have been considered handsome. He had red hair, wide shoulders, below average height, a round pale-white face, blue eyes, and a wart on his forehead and under his right eye, not to mention that one arm was shorter than the other. Some noticed that he was clumsy. However, Otrepyev overcame his physical flaws with his diligent thinking and clever mind, his eloquence — in Russian, Polish and Latin — and his ability to carry himself in a noble and dignified manner.

The sensational and fabricated accounts of what supposedly occurred to Tsarevich Dmitri during the interim between his survival from death and public disclosure varied among the rumors dispersed in the Russian population. Some relate that he found refuge fleeing to Ukraine to his godfather, Pr. Ivan Mstislavski, as a self-imposed exile for his survival as long as Godunov was alive. After the death of Mstislavski, Tsarevich Dmitri supposedly migrated to Poland, where he remained until adulthood and his decision to disclose himself. The flaw in this account is that no Pr. Ivan Mstislavski resided in Ukraine. The pectoral cross that Otrepyev wore and provided as testimony could have been purchased at any Russian Orthodox cathedral or stolen from any important figure, clerical or secular.

How Tsarevich Dmitri was supposedly saved from his murder was likewise unclear. For some, a doctor cared for his wounds and another child that passed away was substituted by the murderers to cover their failure. Another account is that the wrong child was killed during the night (even though the murder was in broad daylight), and the real Tsarevich Dmitri fled that night for his survival in case of another attempt. Otrepyev's own account was that he was wounded and survived, and then later another child was killed by the perpetrators to cover for the failed attempt. Or that Tsarevich Dmitri became aware of a plot to kill him, and when another child killed himself in an epileptic seizure, Tsarevich Dmitri took advantage of the incident to flee the country to save himself from the plot.

Of course the differences between the genuine Tsarevich Dmitri and Otrepyev, as many and as flagrant as they were and noticed by those who knew the real Tsarevich Dmitri after seeing Otrepyev, were not important. Actually, there were no similarities in any respect between the two. Otrepyev had no physical characteristics or resemblances that a person could notice to identify him with either the Nagoi or Tsar Ivan's families. The real Tsarevich Dmitri was 10 years younger than Otrepyev to begin with, but the excuse was that the hard life of refuge and survival took its toll on his physical appearance. Those who were closest to the real Tsarevich Dmitri, such as Bussov and Ivan Basmanov, more than others affirmed the credibility of Otrepyev and the validity of his account of the interim period.

But whether the case can be one or the other of the manner of his purported survival, the greater question is what prompted this person to declare himself Tsarevich Dmitri Ivanovich, heir to the Russian throne, and actually expected it to be granted him, even in the face of Tsar Godunov and the entire Russian nation. Parallel with this quandary is the dilemma whether he decided to undertake this venture on his own free volition, or did another persuade him to do this, and also, did he consciously accept the role as Tsarevich Dmitri and deceive himself to the point that he actually believed it, or did he know all along that he was a pretender and imposter and that the entire endeavor was nothing more than a farce on the people of Russia, Ukraine, Poland and Lithuania.

Otrepyev had self-confidence beyond any of his era. Any that dealt with him were impressed by his passion for attaining the throne of Russia, and no one could not be impressed by his integrity. His right to the throne was noticeable and he was absolutely assured of its proprietorship, referring to himself. When Otrepyev entered Moscow July 18, 1605, he summoned the Boyar Duma to inform them of his usurpation of the throne of Russia. When the crowds asked him to provide testimony, all he replied was, "Ask my mother." The widow-tsaritza Marina Alexandrovna Nagoi knew better, but for her it was the opportunity to be released from captivity imposed by Godunov and take vengeance on the enemies of her family, the Godunov loyalists especially. So much was Otrepyev's self-confidence that when he ascended the throne, he never bothered to satisfy the curiosity of people regarding his whereabouts the years of his survival: 10 years between the murder of Tsarevich Dmitri and the disclosure of his identity in 1602. It was executive privilege, but he knew that any word said would be to his detriment, and what he did say was meager and shallow, only his deliverance by certain noblemen — and he no longer remembered who they were — and his refuge outside of Russia.

More questions arise. Who promoted Otrepyev; who believed that he was actually Tsarevich Dmitri; and to what advantage was it to them to believe and promote it? It was to the benefit of Poland, whose officials supported him. But who initiated the fraud? Not King Sigismund, because he was too cautious a figure to accept such a surprise from an arbitrary mendicant monk having no credentials. For Yuri Mnishek it was a military venture at the expense of Otrepyev and his makeshift army and the opportunity for someone to marry his homely daughter. The most likely person was Lev Sapega, a Lithuanian chancellor. He visited Moscow twice: once during Tsar Feodor's reign; the second time during Tsar Godunov's reign. When Sapega returned from the second visit, he harbored resentment and bitterness toward Godunov. When Otrepyev or the imposter — as he was referred to by those who knew him to be an imposter — appeared at the home of Adam Vishnevetzki, a fugitive from Moscow named Petrovski recognized him to be Tsarevich Dmitri. As Petrovski was a servant of Lev Sapega working for the prince, suddenly Sapega became a strong proponent of King

Sigismund's plans against Moscow and the support of Otrepyev as a manner of penetrating into Russia. There is more basis to suspect Papal Nuncio Claudio Rangoni and the Jesuits of Poland, who had considerable power in the Uniate Church of the region. Their support of Otrepyev would provide a means of introducing Roman Catholicism into Russia and usurping Greek Orthodoxy.

Russian chroniclers relate that Otrepyev was a native Russian and well educated, having a mastery of speaking the Russian language of the Moscow region, and he was able to write well, while knowing little Latin, if any at all. Tsars Godunov, Shuisky and Mikhail Romanov all accused Poland of destroying the Russian government by supporting a native Moskvich (as residents of Moscow are referred to in Russian) as a pretender. If the Russian royalty had the slightest evidence that False Dmitri was Polish, no doubt they would have accused Poland of having one of their aristocrats pose as an imposter and sent him into Russia to usurp the throne (as with False Dmitri II who was a Pole). The Jesuits who promoted Otrepyev also recognized him as a native Moskvich, because of his conversion from Greek Orthodoxy to Roman Catholicism.

Godunov accused the boyars of arranging the resurrection of Tsarevich Dmitri in order to dethrone him, all of them well aware that he was an imposter. Whether the boyars actually did this is disputable because they hardly would have permitted Poland — the perennial enemy of Russia — to finance and create an army and subsequently invade Russia and attempt to convert Russia to Unia. Most of the witness testifies that the idea that Otrepyev could pass himself off as Tsarevich Dmitri originated in Moscow, and that Otrepyev knew while he was still there that he could acquire the support of boyars, although only indirectly, because their goal was to overthrow Tsar Godunov using some third party, but not to elevate the third party. This is why eventually Otrepyev's supporters among the Russian aristocracy turned against him after he became tsar: he was a means to their end. The boyars discarded Otrepyev after the government was stabilized with Tsar Godunov gone and once the evidence presented to the population made it apparent to them that their new tsar — Grigori Otrepyev — was a fraud.

The accounts remaining from Polish chroniclers state that after Tsarevich Dmitri's supposed deliverance from the attempted murder, he was raised in seclusion by some boyars and then was a monk to secure his safety and secret until the time was ready for his discloser to the nation. Another account that circulated was that False Dmitri I was an illegitimate son of Stephan Batori, and he exchanged identities with Grigori Otrepyev when he arrived in Poland from Russia, and then evolved into a False Dmitri. This was the reason for the physical attributes of Otrepyev, hardly appearing as a Russian, as well as his fluency in the matter of Polish government and Roman Catholicism, and the Polish and Latin languages. His skill of horsemanship and military campaigning would have been part of his accrued skills as a son of a monarch, even though illegitimate. Of course, King Sigismund would definitely support an illegitimate Batori posing as Tsarevich Dmitri in order to make inroads into Russia. However the evidence for this final postulation is meager and conjecture at most; its loss of credibility is primarily due to Otrepyev's fear of recognition at Chudovski Monastery and by his relatives, which would not bother a Batori son. Even though every candidate has unanswerable questions relating to their validity as False Dmitri I, this reason probably lies in the inaccuracy of the available documented history compiled by early Russian chroniclers. This history will treat False Dmitri as Grigori Otrepyev, he having the most viable and substantial evidence of all the presumptions.

Beginning of the Polish Invasion

Mnishek assembled for Otrepyev 1,600 men of all ranks from various Polish provinces, most of them volunteers. They joined the makeshift army for a heterogeneous assortment of reasons: riff-raff who sought dignity in defending Tsarevich Dmitri; vagrants and destitute attracted by the enticement of reward; mercenaries seeking excitement; fugitives from Russia, having found the opportunity to take vengeance on Tsar Godunov; Don Cossacks who were suppressed by Tsar Godunov; the bored seeking adventure, and the curious. Ivan Boroshin and 10 or 15 of his retinue that migrated to Lithuania to flee Godunov's reign of terror fell at the feet of Otrepyev and offered their services as his first all-Russian regiment.

Before the army left Poland it grew to 4,000 and Mnishek assigned a weapon to each person. Did they all believe that Otrepyev was who he said he was? Maybe and maybe not. But they all had a reason to join his campaign. Others opposed the venture, knowing that it was a scam on the part of Otrepyev. Not all the displaced and fugitive Russians residing in Eastern Europe joined or supported the campaign. Yakov Pikhachov publicly and right in the presence of King Sigismund denounced the entire venture as a fraud. He said he had discovered the whereabouts of monk Varlaam and had brought him to Krakow to testify. Varlaam offered his testimony because his conscience bothered him, knowing False Dmitri was monk Grigori. Sigismund had both men taken into custody and transferred to Mnishek's military headquarters. He imprisoned Varlaam, while Pikhachov was convicted of conspiring to kill Otrepyev and was executed.

Otrepyev, knowing the character of the Don Cossacks, sent a Lithuanian delegate Svirski with an announcement, which stated that he was the genuine son of Tsar Ivan IV Vasilyevich to whom Christian knights had sworn fidelity, and now he was summoning them to overthrow the criminal and pretender Godunov from the throne of Russia. Two Cossack Atamans, Andrei Koreland and Mikhailo Nezhakozh, hurried to see Otrepyev in person. Cossacks remembered their oppression by Godunov and rushed to join the campaign. If this was not enough, monk Leonid, who earlier accompanied Otrepyev on his migration as a mendicant monk, now assumed the name of Grigori Otrepyev. Leonid could now testify he was monk Grigori so no challenger could attribute the name to False Dmitri.

Loyal messengers of Otrepyev rode on horseback to cities and villages and along the roads of south-west Russia and Ukraine distributing leaflets to Russians, stating that Tsarevich Dmitri was alive and soon to appear to them. The population was amazed as well as perplexed; should they believe or not? But for those living in the border areas, displaced there by Tsar Ivan or Godunov, now their opportunity arose to take vengeance. A new loyalist of Otrepyev, Mikhailo Ratomski, summoned supporters to Kiev to gather there before departing as a unified regiment to meet with the balance of Otrepyev's makeshift army. Many of the Zaporozhski Cossacks — with whom Otrepyev lived learning to fight and survive — joined the campaign.

Before Otrepyev arrived in Lithuania, the rumors he spread in Ukraine that Tsarevich Dmitri was alive and soon to appear reached the ears of Tsar Godunov. In January 1604, Narva official Tirfeld wrote to the Abo city military commander that Tsarevich Dmitri was living among Cossacks. About the same time, news arrived from Lithuania and from Russian commanders in Ukraine about the appearance of Tsarevich Dmitri. Also at the same time, Don Cossacks residing in the lower Volga had attacked and killed Semeon Godunov, a cousin of the tsar who was assigned the post of military governor of Astrakhan. Royal guards at his command post were sent to Moscow with the following message, "Tell Boris that we will soon arrive in the company of Tsarevich Dmitri."

Tsar Godunov, receiving the regular and many reports became agitated and confused. But the more frightened he became, the more fearless he appeared in public. He had no doubt in the murder of Tsarevich Dmitri and so dispatched spies to Lithuania and inquired of new conspiracies against him in Russia. Again he suspected boyars and ordered the widow-tsaritza Marina Nagoi — mother of Tsarevich Dmitri — to Moscow, and she was housed at the Novo-Devichi Convent. Godunov, his wife and Patr. Job visited her and interrogated her, asking her if she was part of this latest conspiracy against him. The widow knew nothing, she claimed. At that moment Godunov's wife took a lamp and thrust it at the widow to burn her eyes or at least her face, but Godunov jumped between the two of them to protect the widow. The widow then admitted that she heard the same rumors as did Godunov, but nothing more. Marina was returned to Nikolai-Viksinski Convent to remove her from public access in case she should say something not to the benefit of Tsar Godunov.

Spies returned to Moscow with the information that Tsarevich Dmitri was actually monk Grigori and former palace aide Yuri Otrepyev whom Godunov had ordered to be exiled to Bel-Ozersk Monastery. Semeik Efimyev was ordered to appear before the tsar. The official was torpid in Godunov's presence and could not answer why he did not obey the tsar's order to exile Otrepyev. Godunov ordered his execution:

he was stretched across a rack and soldiers with their swords hacked his body apart.

Tsar Godunov's Attempt to Suppress the Invasion

Tsar Godunov doubled the size of Russia's guards and troops on the Polish border, hoping to stop any intrusion of either persons or news dealing with Otrepyev. At the same time he realized that silence was not in his best interest as the rumor of Russia's legitimate tsar to return and assume the throne was growing among the population. Godunov then explained the history of the fugitive to the people of Moscow and provided the testimony of monks Pimen and Venedict, a layman Yaroslavetz and an icon painter Stepan. Their testimony was cohesive and clear: Tsarevich Dmitri was monk Grigori, whom they personally knew and traveled with and watched his metamorphosis from palace aide to monk to pseudo king. Such testimony, as truthful and accurate as it was, did not convince the people to abandon their hope in Otrepyev. The variations in the accounts of Tsarevich Dmitri's death that now surfaced did not make matters better. Some said that the murder occurred in 1588, and that he was buried in the Cathedral of the Theotokos, while another account was that the year was 1591 and his body was at the Cathedral of the Holy Savior (Spasski), and there is no church in Uglich with the name Theotokos. Other accounts dated the death 13 or 14 years ago, and none of these rumors were of benefit to Godunov. More rumors circulated: that Tsar Godunov killed his sister Irina, meaning that she did not die of natural causes, and that Godunov was planning to flee to Persia for his safety.

The people of Russia were aware of how unconscionable Pr. Vasili Shuisky was, and the blind devotion of Patr. Job to Godunov. They would hear of the widow-tsaritza Marina Nagoi, mother of Tsarevich Dmitri, but no one had seen her since she was force to become a nun and confined at Nikolai-Viksinski Convent, but now she was temporarily residing at Novo-Devichi Convent. Russians of the provinces, even though they did not have a thorough understanding of the fraud, but loving the tradition of the ancient posterity of the Russian hereditary grand princes and tsars, and listening to fabricated tales of the benevolent deeds of Otrepyev, told their thoughts to each other in secret, that possibly God did actually miraculously deliver Tsarevich Dmitri Ivanovich from the malicious tyrant and usurper to the throne Boris Godunov. Many at least doubted the support of their rulers for Godunov and as a result their own support became marginal. There were also a few Russians that continued to support Godunov, even though they held contempt for him because they felt that treachery and mutiny were not a solution.

What stirred up Poles to further accept the validity of Otrepyev was the increase of Russian troops along the border with Poland, and the distribution of leaflets from Godunov's loyalists stating that even if this was Tsarevich Dmitri he was illegitimate, since Marina was the 6th or 7th wife of Tsar Ivan. But this was a moot point as far as the Poles were concerned, since they were Uniate and not Orthodox and saw no illegitimacy in any of Tsar Ivan's offspring, regardless of his polygamy.

Tsar Godunov became desperate. He dispatched to Poland the uncle of Grigori Otrepyev, Smirni Otrepyev. On his return he mentioned in his reports nothing about Otrepyev, only complaints of Poles and Lithuanians regarding their difficulties at the border areas with the increase in guards. Then Godunov dispatched another official, Posnik Ogarev, with an account of Otrepyev's history in Russia and a demand for King Sigismund to execute him. The Polish King told the official what he wanted to hear just to get rid of him, that Otrepyev was not receiving any subsidy from the Polish government and that any of his supporters would be punished.

Patr. Job dispatched Afanasi Patchikov to Pr. Ostrozhski, to beg him not to assist Otrepyev. The prince sent Patchikov back to Russia without responding to his request. Then Patr. Job sent Andrei Bunakov to the metropolitan of the Polish Uniate Church, for them not to provide assistance for the invasion. Bunakov was restrained by Polish troops at Orsha, the Russian-Polish border, and he eventually returned to Moscow, his mission having failed.

By August 15, 1604, Otrepyev and his makeshift army had gathered at the banks of the Dnepr River and by August 17, they were at Sokolnik, near Chernigov.

Wherever Otrepyev stepped, he distributed leaflets declaring to Russians that he was Tsarevich Dmitri, saved by the providence of God

from the knife of Tsar Boris Godunov, that he was hid in some unde-
termined place all this time until placed back on the Russian theater
as a valiant warrior; that now he hurries to Moscow to acquire what
belongs to him, the legacy of his forefathers: the crown and scepter of
Vladimir Monomakh. Otrepyev tried to convince them to abandon the
corrupt Godunov and serve him as the legitimate sovereign. Otrepyev
promised peace, calm, prosperity, which he claimed they would not acquire during the reign of Godunov. Simultaneously, in the name of King
Sigismund, nobles asserted their confidence in the matter and provided
their testimony — including eyewitnesses — that this was Tsarevich
Dmitri and they recognized him as legitimate tsar of Russia. Such leaflets accomplished their goal. Mnishek and Vishnevetzki on their own
initiative distributed money to Russians and impressed on them a cog-
nizance of their dissatisfaction with the reign of Godunov, so taking
advantage of many easily-manipulative minds.

City governors loyal to Godunov could not curb the distribution of
these leaflets, and more were printed as fast as they could be gathered
and burned by Godunov loyalists. Secret meetings were held between
Otrepyev and the residents of Ukrainian and border cities where his
supporters acted zealously informing the population that their oath
of allegiance to Tsar Godunov was invalid since he was a usurper to
the throne and were deceived by him, telling everyone that Tsarevich
Dmitri was dead. Otrepyev's agents told residents that Godunov knew
all along that Tsarevich Dmitri was still alive and that Godunov had
now gone insane from fear of the inevitable, which he could not have
foreseen. Others informed the people that Godunov was planning to
welcome Otrepyev on his return to Moscow, having waiting for his reappearance some 10 years. People believed it for one reason or another,
or did not know what to believe and were swept away in the excitement. A portion of the noblemen attempted to be neutral, waiting for
further development of events.

On the east side of the Dnepr River, Otrepyev divided his forces.
A smaller half he directed east to Belgorod, while the larger half he led
personally north along the Desna River, which flows through Bryansk.
Otrepyev had no lack of navigators or guides to accompany him north.
On October 16, the army of Otrepyev with Don and Zaporozhski Cos-

sacks crossed into Russia. Only now did Godunov start preparations for a military encounter, sending more troops to forts located near the borders of Ukraine. Noblemen again became military commanders. Princes Dmitri Shuisky, Ivan Godunov and Mikhail Glebovich Saltykov were sent to Bryansk to assemble an army there.

On October 18, Otrepyev acquired his first victory in Russia: the residents and soldiers of the city Moravsk abandoned Godunov and pledged allegiance to Otrepyev, greeting him with bread and salt. The residents took the military governor into custody, tied and handed him to Otrepyev, who took advantage of the situation and freed the governor, stating that it was because of Godunov's deceit that he had allegiance to him. From the Polish border to the city limit of Moscow, Otrepyev gratified the hopes of the people with his personal appearance and his conversations with them (perhaps he learned how to gain the favor of people from Godunov while in his early years at the Kremlin palace). He displayed royal dignity and impressed all he met with the self-confidence of a person destined to be king. The city Olgovich followed the example of Moravsk. On October 26, the famous city of ancient Kievan Russ, Chernigov, accepted Otrepyev. Soldiers and residents greeted him with bread and salt and they handed to him their military governor, Pr. Ivan Andreevich Tatev, who secretly disdained Godunov. Otrepyev likewise freed Tatev, who joined his army. A small regiment of loyal soldiers were left at Chernigov as Otrepyev then hurried to Novgorod Severski[10]. His intent was to be a bloodless victor, to be able to defeat the cities and countryside of Russia along the Desna River and its tributaries north, and without even one casualty. A victory gained from a bloodless war. As Otrepyev traveled north, crowds would be on their knees shouting to him, "Long live our sovereign, Dmitri Ivanovich."

About this time, Otrepyev wrote the following letter to Tsar Godunov.

> It is a pity for you to defile your soul created in the image of God, and now as a result of your obstinacy you are preparing its ruin. It would have been better for you Boris to enjoy what God has

---

10 Presently part of Ukraine, and not to be confused with either the ancient city of Novgorod in northern Russia (also called Velikiy Novgorod) or Nizhniy-Novgorod (Nizhi-Gorod), known during the Soviet era as Gorki.

given you, but you in your opposition to the will of God and with the help of the devil have stolen from me the state. Your sister — the wife of my brother — acquired for you the rule over the entire government, and you took advantage of the situation — my brother for the most part involved in religious service to God — and you deprived certain powerful figures of their life for various reasons, such as the Shuisky princes Ivan and Andrei, and then the best citizens of our capital, and people who were associated with the Shuisky family, and King Semeon [Bekbulatovich] you blinded and his son Ivan you poisoned. You did not even spare the clergy: metropolitan Dionysi you exiled to a monastery, telling my brother Feodor that he suddenly died, but I know that he to this time is alive and that you made his fate easier after the death of my brother. You also destroyed others, whose names I no longer remember, because at the time I was very young. But although I was young, do you remember how many times in directives I reminded you not to destroy my subjects? Do you remember how you dispatched your loyalist Andrei Kleshnin, and who there treated us unkindly because of your intimidation of him? You did not enjoy this at all because I was the obstacle to your attainment of the throne. Now after killing officials you began to sharpen the sword also for me, preparing your officials Mikhail Bityagovski and Nikita Kachalov and Osip Volokhov to kill me. You thought I was alone with them, but also my doctor Semeon was there, and because of his effort I was saved from the death that you prepared for me. You told my brother that I killed myself during an epileptic seizure. You know how sorrowful my brother was over this. He ordered my body to be brought to Moscow, but you persuaded the patriarch to do otherwise, and he confirmed that it was not right for a suicide to be buried along with the anointed of God. Then my brother wanted to travel himself to Uglich for the funeral, but you told him that a plague was affecting Uglich.

From another aspect is the incident with the Crimean Khan. Your army was twice the size of his and you arranged for him to be at the outskirts of Moscow, yet you proscribed any of your own army under threat of capital punishment to attack the enemy. After three days of looking at each other face to face, you released him. The Khan left our country, not harming it at all. You returned home and then waited three days before sending a regiment to pursue him.

When Andrei Klobukov caught some arsonists and they told him that you ordered them to burn Moscow, then you ordered them to blame Klobukov for [the fire], whom you then had arrested and tortured on the rack.

After the death of my brother, which you hastened, you began to bribe the crippled, lame, blind, and they in turn cried for you to be king. But when you began to reign, this charity of yours was noticed by the Romanov, Cherkassky and Shuisky families. Remember all this! And do not prod me with your malice to more wrath. Give to me what is mine and I for the sake of God will absolve all your guilt and assign to you a place of peaceful retirement. It would be better for you in this world to endure this, rather than burn in hell for all the lives you destroyed.

Godunov was perplexed. How should he prepare for a battle where material strength was insufficient? The new enemy was not the Crimean Khan, not the King of Poland or Sweden. Opening the letter listing his crimes against Russia and disclosing his soul, this awesome enemy was summoning Godunov to the judgment of God.

Success of False Dmitri I

Other news encouraged Otrepyev as southern Russia capitulated, city after city, to his forces sent east from Kiev, all of them joining the mutiny against Godunov. The first major city of the region was Putivl, whose governor Pr. Vasili Mikhailovich Mosalski-Rubetz became an ardent leader in Otrepyev's campaign. Their example was followed by other Ukrainian cities and for a distance of 400 miles east to west Otrepyev was recognized as the true tsar. Then other cities capitulated: Rirsh, Komarnitzki, Sevsk, Borisov, Belgorod, Voluiki, Oskol, Voronezh, Kromni, Kivni, Eletz (where monk Leonid was living under the assumed name of monk Grigori). Officials loyal to Godunov were bound and handed to Otrepyev's commanders, who in turn would release them and them impress them into service. Crowds of traitors to Tsar Godunov joined the ranks of Otrepyev's makeshift army. When money was discovered being clandestinely transferred to Moscow in honey barrels, it was confiscated and sent to Lithuania to Pr. Vishnevetzki, for him to use to finance more recruits for the invasion.

To gain the confidence of the people from the religious side, Otrepyev displayed himself as a zealous Russian Orthodox, regardless of his conversion to Roman Catholicism in Poland. He ordered that one of the holiest icons of Russian Orthodoxy to be delivered from Kursk, the Miracle-Working Icon of the Theotokos. He reverently greeted the arrival of the icon and placed it in his tent, and would daily pray in its presence. The icon accompanied Otrepyev to Moscow, where he kept it in his palace.

Making camp 10 miles from the city Novgorod Severski, Otrepyev did not receive any news from inside the city, no invitation to enter, no military governor bound to hand over to him. The hero of the city was Peter Feodorovich Basmanov, brother of the murdered Ivan. He was a valiant man with years of military campaigning and strong leadership, and he no fear of death. Basmanov took charge of the city as a loyal subject to Tsar Godunov, convinced that Otrepyev was an imposter and his entire campaign a fraud. On November 11, 1604, Otrepyev's army approached Severski and was met with bullets and cannon balls; he asked for negotiations. Basmanov stood on the wall of the city and watched Otrepyev's assistant approach with his white flag, telling him that the great king and grand prince Dmitri Ivanovich was ready to become the father of their city if they capitulated to him. If the city proved obstinate, not one living person — male, female or child — would be left alive in Severski. Basmanov replied, "The grand prince and king is in Moscow, and your criminal and you will be impaled together." Russian traitors were sent into the city to convince Basmanov to capitulate, but the attempt was futile. Otrepyev attempted again to attack the city, but his makeshift army was easily repelled: they could not even get close enough to set the wooden walls on fire. They then fired some cannons at the wall, which fragmented them only a little. Many men were killed in the return volleys from Severski and Otrepyev's camp became disenchanted. Basmanov then asked for a two-week delay before making a decision: fight or capitulate, depending on news from Moscow. He hoped that by then the army of Godunov at Bryansk would be notified of the siege and rush to assist him. Otrepyev already considered the city his and Basmanov his captive.

By December 1604, Otrepyev's army grew to 12,000. The sudden and speedy victories — almost bloodless — paralyzed Tsar Godunov and northern Russia. The tsar realized his error in thinking that informing the public of Otrepyev's illegitimacy would keep their allegiance. The new tactic had to be war with a strong and loyal army to prevent Otrepyev from entering Russia and especially to keep him away from the displaced population living along the border areas, who would welcome Otrepyev as a deliverer. The other option was for Godunov to lead the army himself, as he had done on previous occasions, against the

Swedes and the Crimean Mongols. Godunov fantasized that his presence would stir crowds to join his defense of Russia from this imposter, but he was struck with fear because this battle was unlike the others. Godunov elevated Pr. Mstislavski as commander-in-chief in his place and sent him to Bryansk. The prince also indirectly heard that, should he gain the victory over Otrepyev, he would be rewarded with the post of military commander or vice-regent of northern Ukraine. By December 18, 1604, Mstislavski had 40,000 to 50,000 soldiers while Otrepyev no more than 15,000. Mstislavski's disadvantage was that his troops were ill-trained forced conscripts whose sole intent was to survive the battle, rather than gain a victory.

By now, Godunov was informed of the promise that Otrepyev had made to Polish Jesuits and the Papal Nuncio about subjecting Orthodoxy to Catholicism. He ordered all the churches in Russia to sing of Tsarevich Dmitri's eternal memory, a special litany performed to commemorate dead heroes and saints, while priests at their pulpit and ambo were to denounce Otrepyev as a pretender to the throne and a heretic wanting to convert Russia to Roman Catholicism. The crowds reluctantly submitted to the edict, even with the lethargy of the clergy to perform the litany. Parishioners felt the prelates were accomplices in evading Godunov's complicity in the murder of Tsarevich Dmitri, and so no longer had any trust in them, but the fear of excommunication and reprisal compelled the parishioners to perform the litany. Success here was meager, if any, the people more wanting to join Otrepyev than they were to support Godunov.

Godunov then ordered landowners, princes and noblemen to provide recruits for his army, at the rate of one recruit for every quarter-dessyatina of cultivated land,[11] which increased the size of his army by 50%. Godunov demanded haste, noting in his directives that they — landowners, princes and noblemen — lived in palaces and ought to be worried about the invasion of a Polish army and the desecration of the ROC. Godunov threatened those who were slow to respond with horrible tortures and punishment, while the disobedient would be ruthlessly whipped and incarcerated and have their property confiscated. The clergy who were capable of military service, regardless of their

---

11 About two thirds of an acre.

rank, were also to report for duty and under threat of interdict or de-frocking should they delay.

Such edicts and measures created in Bryansk in six weeks only an army of 50,000, as compared to the army of a half-million in 1598 against the Crimean Khan and his Mongol Horde. The troops reluc-tantly marched to Bryansk, and the more they heard of Otrepyev's bloodless victories, the more unwilling they were to fight, convinced that God was with him.

Additional assistance was now offered by Swedish King Charles IX, an enemy of Polish King Sigismund. But Godunov declined the military support, boasting of Russia's previous successful campaigns. Godunov knew that a handful of Swedish soldiers would be of little value to him and would cause him greater detriment should he defeat Otrepyev. An array of princes as military commanders proceeded from Bryansk toward the south: Feodor Ivanovich Mstislavski, Nikita Tru-betzkoy, Andrei Telyatevski, Dmitri Ivanovich Shuisky, Vasili Golitsyn, Mikhail Saltykov, Mikhailo Kashin, Ivan Ivanovich Godunov and Vasili Morozov. Their goal was to delivery Novgorod-Severski from the siege of Otrepyev. The commanders also wrote a letter to Yuri Mnishek, de-manding that he immediately remove his troops from Russia and deliv-er Otrepyev to them for execution. Mnishek did not bother to respond, relying on the possibility that Godunov's army would not actually at-tack or risk battle. Otrepyev thought the same, based on reports from his spies talking to soldiers of Russia's army.

The Russian army drew near to Trubetzk, which had many Otrepyev supporters, and they made camp about four miles from Otrepyev's camp. On December 18, shots were fired at each other's sol-diers. Otrepyev waited for a peaceful surrender since Mstislavski only had 12, 000 troops with him; the balance were still at Bryansk. But only three persons left his camp to join Otrepyev, which disappointed him.

On December 21, Otrepyev left the siege of Severski and attacked the Russian army. At the same time Basmanov and his troops from the city attacked Otrepyev from the rear. The victory was gained by Otrepyev, who claimed the death of 4,000 Russian soldiers, but it was not the victory that he hoped for, because it entailed battle and the death of his own soldiers as well as the enemy's. In the Russian's retreat he noticed their reluctance to fight, while Basmanov returned to Severski with his army. The Russians retreated to Starodub to await reinforcements from Bryansk, while the siege of Severski continued. Nonetheless, the battle discouraged many of the Poles, who were not accustomed to or experienced in actual warfare, and they returned home. Even Mnishek lost hope in Otrepyev and left the camp. To gain strength and remobilize, Otrepyev abandoned the siege of Severski and moved to Komarnitzki and occupied the Sevsk fort.

The Russian commanders were perplexed by his makeshift army and hesitated before sending a messenger to Godunov regarding the battle. On January 1, 1605, Godunov sent Pr. Vasili Shuisky to the front. With the siege lifted from Severski, Basmanov journeyed to Moscow where he received a hero's welcome on entering the city. Tsar Godunov rewarded Basmanov for his loyalty with a solid gold chain, 2,000 rubles in gold coins, and silver goblets, along with an estate and promotion to the rank of boyar. The population of Moscow hailed the new hero, which encouraged them in their support of Tsar Godunov. But these ostentatious displays of reward irritated others and caused more contempt for Godunov. Basmanov received a greater reward and welcome than the actual hero of the battle, Pr. Nikita Trubetzkoy. The choice of Pr. Shuisky to replace Pr. Mstislavski brought no benefit to Godunov either, since Shuisky was an aristocrat with no military experience and was easily intimidated. Pr. Shuisky joined Pr. Mstislavski at Starodub, with a force between 60 and 70,000. The following day some 4,000 Zaporozhski Cossacks joined Otrepyev, increasing the size of his army again to about 15,000.

The largest battle of the campaign occurred on January 21, 1605, beginning at dawn, Otrepyev attacking the Russians at an area called Dobrinitz. The experience of Otrepyev among the Cossacks in earlier years proved its value in the battle, but he was outnumbered, even with the new valiant Cossacks. Otrepyev retreated, losing some 6,000 soldiers in the battle, while the Russians only lost 500. Otrepyev was also captured. Godunov shook with joy hearing the news and ordered a litany of thanksgiving to be performed in churches and all the bells of Moscow rung. Gold medals were awarded to the military commanders and 80,000 rubles was distributed among the soldiers. Godunov hopped the next piece of news would be the end of the rebellion. But the joy of the victors in Moscow was premature as Russian soldiers released Otrepyev on a wounded horse and he fled to Sevsk Fort and then to Rilsk to recover.

The regiment of Zaporozhski Cossacks that recently joined Otrepyev's forces returned to their homes, and he moved on to Putivl, a fort better equipped for his safety. Russian soldiers at Dobrinitz were hanging their captives, or shooting them, or torturing them and the residents of Komorniki were also executed for being traitors to Godunov. They did not spare old men, women or children, which only served to fuel the hatred of the people toward Godunov. As a result, Otrepyev was overwhelmed with despair and deprived of any hope for the future. He planned to join the other war refugees and return to Lithuania secretly, now reduced to having only 1,500 soldiers in his army. His desperate loyalists however refused to allow him to leave, telling him that they had sacrificed everything they had for him. They were also afraid that if they did not fight to the end, they would perish anyway from the wrath of Godunov and in a worse manner. This encouraged Otrepyev and he again summoned recruits form early supporters and any more who would join him. The 4,000 Cossacks returned and more volunteers in the region vowed their allegiance. Otrepyev sent Pr. Tatev to King Sigismund asking for reinforcements to reinforce Putivl at their arrival. He printed more leaflets, again repeating the story of his survival, this time he included a passage of his life in Belarus (White Russia) until he matured and how he secretly spent time in Moscow incognito with Chancellor Lev Sapega, where he saw the usurper — Tsar Godunov — sitting on the throne belonging to him — Tsarevich Dmitri. This second manifest, which seemed to satisfy those who were curious as to how he acquired his knowledge of events in Moscow, increased the size of his makeshift army. His spies told him that the Russians attacked him reluctantly, out of coercion and due to threats, and that the Russian victory was accidental. The survivors of Komorniki, seeing the brutal execution of their countrymen by order of Godunov, fled to Putivl where they offered their lives to Otrepyev.

Godunov's army moved to Rilsk — which had earlier capitulated to Otrepyev — and demanded the city's unconditional surrender. They refused, knowing that execution awaited them by order of Godunov, just as at Komorniki. City officials told Mstislavski, "We serve King Dmitri," and then shot cannons at the Russian army. For two weeks the city was under siege, and then the Russian army returned to Starodub, tired of winter battles, hoping to wait until spring.

Tsar Godunov was infuriated when he heard the news that Otrepyev had been released after his capture. His joy of victory was quenched as he heard that the imposter's army was increasing and remobilizing. Now vexed at Pr. Mstislavski and his commanders, Godunov dispatched Peter Sheremetev and another regiment of Russian soldiers to the front, with words of admonishment. He told them of his disgust with the troops on the front, discrediting them for their negligence in allowing Otrepyev to escape, and that all the victories gained so far were now futile since Otrepyev had time to remobilize. Russian soldiers then complained about the cruelty of Godunov toward the traitors and his unfairness toward them, and toward those who still kept their oath of allegiance to him and risked their lives for him on the battlefield. The opinion of more Russians inclined toward Otrepyev and more soldiers abandoned the Russian army to join him. Contempt toward Godunov increased, even to see him dead. Traveling in the winter snow to the front, more soldiers died. The Russian army was slow in mobilizing and once the army of Sheremetev joined with Shuisky and Mstislavski they began the siege of Kromni, rather than journeying further to Putivl, where Otrepyev was regrouping. The siege was a stalemate after three weeks. An epidemic of dysentery affected the soldiers at Kromni and many of them died in the cold without medical care. Frostbite also took its toll. Eventually, Kromni was set on fire by Russian soldiers, and the supporters of Otrepyev fled the city.

Godunov sent three monks who had known Otrepyev when he was monk Grigori to Putivl to try to expose him. The three were arrested and then tortured until one of them confessed that he had some fatal poison on his person. He was searched and the poison was hid in his shoe. The monk confessed that Godunov promised them great wealth if they could poison Otrepyev. The three were executed.

Otrepyev sent a second letter to Godunov, now reproaching Patr. Job for misusing ecclesiastical authority in supporting the usurper and criminal Godunov. In the same letter Otrepyev admonished the tsar to peacefully abdicate this throne and society, confine himself to a monastery and there live the balance of his life. Otrepyev promised Godunov amnesty if he abdicated without bloodshed or resistance. For Godunov this letter only fortified his drive for defense of his throne.

Death of Tsar Boris Feodorovich and Reign of Feodor Borisovich

In January 1605, Patr. Job sent a directive to all churches in the provinces for a special liturgy to be performed, for God to repulse the enemy, for Him not to deliver the Russian Empire to the plunder and captivity of Poles and Lithuanians, and not to hand them over to Roman Catholicism, which he referred to as the Latin heresy. It was by this time that all Russia, including the northern provinces and Siberia, were aware of the invasion of Otrepyev's army. In Moscow Patr. Job and Pr. Vasili Shuisky were attempting to convince the people to not believe the rumors about Tsarevich Dmitri, telling them that he actually did die in Uglich, and that he — Shuisky — personally buried the boy, and that this person was an imposter named Yuri Otrepyev or monk Grigori. But the people did not believe either the patriarch or Pr. Shuisky, but only muttered to each other, "They are saying this against their will, fearing Tsar Boris. They can say nothing else to us but this. If they say otherwise, all that is left is for them to leave the country and worry about their own heads."

There was also another Godunov that the people did not see or know, a person psychologically devastated, whose mental faculties were overstressed and emotions ready to fracture. Deceived of his victories, watching the inactivity of his army and their negligence, the incapability of his commanders or just their ill-will toward him, Godunov had no other MMMmilitary leaders to assign the command. He suffered as he listened to the gossip of the people, as they spoke reverently of Otrepyev and ill of him. Godunov had exhausted his ability to gain the trust of the people with charity, and now threats and torture would not incline them to him either. Denunciations of him increased daily as Godunov awaited a palace mutiny, feeling his authority as monarch paralyzed, while surrounded by no one whom he would trust. An abyss was in front of him, waiting for his descent into it. The Boyar Duma in Moscow continued business as usual and the palace court was as pompous as ever, but it was all ostensive, superficial. Their hearts were all closed to Godunov, they hid their fear of him, their malevolence, while he forced himself to be dignified in their presence as tsar, lest his true dejected condition surface. Only to his wife Maria did Godunov disclose his emotional despair. He seemed to her deeply wounded and drenched with blood and tears. He would cry in her presence in private, unable to find consolation anywhere or in anything or in anybody. Godunov would go to the palace chapel and pray, but nothing changed. He developed gout due to his rich diet, which drained his strength.

At the age of 53, at what should have been the pinnacle of his life in every respect, Tsar and Grand Prince of all Russia Boris Feodorovich Godunov suffered a massive brain hemorrhage. On April 13, 1605, at one o'clock in the morning, after he had spent the evening greeting some foreign dignitaries and two hours dining with them, and now as he sat and discussed domestic and political matters with the Boyar Duma, he stood up from the table in his Gold Chamber and felt unwell. Blood flowed rapidly from his nostrils, ears and mouth. Within a few minutes he lost consciousness. Two hours later, and in the presence of the palace court, Godunov passed away. The doctors were unable to help. According to the chroniclers of the era, Godunov still managed to bless his son to rule in his place and took the vow of a monk with the new name Bogolepa[12] from Patr. Job, who also was present at the time. The rumor spread that Godunov had committed suicide by taking poison.

Tsar Godunov was buried with all honors due a king in the Arkhangelsk Cathedral. His sepulcher was placed alongside those tsars of royal posterity of earlier generations.

Since Tsar Boris Godunov was a legitimate monarch, it was only naturally for his son to inherit the throne, even though he was only 16 years of age, while mother Maria would act as regent and retain her title. All of Moscow, from Patr. Job and the Boyar Duma to resident and peasant, and with a display of sincerity, pledged allegiance to "Tsaritza Maria and her children, Tsar Feodor Borisovich and Tsarevna Ksenia Borisovna." The oath included provisions "not to betray the royal family, not to conspire against their life and not to usurp the Moscovite

---

12 A name whose derivation means "beautiful to God."

state, not to adhere to the former prince of Tver, Semeon Bekbulatovich, not to the criminal who calls himself Dmitri, not to avoid government service, and not to fear labor or death on its behalf."

Young Feodor inherited the intellect of his father and the goodness of his mother. Even at his age people were impressed with his ability to converse with others and the extent of his knowledge. Tsar Feodor was the first and possible only Russian tsar to have acquired an education in Europe. He quickly learned how to conduct Duma business and — like his father — gain the favor of people by contributing charity. What more could Moscovite Russia want than such a person as monarch? But the cruel shadow of father Boris and grandfather Maluta Skuratov cast a dark cloud and storm over the throne of Feodor Borisovich. Contempt for the father and grandfather was unconsciously routed to the son, and so the people awaited more turmoil the sooner than a return to the prosperity of the earlier years of Tsar Boris' reign.

Needing competent advisors, new tsar Feodor Godunov asked whom he felt were the three that appeared to be the best politicians of his father's era: Pr. Feodor Mstislavski, and brothers Vasili and Dmitri Shuisky. They were to leave the troops at the front and return to Moscow. The exiled and disgraced cousin Bogdan Belski was granted his freedom and asked to return to Moscow, the young tsar returning to him his lost property and reassigning to him a post in the Boyar Duma.

To complete the military victory over Otrepyev, Tsar Feodor selected Basmanov, the hero of Novgorod-Severski and because of his loyalty to father Boris. Basmanov was sent to the front along with Mikhail Katirev-Rostovski and Metr. Isidor of Novgorod, so that the army would in their presence swear allegiance to him — Feodor Godunov — as the new tsar. Calm prevailed over Moscow for the next few weeks now with winter in progress and waiting for spring. Recent news regarding the siege of the city Kromni encouraged the new tsar.

On April 17, 1605, Basmanov returned to Severski and the Russian camp, but neither Mstislavski nor Shuisky were to be found. Basmanov assemble the scattered troops and read to them the declaration of the new and young Tsar Feodor Godunov. He promised the loyal and zealous troops many rewards after the traditional 40-day mourning period for his father. Some were agitated at the son of Boris becoming tsar, while others wept at his demise, but the army, just as with Moscow, pledged its allegiance to Tsar Feodor Godunov. Metr. Isidor returned to Moscow with the good news of the Russian army's continued loyalty. Then something perplexing occurred with the loyalty of Basmanov about this time: his attitude changed toward the young Godunov and he reversed course. As if overnight, Basmanov's loyalty shifted from the newly-crowned monarch Feodor Godunov to the imposter Otrepyev. What could have caused it? Basmanov was the hero of Severski: when all the other cities of Ukraine capitulated to Otrepyev without a drop of blood spilt, Basmanov refused and endured the siege and then fought the army of Otrepyev. Then he accepted rewards from Tsar Boris for his bravery and then accepted command of the Russia army from the son, but all this was now discarded in favor of the imposter gaining the throne of Russia. Maybe Basmanov foresaw the inevitable conclusion of the entire matter, now with the Russian army displaced and its morale low, and the local residents holding contempt for it. The greater loyalty of Basmanov was to himself, his ambition for the future, and he saw greater advantage by having an alliance with Otrepyev than with young Tsar Feodor Godunov, inexperienced and weak. Whether Otrepyev was genuine or an imposter was irrelevant, what mattered most was the greater future of Basmanov: under a Godunov or an Otrepyev oligarchy? Basmanov selected the latter and had his entire army follow his example.

Over the three months since the battle of Novgorod-Severski, Otrepyev in Putivl fortified the city and armed his soldiers. He wrote to Mnishek in Poland that he was planning another invasion of Russia, convinced that he will succeed this time, banking on the low morale of Russia's soldiers and residents with the sudden death of Tsar Boris. While in Putivl, Otrepyev sent gifts to the Khan of the Crimean Mongols seeking a peace treaty with him. He awaited new reinforcements from Galitzia (western Ukraine), while Mikhail Ratomski was able to recruit more soldiers from the local region. By May 1, the majority of Russian troops stationed at Kromni and Severski pledged new allegiance, now to Otrepyev, as a result of the strategy of Basmanov. Other military commanders followed suit: Pr. Vasili Golitsyn, his brother Ivan, and Mikhail Saltykov. The extent of treachery expanded into central Russia: Ryazan, Tula, Kocher, and Aleksin, believing that the only true pledge of allegiance was to Tsar Ivan IV and his descendants and believing that Otrepyev was genuinely Tsarevich Dmitri.

On May 7, Basmanov announced officially that Otrepyev was the legitimate king of Russia, while thousands of his troops declared, "Long live our father, monarch Dmitri Ivanovich." The few Godunov loyalists remaining, princes Mikhail Katirev-Rostovski, Andrei Telyatevski, and Ivan Ivanovich Godunov, fled with a handful of soldiers to Moscow, realizing how many had capitulated to Otrepyev. The makeshift army pursued them and apprehended Ivan Godunov, who was bound and brought to Otrepyev at Putivl as the spoil of war. Realizing their defeat and the seriousness of consequences with the victory of Otrepyev, Godunov's loyalists joined the mutiny, Ivan Golitsyn and Ivan Godunov announced their — and the troops they commanded — allegiance, and that they would accompany him on the return to Moscow and help him gain the monarchy.

On May 19, 1605, Otrepyev, his new retinue of loyal noblemen, military leaders and troops, numbering now about 70,000, along with 70 cannons, departed Putivl for Moscow. Otrepyev passed along the city Kromni, viewing the ashes of the city, having been burned by Russian troops after the siege.

About half-way to Moscow, Otrepyev met with Mikhail Saltykov, Pr. Vasili Golitsyn, Pr. Sheremetev, and Basmanov. The latter pledged allegiance personally to Otrepyev, and expressed his willingness to die for him. At that point and feeling secure in his acquisition of the throne and support of Moscow residents, Otrepyev allocated a month's rest to most of his army; a smaller part he dispatched to Moscow to prepare the event of his arrival, while himself with 2,000 or 3,000 slowly followed behind. Crowds of people and soldiers greeted him with gifts at every city he entered. Forts and cities opened their gates to him and recognized him as their new monarch. From as far away as Astrakhan, committed soldiers brought to Otrepyev their military governor Mikhailo Saburov — a close relative of Godunov — bound in chains. Only a few in Orel refused to acknowledge Otrepyev's validity, and these were arrested and imprisoned. As Otrepyev rode on horseback through the streets of these cities, people rushed to him and kissed his feet. Every city was in joyous turmoil, Otrepyev sensing the materialization of his dream: the victory over Russia without bloodshed.

Moscow Yields to False Dmitri's Forces; Murder of the Godunov Family

In Moscow, the newly-arrived commanders from the field who would not capitulate to Otrepyev: Katirev-Rostovski and Telyatevski, informed Tsar Feodor Godunov of the recent mutiny and events in Otrepyev's camp. The young tsar was in mental anguish, still emotionally immature at 16, pondering his fate. He saw around him few nobles and officials that were sincere, but many that were desperate and perplexed, worried of their own fate once Otrepyev should enter Moscow with popular support. A few tried to console the royal family by mitigating the consequences of Otrepyev's arrival, especially in light of the amnesty he extended toward many and which he had offered to father Boris Godunov. The young tsar offered more rewards to the two commanders, unable to rouse support on his own. The remnants of the Boyar Duma watched their authority dissolve in the massive halls of the Kremlin palace as they heard of Otrepyev reaching the banks of the Oka River and the crowds assembling in Red Square and cheering as they heard of Otrepyev's successes and advance and eager to hear more. To try to curb communication, the tsar's spies apprehended messengers from Otrepyev. The leaflets were burned and the messengers imprisoned. Otrepyev finally guessed that his leaflets were not reaching the residents of Moscow. He ordered two of his loyal officials, Plescheyev and Pushkin to take leaflets and go to the city Krasnoe Selo, and to motivate the residents there, so that they would enter Moscow with the messengers to deliver leaflets. The strategy worked; residents of Krasnoe Selo announced their acknowledgement of Otrepyev as tsar and on June 1, accompanied the messengers into Moscow. Tsar Feodor sent soldiers to try to curb their entrance into the city, but they refused to halt them. Crowds followed the messengers to Red Square to hear the announcement of Otrepyev to the residents of Moscow.

> "You swore to my father to not betray his children and posterity forever, but yet you installed Godunov as king. I do not reproach you. You were under the impression that Boris killed me as a young boy. You were not aware of his guile and could not oppose the person who possessed sole authority during the reign

of Feodor Ivanovich; and he rewarded or executed whomever he wanted. Deceived by him, you did not believe that I — delivered of God — would return to you with love and gentleness. Someone else's precious blood was shed. I feel sorrowful, but without vendetta, because I blame you for your ignorance and fear.

"Already fate has been decided; the city and army is mine. Are you bold enough to start a civil war to gratify Maria Godunova and her son? Let Russia not feel pity for them because they are interlopers who reign. They drank the blood of Severski and want to destroy Moscow. Remember you boyars, what occurred to you because of Boris Godunov, you noblemen and commanders. How many were discredited and endured his dishonor?

"I will return to you what you have lost. How can you refuse? I will not leave you empty-handed. I come with a great army, my own and the Poles. Fear ruin, temporary and permanent. Fear to answer for yourself on the day of the judgment of God. Humble yourselves, and quickly send your metropolitans, archbishops, members of the Duma, noblemen and officials, commanders and merchants, to petition me to be your legitimate king."

The people yielded under the circumstances, regardless of their personal view of whether Otrepyev was genuine or a pretender. As the crowds listened to Otrepyev's messengers the senior noblemen and palace officials agitated in fear in their Kremlin residences. Patr. Job pleaded with the noblemen to act, but himself could not appear in Red Square in his ecclesiastical vestments out of fear for his own safety. He just wept in his cloister at the Chudovski Monastery inside the Kremlin. A few prominent and still loyal noblemen, along with Mstislavski and Vasili Shuisky and Bogdan Belski, left the Kremlin and spoke to the crowds and attempted to take the messengers of Otrepyev into custody. The crowds resisted and shouted at them, "The Godunov era has passed. We have been with him in the depths of hell, but now the sun has risen on Russia. Long live Tsar Dmitri Ivanovich. The oath to Boris is history. Death to the Godunov family."

Shouting, the crowds rushed into the Kremlin and headed for the Palace. Immediately the sentries and bodyguards disappeared and the mob was free to do whatever they wanted. They found the young tsar and grabbed him from his throne. The despairing mother fell at the feet of the angry mob and begged for the life of her son. Mother, son and daughter were dragged out of the palace and into their private residence inside the Kremlin, and sentries loyal to Otrepyev were placed on guard. Relatives of the royal family — Godunovs, Saburovs and Velyaminovs — that did not join the mutiny were imprisoned, their possessions were confiscated and their homes were demolished. The imprisoned families were then exiled to cities distant in Siberia. The odious Semeon Godunov was strangled to death in Pereyaslavl. Foreigners living in Moscow who were business partners with late-Tsar Boris also had their possessions confiscated.

On July 3, 1605, the balance of the palace residents and clergy pledged allegiance, while those that refused — princes Ivan Vorotinsky, Andrei Telyatevski, Peter Sheremetev and others — were accompanied out of Moscow and to Otrepyev, now residing temporarily at Tula. The messengers Plescheyev and Pushkin by now returned to Tula and related to Otrepyev all that had occurred in Moscow the previous few days. Otrepyev then dispatched Princes Vasili Golitsyn, Vasili Mosalski and Sutupov with a secret mission to terminate the royal family, while Basmanov took a small regiment of soldiers to deal with Patr. Job. The group was greeted by Moscow officials and residents as though having full investiture of royal authority. Basmanov and his regiment went to visit Patr. Job, who presented them with a petition, hoping to gain amnesty and save his own soul by offering to perform the coronation of Otrepyev. However, Otrepyev was not about to accept his superficial repentance and grant him a reprieve, especially for his role in white-washing the murder of Tsarevich Dmitri. Otrepyev knew better than to trust or condescend to his former mentor to crown monk Grigori as tsar of Russia. Basmanov's group left the patriarch and began agitating the crowds, implicating him in the crimes of Tsar Boris Godunov and that he must no longer be patriarch. Shortly thereafter, while Job was performing liturgy in Uspenski Cathedral, a mob of furious rebels holding spears and clubs rushed in. They grabbed Job at the altar and shook him side to side tearing off from him his ecclesiastical vestments. The mob dressed Job in a plain monk's frock, drug him about the cathedral, and out the door into the square with the intent of beating him to death, but guards intervened. Job was then brought to Red Square for execution, but his life was spared at the last minute by Otrepyev, who did not want to begin his rule as tsar with the patriarch's blood on his hands. Job was thrown in a carriage and taken to Staritzki Monastery.

Tsaritza Maria Grigorievna, young Feodor and Ksenia, as a result of their confinement in their private residence, were unaware of events that occurred that week on the streets of Moscow and in Red Square. On June 10, 1605, Pr. Vasili Golitsyn with Vasili Mosalski and Sutupov, along with officials Mikhail Molchanov and Sherefedinov and two royal guards, entered the private Godunov residence where the three were sitting next to each other on a sofa. The two children were taken into separate rooms. Tsaritza Maria Grigorievna was strangled to death. Young Feodor, a strong 16-year-old, fought as hard as he could with the guards, until one of them injured him in the testicles and then Molchanov strangled him to death. Ksenia was left to live and given to Vasili Mosalski as a mistress. The princes announced to the residents of Moscow that mother Maria and son Feodor had committed suicide by taking poison, although signs of physical damage as a result of the struggle were obvious on their bodies. The crowds viewed their bodies in the coffins before the funeral, purposefully displayed to impress on the populace the fear of their new False tsar Otrepyev. Some people viewed the bodies out of curiosity, others due to perplexity or else despair for their own safety. Some felt it was due Tsaritza Maria as the daughter of the odious and loathsome henchman Maluta Skuratov; others felt she was innocent and implicated due to circumstances beyond her control as the wife of Tsar Boris. The most sorrow was expended on the young Feodor Borisovich, whom the people felt could have installed a new era for Russia after the horrors of previous decades.

The body of Tsar Boris Godunov was exhumed from his sepulcher in the Arkhangelsk Cathedral and placed in a wooden coffin. Boris, wife Maria Grigorievna and son Feodor were buried together at the Convent of St. Varsonofei, next to Sretenski Monastery in Moscow at some isolated part of the cemetery.

6. The Era of Tsar False Dmitri I

False Dmitri I Enters Moscow

Tula had the appearance of a busy capital, filled with triumph and joy. Over 100,000 soldiers and officials, merchants and residents from nearby cities and villages, gathered there. Prominent members of the Duma followed princes Vorotinsky and Telyatevski, who were dispatched from Moscow with a petition to Otrepyev on behalf of the city. The many officials of Moscow including Mstislavski and the Shuisky brothers, were now to devour the fruits of their cowardice: contempt by the one to whom they sacrificed all they had, except for their rank and wealth. Along with the crowds more Cossacks, new fugitives from the Don River basin, visited Otrepyev at his Tula palace. He stretched his hand to them and with a smile, but the boyars later he greeted with anger because of their lengthy obstinacy. Right in the presence of Otrepyev Cossacks reviled the humiliated nobles and especially Pr. Andrei Telyatevski. However the noblemen presented to Otrepyev the state seal, the key to the state treasury, clothing, royal armor, and a number of palace servants to attend to his needs.

The reign of the imposter had now begun, whether by the insistence of counselors or due to his personal drive. Otrepyev immediately took charge acting without apprehension and decisively, as if he was born upon the throne of Russia and accustomed to possessing such authority. Not yet hearing the news regarding the murder of the Godunov mother and son, on June 11, 1605, Otrepyev wrote a letter to all the major Russian cities including those in Siberia stating that he, having been sheltered by a secret power from the evil-minded Boris Godunov and having matured to full adulthood, now assumes authority over the Moscow sovereignty as the rightful heir, and that all the clergy, nobles officials and residents have sworn loyalty to him. Otrepyev requested the city commanders to immediately require such an oath from all people in their jurisdictions, to swear loyalty to the widow-tsaritza Marina Nagoi and to himself, her son, Tsar Dmitri Ivanovich, with the absolute necessity to faithfully serve him and at the same time not to associate with the surviving family members of the Godunov family. The letter was appended with a few remarks about their conducts as citizens: not to take vengeance, not to kill anyone without an order from the state, to live in peace and quiet and to serve the state courageously.

Otrepyev also sent couriers to rendezvous with the English delegate Smith, who had just left Moscow with the intention of returning to England. The couriers were to confiscate letters that Tsar Boris Godunov had written and replace them with new letters from himself. The letters dealt with the mercantile arrangements for English trade in Russia, now Otrepyev promising the English new benefits for trade and that he would dispatch a Russian official to London after his coronation to conclude a trade agreement with King James.

Having heard that his orders were enacted in Moscow: the patriarch exiled, the wife and son of Boris Godunov cold in their graves, their close associates either exiled from the region or had become now loyal to Otrepyev, Moscow calm from the upheaval, and the populace awaiting impatiently Dmitri Ivanovich as though resurrected from his grave, Otrepyev left Tula on June 16, and encamped in the meadows of the Moscow River near the village Kolomensk. Prominent residents and officials greeted him with the traditional bread and salt, gifting him gold goblets and furs, while boyars gifted him beautiful ornaments from the tsars' collections. In unison and superficial condescension they said to Otrepyev, "Come and reign over the legacy of your forefathers. The holy cathedrals, Moscow, and the chambers of your father Ivan Vasi-lyevich await you. No more criminals are to be found, the ground has swallowed them. The time of peace, love and joy has arisen." Otrepyev replied, saying that he will forgive the guilt of the children, and not act as an formidable or harsh sovereign, but as a gentle father of Russia.

Germans living in the suburbs of Moscow approached Otrepyev with a petition. The explained their loyalty to Tsar Boris and their re-fusal to engage in any mutiny against the government, since they were expatriates. They requested Otrepyev to accommodate them under the circumstances, saying in their petition, "We honorable fulfilled our oath of loyalty and as we served Boris so are we ready to serve you as the legitimate king." Without hesitation, Otrepyev accepted their peti-tion and oath of loyalty.

On June 20, 1605, a sunny and beautiful summer day, Otrepyev en-tered Moscow triumphantly and pompously. Ahead of the Polish del-egation were kettle-drummers and trumpeters, then a cavalry regiment and infantry regiment, and chariots and carriages pulled by six-horse teams decorated for the occasion. Next were more drummers with Rus-sian soldiers and horsemen with steeds from the tsar's stables and cler-gy in their best of ecclesiastical vestments, then followed by Otrepyev riding on a white horse (the value of the jewels and pearls brilliantly and majestically woven into his clothing is recorded as 150,000 20-ru-ble gold pieces). Surrounding him were 60 nobles and princes. Next in the parade was a Lithuanian military regiment and Germans, Cossacks, and Russian Royal Guards. All the bells of Moscow rang. The streets were filled with innumerable crowds of people, along with specta-tors on the roofs of buildings and churches, towers and walls. Seeing Otrepyev the crowds fell prostate and cried, "Greetings our father, sov-ereign and grand prince Dmitri Ivanovich, saved by God for our pros-perity. Shine in splendor, sun of Russia". Otrepyev greeted the people with a loud reply and referred to them as his trustworthy subjects, tell-ing them to rise and pray to God on his behalf. However Otrepyev did not trust Moscow residents and so he had his spies wandering through the crowds street by street listening to conversations and regularly re-porting to him the people's gossip. Even with the fanfare all was calm in the city during his entrance parade.

One incident noted by the chronicles occurred as the entourage of Otrepyev was crossing the Moscow River into Red Square and a whirlwind upset the parade. The column of dust interfered with the procession a few minutes. The superstitious crowds discerned the whirlwind as a bad omen and, while making the sign of the cross, cried "Save us Lord from disaster. This is a bad omen for Russia and Dmitri."

When Otrepyev met with Moscow's prelates and clergy at Red Square near the Cathedral of St. Basil the Blessed, Otrepyev descended from his horse to approach icons they were holding. The prelates and clergy gathered for this holy rite were alarmed at what was occurring, the Lithuanian musicians continued to play their trumpets and beat their tambourines, deafening the chants of the outdoor liturgy. More inconsiderate actions occurred as Otrepyev followed the clergy into the Kremlin and into Uspenski Cathedral. Otrepyev brought with him inside the cathedral individuals that the ROC clergy considered heterodox and heretic as well as Polish gentry and other Europeans. Such an action was never attempted by a previous Russian monarch and which seemed to the people as desecrating their sanctuary. Beginning with his arrival into Moscow Otrepyev's actions caused the ROC clergy to be suspicious of his orthodoxy.

From Uspenski Cathedral, Otrepyev hurried to the Archangel Cathedral where, with a superficial display of pious humility, he prostrated himself at the sepulcher of his supposed father Tsar Ivan IV, poured out tears and cried, "O my beloved father, you abandoned me as an orphan amidst persecution, but as a result of your holy prayers I am whole and have obtained the sovereignty." Such an artificial spectacle was not without its intended benefit: the crowd wailed and shouted, "You are the true Dmitri." Finally, Otrepyev entered the palace of the tsars and sat upon the throne of the previous rulers of Moscow.

While Otrepyev was inside the Kremlin, several officials gathered in Red Square among the massive crowd, among them Bogdan Belski, cousin of Boris Godunov. He stood in the center of the square, removed from his chest the icon of St. Nicholas the Wonder Worker — the patron Saint of Russia — kissed it and swore to the residents of Moscow and gathered crowd that the new sovereign was really the son of Tsar Ivan, preserved by the intercession of St. Nicholas. Belski attempted to convince the assembled crowd to love him who is beloved of God and to serve him faithfully. The assembled crowd responded in unison, "Long live our sovereign Dmitri. May his enemies perish." The celebration seemed sincere with the inclusion of all who were in Moscow at the time. Otrepyev and his officials and clergy feasted in the palaces while the residents dined in the city square and in their homes, eating and drinking late into the night.

Pr. Vasili Shuisky, who led the investigation into the death of the child Dmitri some 13 years earlier and confirmed his death, took a different stand shortly after the execution of the Godunov family and recanted his testimony, no doubt in despair for his own life. Now with the public acceptance of Otrepyev, Shuisky again changed his attitude and began to voice his original testimony and related to several individuals that their new tsar was an imposter, and the news spread. Basmanov heard of the statements and reported this to Otrepyev. On June 23, Shuisky was apprehended along with his brothers, all of whom had related to residents that their new tsar was an imposter, heretic and an instrument of Polish gentry and Catholic Jesuits. Otrepyev gathered a jury of local riff-raff and derelicts and conducted a monkey trial which resulted in the death sentence for Vasili Shuisky. During the calumnies directed at him by the prosecution the prince held to his convictions and witness to the death of the child Dmitri. Shuisky was tortured but refused to recant.

On June 25, Pr. Shuisky was brought to the center of Red Square and his head was placed on a block with the executioner and axe alongside him. Surrounding him were a regiment of soldiers, Royal Guards and Cossacks, while more soldiers stood on the walls and towers of Kremlin to impress the fear of Otrepyev and his authority on the populace. Peter Basmanov read the conviction of behalf of Otrepyev, "Great nobleman, Pr. Vasili Ivanovich Shuisky has betrayed me, your legitimate sovereign of all Russia, Dmitri Ivanovich. He is insidious, sinister and has discredited me and turned you, my faithful subjects, against me, calling me a false tsar and wanting to dethrone me. For this reason he is sentenced to death; let him die for his treachery and betrayal." The crowd was silent in great sorrow, having loved Pr. Vasili all his life. The crowd shed tears as the condemned prince, awaiting the raised executioner's axe, loudly shouted to the spectators, "Brethren, I die for the truth, for the Christian faith, and for you." As Pr. Shuisky's head lay on the block, a voice was heard in the background, crying "Stop!" They saw a royal official running from the Kremlin to the center of Red Square holding a paper. "They have announced a pardon for Shuisky!" Suddenly the entire crowd in Red Square sighed with indescribable joy. The supporters of Otrepyev, who for a moment were questioning the wisdom and sincerity of their new sovereign, complimented him, acceding to him more right to the throne and their loyalty. A few of them kept their thoughts to themselves, fearing likewise prosecution should they voice the same testimony as did Pr. Vasili. Others wondered whether Pr. Vasili would really forget the incident and recognize the imposter as tsar.

Later, Pr. Vasili discovered that it was not the vacillating Otrepyev whose heart was touched by an unabated magnanimity but it was the widow-tsaritza Marina Nagoi who had sent a message to her pseudo son imploring him not to execute his enemy, knowing it would ruin his reputation in Moscow because of the high regard of the populace for their prince. As other officials attached themselves to the petition of Marina Nagoi, Otrepyev had to face the political necessity of complying with their request, realizing that it was in his best interest. But Otrepyev was not about to liberate the three Shuisky brothers, princes Vasili, Ivan and Dmitri, as a result of the public confessions they made that were detrimental to his career, and so he ordered their exile to Galitzia, while their property and possessions were confiscated and allotted to the state treasury.

Pardons were granted by Otrepyev to others, although for political expediency. The Nagoi family, who were impoverished and exiled by Tsar Boris, had their freedom, ranks and estates returned to them, a gesture of Otrepyev to recognize his pseudo relatives. Mikhail Nagoi was promoted to the rank of Cavalry Master, while his brother and three nephews, and Ivan Nikitich Romanov, three Sheremetev princes, two Golitsyn princes, Dolgoruky, Tatev, Kurakin and Kashin were all promoted as boyars. Vasili Schelkalov became a chamberlain. Vasili Golitsyn was designated great palace-member, Bogdan Belski became great knight; Pr. Mikhail Skopin-Shuisky became great sword-bearer;

Pr. Likov-Obolenski became great cup-bearer; Pushkin became great falconer; petty-official Sutupov became great secretary and printer, while Vlasyev became great secretary and court treasurer. Otrepyev introduced new ranks for his political supporters at his whim as well as introducing into Russian ranks titles that were derived from Polish gentry.

Otrepyev summoned the humiliated and disgraced monk Filaret — Feodor Nikitich Romanov — from the Seiski Hermitage and elevated him to metropolitan of Rostov. Filaret was glad for the pardon and the opportunity to again see his wife and son, the future tsar Mikhail Romanov, and the two were allowed to live in the Rostov diocese near Kostroma at the Monastery of St. Ipatie (Ipatiyevski), where the young Mikhail was raised and received his education.

Semeon Bekbulatovich was also granted a pardon by Otrepyev, even though he was blind. He was admitted to the palace and allowed to reside there and his previous title of Prince of Tver — although honorary — was again assigned to him. Other officials disgraced by Tsar Boris and exiled to Siberia were released and were assigned duties in provinces of Siberia and other distant regions of Russia. The dead were also not forgotten by Otrepyev: he exhumed the bodies of his Nagoi pseudo relatives and others who were executed by Tsar Boris, brought their bodies to Moscow or their hometowns, and reburied them with the greatest of honors alongside their forefathers.

Having pleased Russia with his pardons toward the innocent sacrifices of the tyranny of Tsar Boris — both the living and the dead — Otrepyev now began to initiate measures to please the general population. He doubled the income of petty officials and soldiers, ordered all debts of his pseudo father Tsar Ivan IV to be paid out of the royal treasury; removed many taxes and fines from judicial convictions; sternly prohibited all bribery and punished many unconscionable judges who were apprehended. Otrepyev announced that he would personally in Red Square, every Wednesday and Saturday, accept petitions from residents and citizens. His edicts on behalf of serfs and peasants also gained him popularity. He ordered serfs to return to their estates and landowners, except for those that fled during the famine of Tsar Boris, while serfs that were impressed into service at state-owned estates were permitted freedom. In order to further gain the trust of his Russian subjects, Otrepyev released his foreign bodyguards and Polish gentry from service, allotting each of them compensation for their service in the amount of 40 gold coins each and a bag. The exercise failed because the amount did not satisfy the greed of the bodyguards and gentry, and so they refused to leave Moscow. The money was then squandered on drinking and feasting.

Still captivated by the customs of the lands of Lithuania and Poland where his career as Dmitri Ivanovich was initiated, and which Otrepyev considered more excellent and couth in comparison with Russia's, the new monarch became disenchanted with the composition of the State Duma and so altered its membership. In addition to the specific boyars of high standing and the irregular appearance of the patriarch on important matters, Otrepyev added clergy to the Duma to gratify the secular ambitions of certain ROC prelates. He added four metropolitans, 7 archbishops, and three bishops. The titles of the members also changed following the Polish custom and the Duma members were now designated senators and he increased their number to 70, as opposed to as little as five and as many as 20 under previous tsars. As opposed to the appellation of Duma, the supreme legislative council now became known as the Senate. Otrepyev likewise regularly attended the sessions, heard the issues and decided matters with unusual ease. Otrepyev had a gift of eloquence and impressed the Duma members with his advice; he was very verbose and was able to articulate his opinions clearly and precisely. He loved to compare, often referring to history or what he saw in his travels, or in Poland and Lithuania. Otrepyev would tell of his high regard for the French King, Henry IV of Navarre, and would boast of himself in their presence, boast of his kind-heart, humility, magnanimity and his ability to encourage others. Once Otrepyev stated at a Duma session, "I can retain the throne in two manners: using either tyranny or mercy. I would prefer to use mercy and so fulfill the promise I made to God: not to spill blood."

Otrepyev was lauded by the populace. Proto-pope Terenti of the Moscow Blagoveschenski (Annunciation) Church composed a commendation on his behalf lauding Otrepyev as a valiant king with charity impressed on his lips. The Patriarch of Jerusalem wrote a letter to

Otrepyev informing him that all Palestine rejoices over the deliverance of the son of Tsar Ivan, and that three lamps were dedicated to the memory of Tsar Dmitri at one of the Jerusalem churches. The effort was not without purpose, the patriarch hoping that Otrepyev would assemble a Russian army to defeat Islam, now occupying most of the Eastern Orthodox sees.

People closest to Otrepyev advised him to quickly and formally have the coronation performed, which had not yet been accomplished. This would solidify him as tsar and grand prince of Moscow and all Russia. The coronation would be performed by the Patriarch of Moscow, but because Otrepyev did not trust any of the Russian clergy — most of them knowing him as monk Grigori from his earlier assignment at Chudovski Monastery — Otrepyev decided to install a new patriarch who was not Russian in place of the defrocked Job, the sycophant of Tsar Boris. The selection was a Greek, Ignatius, formerly archbishop of Cypress who abandoned his diocese when the island fell under the occupation of Ottoman Turks. Ignatius lived a short while in Rome and then arrived in Russia during the reign of Tsar Feodor Ivanovich. He was able to gain the favor of Tsar Boris and was installed as archbishop of Ryazan in 1603.

While Otrepyev was residing in Tula, Ignatius sought his favor and Otrepyev recognized a perfect candidate for the patriarchate: Ignatius had no genuine moral convictions, no loyalty to Russia, no shame, and that he could be used as an instrumental part of Otrepyev's deception of Russia. Ignatius was installed as patriarch of Moscow without a moments delay and he began to prepare for the coronation while Otrepyev was preparing himself for the triumphant pinnacle of his fraud: to wear the crown of Monomakh as the son of Tsar Ivan IV Vasilyevich that would confirm him as Tsar of Moscow and all Russia, which would also affirm his right to the throne before the entire population of Russia and the sovereigns of other nations.

So far the military, senate and all state officials recognized Otrepyev as Dmitri Ivanovich, all except his False mother, whose testimony was important and a political necessity. Otrepyev had now resided in Moscow a month while the populace had yet to see his False mother Marina Nagoi, living about 350 miles away at the Nikolai-Viksinski Convent.

But Otrepyev was unsure whether she would agree to and collaborate in the fraud, which would have been objectionable to the holy calling of a nun as well as her motherly instincts; her age was about 40 at this time. From the one side she was offered a royal life-style should she cooperate, from the other, the threat of torture and death should she betray him. Should she be obstinate, which Otrepyev feared, his agents could quickly strangle her and inform the public that she died of some illness and she would receive a pompous and dignified funeral worth a tsaritza, and so also calm any doubts people may have.

Confined to a convent as a nun and always under surveillance and still an able woman, Marina remembered the gaiety of society, the royal court and the extravagance of being wife of the tsar of Russia; but now for 13 years she wept in humiliation due to the indignity she suffered with the murder of her son and a hopeless future. Then Otrepyev publicly sent Pr. Mikhail Vasilyevich Skopin-Shuisky and other dignitaries with a pleading petition from a dear son wanting her blessing at his coronation. Marina agreed to their proposition and she was moved from the convent to the village Taininski, a short distance outside of Moscow.

On July 18, Otrepyev met Marina Nagoi, his False mother. Along the road a large tent was erected, and both mother and son entered the tent in view of the accompanying royal court and curious crowd that gathered for the historic event. The artificial and hypocritical display had its definite positive impact on the spectators: their rendezvous appearing so natural and sincere, False mother and son were alone in the tent and only their shallow voices were heard with no clear recognition of their subject matter or content. Then the two exited the tent displaying joy and love, intimately embracing each other, tears flowing on each of their cheeks, so indicative of a long-awaited meeting after 13 years of absence and the resurrection of each. The considerate crowd wept with the royal parent and child convinced of the sincerity and trustworthiness of the historic event. Otrepyev placed Marina in a decorated carriage while he and the other dignitaries walked behind. After a mile or so, Otrepyev mounted his horse and sped ahead to the Kremlin to again publicly greet his mother in view of the court at the entrance to her former residence at the palace. Marina only resided a short time at the Kremlin and then she was moved to new quarters at the Novo-Devichi Convent along with some royal servants to attend to her needs. Otrepyev felt that distance was best after the superficial theatrics of their meeting, while Marina could also be kept in seclusion and surveillance at the convent. Otrepyev visited with her daily at first, appearing as a submissive and considerate son until he was satisfied that she would not betray their fraud. Visitors were also forbidden to meet with Marina in private and conversations with them were limited even if in public, lest she change her mind or say something disclosing the fraud.

Coronation of Tsar False Dmitri I and the Polish Intervention

The coronation of Tsar False Dmitri Ivanovich was performed at Uspenski Cathedral on July 21, 1605. Patr. Ignatius, in the presence of an ecclesiastical assembly, the Boyar Duma, and both Moscovite and provincial noblemen, along with representatives of major cities, crowned Grigori Otrepyev according to the traditional rite and he became tsar of Moscow and all Russia. However, after the sacred service, the Russian attendants were astonished when Jesuit Nikolai Chernikovski congratulated the newly-crowned monarch in Latin, a language foreign to them and then read letters from Pope Paul V to all attending. After the coronation the assembly moved to Arkhangelsk Cathedral where Otrepyev kissed the sepulchers of his False ancestors — the earlier tsars and grand princes — and accepted the crown of Vladimir Monomakh from the Greek Archbishop Arsenius of Elasson, placing it upon his head. Otrepyev then announced his soon marriage to Marina Mnishek, Polish military commander Yuri Mnishek's daughter. Officials, clergy and his False family feasted that day to celebrate the occasion, even though many were aware of the fraud.

Otrepyev's character began to change after the coronation: he became his greatest enemy; having become quick-tempered, arrogant, careless and inconsiderate as a result of his success. Even though he impressed the boyars with his acute mind and lively debates in state affairs, he often forgot himself and would insult them with jokes, insult their lack of intelligence, irritate them by flaunting the capabilities of foreigners and insisting that Russia become the pupil of foreign nations in order to improve their own education and culture. Poland was always on the tip of his tongue, and to further insult the Russian officials Otrepyev assigned two Polish gentry — the Buchinski brothers — to positions of private royal secretaries. As a result, the boyars were no longer able to draw close to their tsar, having lost their titles and rank in the Duma and they felt embarrassed. Only one Russian from beginning to end had the trust and friendship of Otrepyev: Basmanov, the guiltiest one of them all for capitulating to the fraud. But Basmanov likewise erred in his relationship: he considered himself the sole favorite, although Otrepyev discarded most of the advice provided by Basmanov and at times just to irritate Basmanov and impress on him that Otrepyev was not going to be the pupil but the preceptor. Irritating the boyars with his lack of manners and uncouth attitude toward them, Otrepyev soon lost their respect.

In time the Russian populace likewise turned a cold-shoulder to him as a result of his imprudence. Although Otrepyev acquired some education in school and more while in the company of Polish gentry, he would laugh at the superstitions of the Russian devotion to their religious idiosyncrasies. Otrepyev did not make the sign of the cross in front of icons, did not allow his confessor to bless or sprinkle his meals with holy water, and he would sit at table to eat without allowing the priest to first pray, but preferred music played by his Polish orchestra. Devoted Russians were insulted by Otrepyev's favoritism toward Catholic Jesuits, whom he settled in the best rooms inside the Kremlin and allowed to conduct Catholic mass in Latin. Passionate toward foreign customs it never came to the thoughtless mind of Otrepyev to observe Russian customs, but in the manner he dressed and styled his hair, walked and moved his body, he preferred those of the Polish gentry. Otrepyev ate veal, which was proscribed and considered base by Russian culture. He never visited the steam bath and would not take a nap after dining, as did previous Russian monarchs, but preferred to take a walk. Regularly Otrepyev would stealthily leave the palace, alone or with a companion, and visit artists, goldsmiths, the apothecary, while palace servants would chase him down in the Moscow city streets. The populace expected their monarch to only display himself publicly in dignity and pomp, surrounded by royal servants, and it annoyed them to see him dressed as a common denizen.

Even Otrepyev's amusements and sport seemed strange; he enjoyed riding wild horses and personally boxed bears with his bare hands in rings with both royalty and rabble attending. Otrepyev would personally test new guns and shoot at a target, although seldom with good aim. Participating in such crude activities Otrepyev would seem to have forgotten his rank. At the same time, he would personally ruthlessly beat any official that would snicker or ridicule him if he should fail or flounder during sporting activities. Although Otrepyev rode horse back as often as he could, even to church, he possessed a large number of chariots for warm weather and sleds for cold. They had silver ornaments on them and were covered with velvet and furs. The bridles on his pride Asiatic steeds were made of gold, and the saddles were gold-leaf with embedded sapphires and rubies. His horsemen were dressed as well as the best state dignitaries. New buildings were also erected by Otrepyev. He demolished the palace of Tsar Boris Godunov and built a new one for himself near the Moscow River. The walls he covered with Persian embroidery and the window frames were of silver.

Otrepyev was criticized for his excessive spending and squander of the royal treasury. He distributed money and rewards insanely. For example, he would pay his foreign musicians more than the primary state officials. Otrepyev loved pomp and luxury and buying expensive goods, and in the first three months after his coronation he squandered over 7 million rubles. The Russian populace disdained such a spendthrift, fearing taxation to compensate for the depletion of the state treasury. Describing the brilliance of the Moscow court and Kremlin, foreigners in amazement spoke of Otrepyev's throne, cast from pure gold, inlaid with clusters of diamonds and pearls, and setting upon two silver lions. Above the throne hung a gold globe and the emblem of the two-headed eagle, also cast gold.

Otrepyev did not lack in promiscuity and regularly violated married women and young girls whom he brought into the palace during the night and who left before sunrise, or else he would patronize brothels in the cover of darkness. A brood of mothers surfaced after the death of Otrepyev, testifying to their clandestine affairs with their pregnancies or newly-born babes. To complete the pinnacle of his amoral excess, Otrepyev took Ksenia, daughter of Tsar Boris, away from Pr. Vasili Mosalski and she became his concubine. It was a decadent manner of Otrepyev's display of his triumph over Boris Godunov. In December 1605, with the arrival of his bride Marina Mnishek from Poland and at the threat of his father-in-law, Otrepyev had Ksenia confined to a convent near Kirillo Monastery at Beloye Ozero and forced her to take the veil as a nun with the new name of Olga.

Since it was the desire of the Russian populace to have someone of the royal posterity to sit on the throne of Russia, even with many character faults, Otrepyev could have continued his fraud longer if his facade did not collapse in their eyes. Because it was deceit that elevated Otrepyev, it would be truth that would dethrone him. Even ex-patriarch Job remembered the Chudovski fugitive monk from earlier years, and so Otrepyev was doomed to play the part, deceiving himself more than anyone so as not to allow doubt in anyone's mind that he was the true Dmitri Ivanovich delivered from death. However he refused to enter Chudovski Monastery, fearing someone would recognize him or that the memory of his earlier residence there would somehow slip and betray him. Nonetheless, beginning with his entrance into Moscow, people whispered under their breath one to another about the physical similarities between their tsar and monk Grigori. The whispers eventually turned into shouts from the roof tops. One Chudovski monk who had attended school with Grigori Otrepyev and knew him from childhood publicly voiced his opinion that this was the same Otrepyev. The monk vanished from sight and was secretly executed in some Moscow dungeon.

Quickly the witness of many Ukrainians, native Russians and close associates of monk Grigori echoed throughout Moscow. His uncle, brother and even mother, the good-natured widow Varvara ,saw him and recognized him, and they could not remain silent. Mother and brother were locally incarcerated while uncle Smirni-Otrepyev was exiled to Siberia. Arrested also were the nobleman Peter Turgenev and the commoner Feodor, both of who publicly aroused people against Otrepyev. The imposter ordered that they both be executed, and noticed to his satisfaction that the gathered crowd, which was earlier grateful for his pardon of Shuisky, did not display any repulsion or empathy toward the two martyrs. Both were led to their death without fear or regret, shouting aloud that Tsar Dmitri was the antichrist and satan's sycophant; they voiced their sorrow for Russia and foretold further calamity as a result of the presence of Otrepyev. The mass of spectators — the lower class residents of Moscow — reviled the condemned men, but the incident did not suppress the reports, whether true or false. All who voiced their doubts about the validity of Otrepyev's claims were apprehended and taken into custody and the reigns of terror of Tsar Ivan IV and Boris Godunov were repeated. The victims were tortured, executed, strangled in dungeons, deprived of their possessions, or exiled, just for one spoken work of doubt regarding the validity of Otrepyev as legitimate tsar of Russia. The monks and other residents of Chudovski Monastery were exiled by order of Otrepyev to distance hermitages in forsaken areas, although he left unmolested Metr. Pafnuti of Krutitzk, sparing him only due to his high rank and influence in the ROC, even though he recognized monk Grigori at first glance. The effort was able to achieve its goal and silence descended over Moscow, every person fearing to say anything that might jeopardize their life.

Not trusting Russians, Otrepyev selected 300 Germans as his new bodyguards and divided them into three regiments. He armed them with halberds, spears, hatchets and battle axes, all having the Russian eagle on the handle imbedded with gold and silver. The bodyguards were allotted from 40 to 70 rubles salary per year along with free room and board. Beginning at this time Otrepyev did not go anywhere alone, but was always accompanied by formidable bodyguards and then boyars and other court officials followed behind, but Otrepyev was wrong in his assertion that a handful of guards could protect him from the rise of a hundred-thousand Russian soldiers under the authority of the boyars and landowners.

Meanwhile Otrepyev wanted joy: music, dancing and gambling were daily events at the court. To gratify Otrepyev's taste for elegance, court officials dressed up and every day was a festivity, but it was different in the city. As one chronicler related, "Many wept in their homes, although on the streets they seemed joyous and dressed for a festivity."

The disenchantment toward Otrepyev spread slowly as a virus through the body of the Moscow populace.

In Poland, no one more served the interests of Otrepyev in his absence than the papal nuncio Rangoni, who wrote flattering letters to him after his ascension to the throne. Rangoni's hope was that Otrepyev would likewise fulfill their agreement to install Unia in Russia, for the ROC to become subject to Papal authority in Rome. Soon after Otrepyev's coronation Alexander Rangoni, nephew of the Papal nuncio, arrived in Moscow with an apostolic blessing from Pope Paul V, who was eager to see himself at the head of Catholicism expanding into Russia. The effort on the part of Otrepyev was slow in regards to converting Russia to Unia, because of more pressing state matters. The subtle King Sigismund, the primary benefactor of Otrepyev, soon realized that the good-fortune of Otrepyev had changed his character; he who earlier had kissed the hands of Sigismund while condescending to him like a servant had now ascended to the throne, which contributed to his change in attitude. Having been the immediate reason for the success of Otrepyev, providing the fugitive-monk and imposter money, soldiers, and recognition of his person as Dmitri Ivanovich, Sigismund naturally expected some gratitude. But Otrepyev responded to Sigismund's delegate Alexandr Gosevski (or Gonsevski) coldly because Sigismund only referred to him as Master and Grand Prince in his letters, but not as Tsar. Otrepyev expected Sigismund to treat him as an equal, but Sigismund knew better and refused. Such arrogance on the part of Otrepyev infuriated Sigismund when he heard of it, and he pressed Otrepyev to make good on his promises.

Turbulent Reign and Marriage of Tsar False Dmitri I

Having calmed, or so he thought, Moscow, Otrepyev hastened to fulfill his promise to Marina Mnishek, to take her hand in marriage and bestow on her the crown as tsaritza of Russia. Otrepyev felt she had earned this honor as a result of her support of him since their initial meeting in Poland. Communication had been steady between Otrepyev and Yuri Mnishek, his designated father-in-law. Otrepyev would regularly inform Mnishek of his successes, referring to him as father and friend, having written to him from Putivl, Tula and Moscow. Mnishek

wrote in reply not only to Otrepyev, but also to boyars and court officials requiring their recognition of Otrepyev as the legitimate monarch
and genuine son of Tsar Ivan IV.

In September 1605, Otrepyev dispatched secretary Afanasi Vasilyev
to Krakow, Poland, to complete his engagement to Marina Mnishek,
along with a letter to Polish King Sigismund. Otrepyev did not discuss
the matter of his marriage with the Boyar Duma, as previous tsars and
grand princes had done, but only told them that his correspondence
was with Polish gentry. The selection of a wife for the tsar was not a
private matter, as in most marriages, but was a national matter since
she would also be crowned as tsaritza or queen.

On November 1, 1605, Afanasi Vlasyev arrived in Krakow with a
large retinue of court attendants and met with Sigismund. Vlasyev
spoke of the successful coronation of the son of Tsar Ivan IV, of his
intentions to rage war and overthrow the Ottoman Empire, and occupy
Greece, Jerusalem, Bethlehem and the balance of the Holy Land (at the
time under Ottoman occupation), and the desire of Otrepyev to share
his throne with Marina Mnishek because of the assistance provided to
him by her father.

The engagement was performed November 12, 1605, in the presence of King Sigismund, son Wladyslaw, and sister Anna the Swedish
Queen, the liturgy being performed by a Jesuit priest named Grokhovs-
ki. Marina with a crown on her head and dressed in white, and weighed
down by the weight of the jewels woven into her dress, glistened in
beauty and elegance. Afanasi Vlasyev stood in for Otrepyev, and father
Yuri Mnishek blessed his daughter for both the marriage and her coronation as tsaritza of Russia. Lithuanian chancellor Lev Sapega gave a
long address, as did the cardinal-bishop of Krakow. Vlasyev placed a
large diamond ring on the finger of Marina to complete the ceremony.
During the celebration dinner, Marina sat next to King Sigismund and
accepted gifts from Russian dignitaries given on behalf of Otrepyev: a
writing pen of ruby, a hyacinth bowl, a gold ship encrusted with jewels,
a gold ox, pelican and peacock, a clock (a novelty for the era and region)
with flutes and trumpets engraved on it, along with 7 lbs of pearls, 640
furs, and bundles of velvet, brocaded cloth, silk and satin, and on and
on. On behalf of future mother-in-law Marina Nagoi, an engraving of

the Holy Trinity in a precious setting was given, a sign of her blessing of the wedding. Vlasyev the vicarious groom was somewhat embarrassed and attempted to be courteous, but he refused to sit alongside Marina at the table, and it annoyed him to the bone when the guests were already toasting for the health of the tsar and tsaritza, although this was only an engagement ceremony. After dinner the guests and dignitaries danced with Marina, but Vlasyev refused to do so.

On the following day, the engagement ring for Otrepyev as a gift from his bride was dispatched to Moscow along with her portrait painted by a Polish artist. Vlasyev, who was also to accompany the Mnisheks to Moscow, remained in Krakow until December 8, and then moved to Slonim (in the present Belarus), there to meet the Mnisheks on their departure from Poland.

Having sacrificed a substantial portion of his wealth to the cause of Otrepyev Yuri Mnishek was not at all satisfied with a few gifts, but wanted more money and enough at least to compensate him for his losses and to pay creditors, and he was not about to leave Krakow to Russia until Otrepyev satisfied his debt. Mnishek was alarmed by what he heard was occurring in Moscow, the disdain of Russians toward Otrepyev and many not willing to accept him as the actual son Dmitri Ivanovich delivered from death or the testimony that was provided. Poles in Krakow were not ignorant about the talk in Moscow and they warned Yuri Mnishek. Even the False mother Marina Nagoi clandestinely dispatched a Swedish messenger to King Sigismund to inform him that False Tsar Dmitri was not her son. Russian officials whispered into the ears of the curious about the escapades and sport of Otrepyev and their opinion that his reign would be short. But King Sigismund and Yuri Mnishek refused to acknowledge the validity of such reports, brushing it off as libelous gossip from envy or else circulated by friends of the Godunov and Shuisky families. But it was too late in the game to sever the connections between Poland and Otrepyev, and the Mnisheks pressed their demands. Finally in January 1606, secretary Yan Buchinski brought 200,000 gold ducats from Moscow to Yuri Mnishek and King Sigismund to compensate them for their investment. Mnishek still procrastinated, using as an excuse the poor roads and traveling condition of winter.

Having surrounded himself with foreign bodyguards and noticing calm in Moscow and the ambivalent attitude of court officials, Otrepyev was drawn to believe some seer's prediction that he would reign for 34 years. Otrepyev would feast with boyars and allow them to select their own brides and marry. The popular Boyar Pr. Feodor Mstislavski, although now a mature person, took advantage of the ease of restrictions on this issue and married Praskovya Ivanovna, a cousin of the widow-tsaritza Marina Nagoi. To gain the favor of Moscow residents, even with his clandestine reign of terror in force, Otrepyev poured money into public dinners and festivities, people taking advantage of his generosity, although superficially. Otrepyev forgave the Shuisky brothers, returning them from exile after six months and returning to them their wealth and rank, which was to the satisfaction of their many friends.

People lauded Otrepyev for the pardon, but this only blinded him to their real intentions since Vasili Shuisky was a dedicated Russian statesman and idolized by people as well as being a descendent of the ancient royal princes of Suzdal and Vladimir. His rebuke of Otrepyev, his sentence to death, his survival from exile and endurance of torture, made Vasili Shuisky appear as a brilliant hero and survival-martyr, incomparable with any other living person in Russia at the time. No one at the time had such influence over the minds of Russia as did Vasili Shuisky, as well as being personally ambitious and bold, yet dedicated to the prosperity of Russia and every citizen. Pr. Vasili Shuisky signed a codified oath of loyalty to Otrepyev and so returned to Moscow as a different person, appearing to be appreciative of Otrepyev for not executing him and only sentencing him to six months exile. But only a fool such as Otrepyev would actually believe Shuisky was sincere in his oath of loyalty. Now Shuisky had to take one of two courses of events: destroy Otrepyev or be destroyed for sure by Otrepyev. Upon the return of Vasili Shuisky from exile Otrepyev insisted that he take a wife, so Shuisky selected Princess Maria Buinosova, daughter of Pr. Peter Ivanovich Buinosov of Rostov, related to the Nagoi family, and the wedding date was set a few days after the planned wedding of Otrepyev and Marina Mnishek (however, the wedding did not occur until several years later).

Otrepyev continued to vex the Russian populace as a result of his thoughtless actions and uncultured attitude. As a result, xenophobia developed among Russians toward the Germans, Poles and Lithuanians that Otrepyev brought with him. The foreigners would attend ROC services with weapons at their side, and would lean or sit on the vaults containing the remains of saints. The conduct of the Cossacks loyal to Otrepyev — who followed him to Moscow from the Ukraine — likewise brought him contempt from the Russian populace. Otrepyev would also humiliate the ranks of monasticism, discredit monks at every chance available, appropriate money from monasteries to fund the state treasury and his opulence, and then demand an account of all monastic income in order to know how much more he could appropriate to compensate for his private army. As the funds in the state treasury declined Otrepyev began to appropriate money from monasteries: 3,000 rubles from Joseph-Voloko-Lamsk; 5,000 from Kirillo-Belozersk, and 30,000 from Troitse-Sergieva. Such appropriations caused the ROC clergy to become his most formidable enemy. Otrepyev banished the Arbatski and Chertolski priests from their homes and used them to house his bodyguards. As ROC priests conducted services in their churches and publicly prayed on behalf of Otrepyev, they would secretly curse him in private and whisper to parishioners that he was persecuting the ROC and was actually a heretic, inferring his bias towards Catholicism. Otrepyev permitting Lutherans to conduct services in their churches in the German Quarter caused him to lose more respect with ROC clergy.

About this time, another imposter surfaced, who was of no benefit to the credibility of Otrepyev. Noticing the success and honor attributed to the Don Cossacks who accompanied Otrepyev to Moscow, the Volga and Tersk Cossacks nominated one of their own, a young man named Eleika, and identified him as Peter, a son of Tsar Feodor Ivanovich. The fraud was that Irina Feodorovna in 1592 actually gave birth to a son, whom Boris Godunov exchanged for a girl, Fedosia, while the boy went into hiding. Some 4,000 Volga and Tersk Cossacks joined the procession from southeastern Russia to central Russia with their newly-designated tsar Peter Feodorovich. Every city they passed from Astrakhan to Kazan was plundered, resulting in a total of some 300,000 rubles worth of spoils.

Otrepyev did not interfere with their journey and rather wrote to pseudo-Peter, inviting him to Moscow and urging him to hasten his arrival, and saying that he would be accepted with honor in Moscow. No one believed the new imposter, although some felt collusion between the two imposters had been arranged and that the spoils would be used to further the agenda of Otrepyev. The journey of pseudo-Peter — Eleika — moved slowly, and by the time the company reached Sviazhsk Otrepyev had been murdered and so the Cossacks dispersed.

The anxiety regarding Otrepyev increased and his greatest supporter Basmanov even admitted that Otrepyev was not the son of Tsar Ivan, but his justification was that because Otrepyev was tsar, and the populace accepted him as tsar, having sworn an oath of loyalty, than they had the obligation to observe their loyalty. So did Basmanov justify himself, while others felt that the oath was invalid because the oath was directed towards the son of Tsar Ivan IV, their legitimate tsar, and not to an imposter. This was the thinking of the boyars and Russian aristocracy. Some were even willing to take the chance and accept pseudo-Peter in lieu of Otrepyev. Eventually the thread of conspiracy ran from the senior members of the Boyar Duma — the Shuisky, Romanov and Mstislavski families — through all the levels of the government to the general population, including these that knew Grigori Otrepyev in earlier years. It was also common knowledge that Otrepyev intended to convert Russia to Unia, subjection to the Pope, after his wedding. The conspiracy to overthrown Otrepyev was postponed until after his wedding and the coronation of Marina, the conspirators knowing that the event would agitate the people to a point of frenzy and so guarantee success. Rumors were circulated to the detriment of Otrepyev, some true, some not: one was that he was preparing for war against Europe; another, a war against Islam. Otrepyev had already irritated the Sultan Shah Abbas by sending him as a gift a coat made of pigskin, an animal considered unclean by Islam. On the other hand, Otrepyev kept good relations with the Khan of the Crimean Mongols, Kazi-Geri.

Yuri Mnishek meanwhile procrastinated in Minsk, awaiting further funds from Moscow. Otrepyev forwarded to him 5000 more 20-ruble gold pieces and 5,000 rubles in gold, and 13,000 thalers for Marina. On April 8, 1606, Yuri Mnishek, his daughter Marina, and a large retinue of 2,000 Poles and Lithuanians, crossed into Russia. Marina wept the entire journey from Krakow to Moscow because of anxiety and premonitions of sorrow in the future and could not be comforted by the assurances of Afanasi Vlasyev who kept reminding her that she will be crowned as tsaritza of Russia. Marina rode in a carriage pulled by 12 white horses and was accompanied from the border to Moscow by False uncle Mikhail Nagoi and Pr. Vasili Mosalski. Every city and village the procession passed greeted the royal bride with the traditional bread and salt and priests carrying icons. Residents of Smolensk, Dorogobuzh and Vyazma brought expensive gifts, all urging for the favoritism of the bride once installed as tsaritza. The attitude of the Polish gentry and officials of the group was otherwise: they were awaiting the extension of their borders into Russia, back to the period when Lithuania was at its pinnacle of power and expansion in the 15th century, while Russia wallowed under Mongol occupation.

On April 25, having arrived in Moscow, Yuri Mnishek was in ecstasy when he saw his future son-in-law on his majestic throne, with the patriarch and bishops at his right and boyars and other state officials at his left. Mnishek kissed Otrepyev's hand and could not find words sufficient to describe his good-fortune to be at the royal court. Otrepyev listened attentively to Mnishek's words of appreciation and even wiped a tear or two from his cheeks with a handkerchief. That evening Mnishek dined with Otrepyev at his new palace, where the Polish guests lauded the wealth and food; Mnishek, his son, and son-in-law Adam Vishnevetzki, ate from gold plates. (Marina remained behind in a village 10 miles from Moscow with her personal retinue.) During the dinner Otrepyev boasted of the immeasurable expanse of Russia and its diverse population, consisting of several cultures and languages. That evening they listened to a Polish orchestra while the guests danced. For five days straight Yuri Mnishek and his family and Polish officials were subject to continuous lunches and dinners and hunts for wild animals. Otrepyev impressed them with his abilities and boldness as he beat a bear with a metal rod and then decapitated the bear with a sword, while the spectators would laugh and shout, "Hail the king."

While Marina Mnishek was still in Krakow, Otrepyev wrote to her that she as tsaritza of Russia was obligated to observe the rites of the ROC, have respect for the national religion, and to observe the customs and traditions of Moscovite women in the manner princesses and tsaritzas have in the past. The papal nuncio Rangoni replied with his objection, that the autocrat himself has no obligation to observe — as he labeled it — the superstition of the ignorant populace, and that no law prohibits marriage between a Catholic and an Orthodox, while requiring the wife to sacrifice her religion in favor of the husbands. The compromise to permit the marriage made between Otrepyev and ROC prelates was for Marina to attend ROC services and take communion from the patriarch once a week, while she would be allowed to practice her Catholic rites at a private chapel in the tsar's palace. Patr. Ignatius did not make conversion or baptism in the ROC a mandatory requirement for Marina to marry in an Orthodox Church or be crown as tsaritza. Out of fear for their own security prelates consented. However some conservative prelates objected and voiced their concerns, but not without the expected repercussions. Metr. Hermogen of Kazan and Bishop Iyosef of Kolomensk were both exiled for confirming ROC statutes that required the bride to be baptized into the ROC, or the wedding would be illegitimate. Nonetheless, wedding arrangements proceeded when the wedding party arrived in Moscow.

On May 2, 1606, Marina Mnishek and her personal retinue entered Moscow watched by some 100,000 spectators; she had 13 carriages filled with her personal belongings. A Polish marching band was at the tail end of the procession following her. Marina was greeted by Pr. Mstislavski, who gave a public speech of welcome, while the balance bowed low to ground as a sign of respect. Bells rang, guns were fired, drums were beat, and trumpets blown to greet the arrival of Marina Mnishek into Moscow. The attitude of Moscow's populace was diverse: some were happy, others were curious at the Polish import, while others were sorrowful that she was not Russian and the sight of more Europeans entering Russia — her personal retinue — was a premonition of worse to come. ROC prelates greeted the Catholic bride at the gates to the Kremlin to welcome her, as if she was one of their own; an event unheard-of in Russian history. The bride was housed at the Novo-Devichi Convent where she met the widow-tsaritza Marina Nagoi, her future False mother-in-law, and also Otrepyev, whom she had not seen in some two years.

The Moscovite aristocracy and episcopacy were seething in the meanwhile. Having housed Yuri Mnishek in Tsar Boris Godunov's former residence in the Kremlin, assigning the best homes in the Eastern and White Quarters for their companions, while displacing the original residents, people were annoyed. The thousands of Europeans that had arrived with Otrepyev and subsequently with the wedding party, most of them armed — an unknown situation in Moscow society where few carried a weapon — intimidated Moscovites and they wondered whether the Europeans were planning to occupy the city. The boyars discovered the secret arrangement for transfer of the Smolensk and Severski (northwest Ukraine) regions once Otrepyev was to ascend to power. Otrepyev called a special session of Boyar Duma to convince them that not even one handful of Russian soil would be yielded to any European country during his reign, but the boyars were not to be fooled by a new deceit.

Moscovite women had one eye on Marina Mnishek. Supposedly she was learning how to be Russian while at Novo-Devichi Convent, but nothing of the sort. She isolated herself in her cloister with her personal attendant. Otrepyev would smuggle musicians and clowns into her cell to amuse her, which seemed to the monastic residents to desecrate the sacredness of their sanctuary. Marina refused to eat the bland dishes served at the convent, and Otrepyev had a Polish cook at the Kremlin cook special dishes and bring them to her cloister in secret. Moscow seethed with disgust at hearing of these occurrences.

Over the one month between the arrival of Yuri Mnishek and the wedding day, Otrepyev squandered over 800,000 rubles on hosting his guests, plus 100,000 gold ducats paid directly to Yuri Mnishek for his role in supporting Otrepyev. Two days before the wedding, Otrepyev bought for his bride a richly ornamented jewelry box at the cost of 50,000 rubles. The gifts purchased for the retinue of the Mnisheks, as well as the cost for their lodging and dinner, depleted millions from the state treasury just in the one month, and many Poles were planning to remain in Moscow at the expense of Otrepyev. The populace became incensed as they saw the state treasury — the proceeds of which was due to their effort and that of previous tsars — funneled into catering to the immemorial enemies of Russia, the Poles and Lithuanians.

From the Novo-Devichi Convent Marina was moved to the Voznesenski Convent inside the Kremlin a week before the wedding. Patr. Ignatius issued strict instructions to the nuns for Marina to observe Orthodox canons in food and clothing, and that she learn the conduct and protocol expected of her as wife of an Orthodox king. Under orders of Patr. Ignatius, no Catholic priest, and especially any Jesuit, was allowed into the convent. During the night of May 7/8, 1606, Marina was moved from the convent to the palace, and the wedding was set for May 9.

That morning the tsar and Marina met at the Granite Chamber, where feudal princes and noblemen were gathered. Otrepyev sat on the tsar's seat and Marina was invited to sit on the seat next to him. Officials entered the Granite Chamber bringing with them the symbols of imperial authority: the crown of Vladimir Monomakh, a pectoral cross, a gold chain, and a small cape that hung over the shoulders interwoven with jewels. Otrepyev arose and kissed the cross and crown, while his confessor recited words to the prayer, "Worthy is the Lamb." Marina descended from her seat and down three steps, as a sign of condescension and likewise kissed the Orthodox cross and crown, and then returned to her seat. Royal emissaries then lined up to offer their congratulations to the tsar and tsarevna, while the assembly awaited indication that clergy were ready for their marriage and her coronation. An official then made a sign, which was relayed to the bell ringer at the palace. Once the Kremlin bells began to ring, all the bells in Moscow joined in until the entire city resonated from the sound of church bells. Otrepyev and Marina arose from their seats and moved toward Uspenski Cathedral.

The doors of the cathedral opened and Patr. Ignatius and a procession of prelates exited into the Kremlin courtyard, all of them wearing full sacerdotal vestments. Tsar and tsarevna walked arm in arm wearing long Russian-style robes having wide sleeves and made of pink velvet. The cloth, which the robes were made of, could hardly be seen under the massive layer of smoothly polished diamonds, emeralds, sapphires and rubies in gold settings. Setting on the head of Marina was a Russian-style headdress, embedded with diamonds, the value of which was 500,000 Dutch gilders. On Otrepyev's side walked his father-in-law Yuri Mnishek, and on Marina's side walked Praskovya Ivanovna wife of Feodor Mstislavski. Directly behind them walked the two men who were coincidentally planning Otrepyev's murder: princes Vasili Shuisky and Vasili Golitsyn (these two men's wives were also cousins). To hide their preconceived scheme, the two of them superficially participated in all coronation and marriage rites. The balance of the Boyar Duma followed behind.

Having entered Uspenski Cathedral, Otrepyev kissed the icon of the Vladimir Theotokos and the icons of the metropolitans of Russia. Shuisky then brought Marina up to the icons, and she fell upon her knees in front of them and kissed them. Patr. Ignatius formally greeted the tsar and tsarevna, blessed them, and with great celebration placed a crown on Marina's head, a mantle over her shoulders, and hung a cross around her neck, all of this signifying her as the new queen or tsaritza of Moscow and all Russia. The marriage rite then followed. After performing the marriage liturgy Patr. Ignatius anointed her with holy oil as a sign of her ROC membership and allowed her to partake of the Eucharist. The assembly then vacated Uspenski Cathedral. As they exited, gold coins minted especially for the occasion were distributed to the crowds by the elderly Feodor Mstislavski. To the amazement of the crowds their Polish tsaritza was holding the arm of Pr. Vasili Shuisky as she exited the cathedral! The tsar and his new wife-queen were led to the palace and the festivities of the day ended.

Murder of Tsar Yuri Bogdanovich Otrepyev and the Polish Massacre

Although the day was majestic and pompous for Otrepyev and even more so for Marina it only increased the contempt of the people toward them once the populace saw a foreigner and heterodox as their queen, which gave them more impetus to recognizing their tsar as an imposter and possibly not even Russian, but a member of the Polish gentry. Some traditionalists felt Marina's veneration of the holiest icons of Russia to be sacrilegious, since she was still Catholic, having refused baptism, and these traditionalists felt Patr. Ignatius to be responsible for such a reprehensible action. None of the earlier tsaritzas were celebrated or flaunted as was Marina: not Anastasia Romanova (first wife of Tsar Ivan IV), or Irina Feodorovna (wife of Tsar Feodor Ivanovich), or Maria Grigorievna (wife of Tsar Boris Godunov). Seeing the crown of Monomakh on her head tore into their hearts, especially hearing that only a few Russians were allowed into the cathedral while the majority were Poles. That evening while the nuptials were enjoying their wedding night, several Russian generals of the Novgorod and Pskov regiments, commanders of the Royal Guards (Streltzi), and other influential men of Moscow gathered at the home of Vasili Shuisky to plot the overthrow of the impostor, and so deliver both Russia and Orthodoxy from further decay or betrayal. They, at the same time, would also execute all the foreigners — Poles and Lithuanians — who were part of Mnishek's retinue.

The feasting and revelry of the wedding and coronation festivity continued the following few days with drinking and dancing every evening. It was not until May 15, that state business surfaced on the agenda of Otrepyev as he met with the Boyar Duma. Later that day Otrepyev planned more amusements for himself and his wife's family.

The postponement of Pr. Shuisky's coup until after the wedding proved its value as the populace was now incensed with Otrepyev and the Catholic Europeans now having infiltrated Moscow with no intention of departure. People also surmised that Otrepyev was a puppet of King Sigismund, and not an independent Russian monarch having Russia's interest as his prime concern. Drunk Poles at the wedding festivities boasted to Russian officials, "We have provided you your king." Russians seethed with odium and whispered to one another, "Vengeance is near." Evenings during the week of wedding festivities drunk Poles and Cossacks killed Moscovites arbitrarily and raped women: forcing them out of carriages or breaking into their homes. People demanded justice. The clandestine terror of Otrepyev continued: the royal guard Grigori Mikulin under orders of Otrepyev personally executed other guards who dared to say that Otrepyev was an enemy of the ROC. Timofei Osipov was executed for stating that their tsar was actually Grigori Otrepyev.

Beginning May 12, Pr. Vasili Shuisky was discussing the arrangements for the coup in close association with Pr. Vasili Golitsyn and Boyar Ivan Kurakin, and a number of noblemen, state officials, military commanders and civic leaders. As the conspiracy grew more Russians were being arrested and interrogated by Otrepyev's bodyguards, but they refused to divulge information and Otrepyev knew something was amiss. By May 16, stores in Moscow were completely closed to foreigners and gunpowder was nowhere to be purchased — it was all being saved for the coup.

It was during the week following his wedding that Otrepyev made plans for the betrayal of Orthodoxy to Catholicism. On May 16 he wrote a letter to Pr. Konstantine Vishnevetzki stating that the time had arrived and he was ready to convert Orthodoxy to Unia. Otrepyev's intent was to create an artificial rebellion the following Sunday, May 18. He would use his Polish and Lithuanian troops that were quartered in the city to suppress it by executing a number of boyars, state officials and Royal Guards. The Jesuits would then arrest Russian prelates and demand Moscow residents to swear allegiance to the Catholic pope. However, Sunday was never to arrive because Vasili Shuisky and his confederates were organizing the Royal Guards for an assault on Saturday.

On the night of May 16/17, some 18,000 Russian soldiers stealthily entered Moscow through its gates, with a few surrounding the city stationed in meadows. All 12 gates were guarded by soldiers loyal to the conspirators, not allowing any to enter or leave. Otrepyev was unaware and blind to the movements of Russian troops about Moscow as he sat with friends in his royal chamber enjoying music. The balance of Europeans were sound asleep as the conspirators were reciting a list of targets for the Russian soldiers once the coup began. The Royal Guards in the Kremlin agreed not to interfere with the coup, while city officials were spreading word house to house of the rebellion to begin at dawn.

It was four o'clock on May 17, the most beautiful of spring mornings, when the first bell began to ring at the Cathedral of St. Elijah, and then the other bell towers followed. Residents streamed into Red Square with staves, spears, swords, knives, and handguns, as well as government officials, Royal Guards, merchants and artisans, regular residents and the city rabble. By that time boyars were mounted on their horses and led the crowd into the Kremlin through the Spasski Gate. Vasili Shuisky at the forefront held a sword in one hand and the traditional ROC cross in the other as he entered the Kremlin, and told the crowd, "In the name of God proceed against this evil heretic," pointing at the palace.

Awakened by the alarm bells, Otrepyev arose from his bed in bewilderment and hurried to dress; he asked his servant the reason for the alarms. The servant answered that it was probably a fire, but as Otrepyev looked out the window he heard a ferocious cry from the crowd and their swords and spears held high. Otrepyev called for Basmanov, who spent the night in the palace, and asked him to find out the reason for the alarm. Basmanov went to meet the crowd, asking them the reason for their assembly, and several shouted at him, "Lead us to the imposter, hand the vagrant over to us." Basmanov jumped back and slammed the door, ordering the bodyguards not to allow the insurgents inside. Running to the tsar's chamber, Basmanov told him, "All has ended. Moscow is rioting and they want your head. Save yourself." Otrepyev grabbed a halberd from a bodyguard and went to face the crowd, telling them, "I am not your Godunov." Shots were fired at Otrepyev and the bodyguards pulled him back into the palace and slammed closed the doors. Basmanov again walked out and faced the crowd, now seeing among them several boyars and princes Golitsyn and Mikhail Saltykov. He tried to talk sense into them, to convince them that their treachery, mutiny and anarchy were wrong. Mikhailo Tatischev interrupted him, saying, "Criminal, go to hell," and thrust a knife straight into Basmanov's heart. He fell dead off the porch onto the steps.

By this time some of the crowd had rushed into the palace, disarmed the bodyguards and were searching for Otrepyev, who had thrown down the halberd and was running away room by room to try to escape his unavoidable fate. Having found himself cornered in the last room, Otrepyev jumped out the window. Landing on the stone pavement, he broke his leg and chest, and struck his head; a pool of blood quickly formed. Some of his loyal bodyguards picked him up and Otrepyev regained consciousness. Immediately he begged for their loyalty and defense, promising them money, rank and women, but it was to no avail, since the rioters by now were surrounding him.

Meanwhile, the widow-tsaritza Marina Nagoi had been summoned from her cloister at the Chudovski Monastery where she had been staying since the wedding. She announced to the riotous crowd that her son Dmitri died in her arms in Uglich, and that she — a frail woman — was threatened and intimidated into the lie and deceit, to admit that this stranger was her son. Other Nagoi relatives were summoned that morning and they likewise testified that Dmitri had died and that to save their own life they sided with Otrepyev. Marina Nagoi showed the crowd a portrait of her son and which had no resemblance to Otrepyev.

The bodyguards handed Otrepyev to the vigilantes, who drug him back to the palace. Some rioters asked him, "Who really are you?" Otrepyev answered, "You know, I am Dmitri." Ivan Golitsyn told Otrepyev about the widow-tsaritza recanting her testimony, which was as good a sentence for his execution as any. Otrepyev tried again to gain time so he would explain his situation to them and prove his credibility. The impatient crowd could tolerate no more and two shots from the noblemen Ivan Voikov and Grigori Voluyev terminated Otrepyev's life. The unrestrained crowd mutilated Otrepyev's corpse, stabbing it with their spears and swords and then throwing the body off the porch on top of the body of Basmanov. The bodies of Yuri Bogdanovich Otrepyev (monk Grigori) and Peter Basmanov, naked by this time, were drug out of the Kremlin into the center of Red Square and dumped there in public view.

According to another account, as the Royal Guards encircled Otrepyev with their weapons, Grigori Voluyev told them, "We don't need to let the heretic try to justify himself, I will myself bless this Polish pipe-piper," and then shot him. The Royal Guards plunged their rapiers through his body, and then they carved his torso apart with their halberds. His feet were tied together and he was drug by a horse about the Kremlin courtyard while the crowd threw rocks and dirt at his corpse. Then he was dragged into Red Square.

Some boyars meanwhile were attempting to rescue Marina Mnishek in case the riotous crowd would do to her what they did to her husband. Having heard of his death she in her nightgown ran from the palace onto the porch where the crowd, not recognizing her, knocked her down. Marina then ran back into the palace. The rioters followed her and killed her personal servant Osmulski, but the boyars followed right behind them and stopped them from killing Marina.

At the sound of the initial alarm bell and while the Europeans were still sleeping Russian soldiers surrounded the homes of the Polish gentry, barricaded main streets, and closed the gates. Yuri Mnishek and his family were awakened by the cry, "Death to the gentry," and hurried to arm themselves and their servants, not knowing the intent of the Russian soldiers. Boyars intervened to save their lives. Yuri Mnishek, his son and son-in-law were accompanied to the Kremlin by Royal Guards under the auspices of Pr. Shuisky. Yuri watched as the crowd surrounded them with their swords and spears and noticed the corpses of their countrymen littering the streets.

The raging crowd killed all the members of Otrepyev's Polish orchestra, plundered the residence of the Jesuits and tortured to death the Catholic confessor of Marina Mnishek. They then left the Kremlin and headed for the Eastern and White Quarters of the city, and massacring most every European they could find. There was nowhere to flee, no place was safe, and no pleading with the Russians could save them. They were slaughtered defenseless in their homes and in the streets, which were barricaded with spikes and poles. The confederates and associates of Otrepyev fell at the feet of the Russians and kissed them, begging for mercy in the name of God, on behalf of their innocent wives and children, and offered their possessions as a ransom, and promising more, but it was to no avail as they were killed by sword or spear or knife on the spot.

Russian monks and priests urged the riotous crowd to further their murderous rage, shouting, "Kill the enemies of our religion." Cannons were brought from the arsenal and used on doors that were barred or chained closed from the inside. Not one person remained alive of all the Poles, Lithuanians and Germans that the rioters felt were part of the company of Otrepyev. Polish soldiers and noblemen, doctors and priests, merchants and jewelers, all suffered the same fate, between 1,500 and 2,000 Europeans with about 300 Russians died within hours of Otrepyev's execution. The wives and daughters of the Poles were raped and several were kidnapped as slaves. After hearing that a few of their own Russians had been killed in the frenzy, mainly those wearing Polish-style clothing, princes Mstislavski and Shuisky on their horses raced through the streets telling the vigilantes to cease.

Plunder of the homes of those murdered continued the balance of the day. Russians living in nearby villages rushed to Moscow after hearing the alarm bells and entered the city once the slaughter was done and the gates were opened. No home resided by a Pole, Lithuanian or Catholic was spared of its possessions, and not until 11 o'clock that morning did the city rest. The few confederates of Otrepyev that survived were taken into custody. The brutality lasted 7 straight hours, until Moscovites returned to their homes to discuss and celebrate their victory. Some went house to house congratulating each other on their vicious achievement to save Russia from Poland and Orthodoxy from Catholicism. The Germans were spared for the most part, those living in the German Quarter, except for the Augsburg merchants and those who lived in the same streets as the Polish gentry. The Eastern and White Quarters were drenched with blood and filled with mutilated corpses by the end of the day, but this affected the residents little.

7. THE ERA OF TSAR VASILI SHUISKY

Coronation of Tsar Vasili Shuisky and Cremation of Otrepyev

At the close of the day, Pr. Vasili Shuisky stepped forward to fill the void of a supreme ruler over Russia. The eldest and most-respected noblemen, Pr. Feodor Mstislavski declined to press for the throne of Russia, already exhausted by the events and his public service over the years during the reigns of Tsars Ivan IV, Feodor Ivanovich, Boris Godunov and now Otrepyev. Some felt that Pr. Ivan Golitsyn should attempt to ascend the throne, but his ancestry was with the Lithuanian Gediminov clan, and not from either Moscow or Suzdal. Pr. Shuisky took the initiative again, now to summon and reorganize the Boyar Duma for a session the next morning. In Red Square he spoke to the crowds that evening, promoting himself as the candidate most legitimate and qualified as the subsequent tsar and with the capability to stabilize the country. Some felt an Estates (Zemski) Duma was in order, as with the approval of Boris Godunov as tsar, but the crowd agreed that either way it was Pr. Shuisky who would be the best candidate.

The following day, May 19, at two o'clock in the afternoon, the Boyar Duma, a number of prelates and a crowd of Moscow residents assembled at Red Square and approved the selection — or at least did not refuse the selection — of Pr. Vasili Ivanovich Shuisky as tsar of Russia. Again bells rang throughout Russia to celebrate the event. At the very spot where just a few months earlier Vasili Shuisky's head laid on a chopping block as the executioner stood next to him with his axe raised the assembled crowd congratulated him for his victory over the Poles and Catholics, for saving Russia and for accepting the throne over Russia. Just a few feet away, the exposed corpse of Grigori Otrepyev decayed.

In his modesty, Pr. Shuisky suggested an ecclesiastical council to first select a new patriarch for the ROC in place of Ignatius, who would perform the coronation. The crowd responded, "We need a monarch more than a patriarch for our Fatherland. No council is required, Moscow represents our sovereignty. Shuisky will be tsar." The crowds followed the assembly of boyars and prelates inside the Kremlin to secure his nomination by the next leading prelate in Russia, Metr. Isidor of Novgorod. Fearing Semeon Bekbulatovich would be a threat to his possession of the throne, Tsar Shuisky ordered his exile on May 29, to Solovetski Monastery in the far north and forced him to be tonsured as a monk, even though he was blind.

Vasili Ivanovich Shuisky was crowned June 1, 1606 at the Uspenski Cathedral in the Moscow Kremlin, following the same format of previous tsars with the crown of Vladimir Monomakh placed on his head by Metr. Isidor of Novgorod. Under duress Isidor and a number of prelates blessed the murderer of his predecessor as his successor. Russians outside of Moscow were offended because of the haste to coronate Shuisky as tsar and felt slighted. This insult — as they outside of Moscow considered it — would later serve as a reason for their later rejection of Shuisky as tsar and to justify their mutiny. As part of the city was celebrating the coronation of Tsar Shuisky, the balance was carting corpses outside the city to be buried in mass graves. The body of Basmanov was given to relatives, who buried him at a cemetery alongside the Church of Nikolai Mokroi, next to a son that had died in infancy.

The body of Otrepyev laid exposed in Red Square for three days, the object of ridicule and curiosity, until it was taken outside the city and buried at a cemetery for paupers alongside a poorhouse. A few days later and after another superstitious premonition of catastrophe — visions seen atop his grave and a sudden change in weather from May 18 to 25 — the body of Otrepyev was exhumed and cremated in a bonfire. The ashes were gathered and mixed with gunpowder and inserted into a cannon. The cannon fired the ashes towards the east, in the direction of Poland, and the wind blew away the dust.

Tsar Shuisky's Effort to Restore the Rule of Law in Russia

Vasili Ivanovich Shuisky was the 7th generation from Pr. Dmitri of Suzdal who fought the famous Dmitri Donskoi of Moscow over the title of Grand Prince in 1360. He was also grandson of the hated but respected oligarch Andrei Mikhailovich Shuisky, executed by Tsar Vasili III. Tsar Shuisky wanted the best for his homeland and without doubt had sincere concerns to provide for and please his Russian countryman. Having seen the amount of misfortune resulting from unlimited autocratic authority, Tsar Shuisky wanted to restrain his own monarchial authority by subjecting it to laws and the Boyar Duma. After his coronation, after noblemen, court officials and residents swore loyalty to him Tsar Shuisky promulgated the following laws. (1) No executions to be performed without a boyar court trial. (2) The property of criminals was not to be confiscated, but would remain with the wife or children. (3) Any accusations or investigations would be accompanied by a personal appearance of all parties for a face to face confrontation. (4) Any person convicted of perjury or false-witness would receive the same sentence as that intended for the person falsely accused. Tsar Shuisky kissed a ROC cross in public and swore to uphold the law in all good conscience. With these initial few promises Tsar Shuisky hoped to deliver Russia from the political plagues that infected Russia during the reigns of Tsars Ivan IV and Boris Godunov as a result of false or unsubstantiated accusations made in private. Shuisky wanted to begin his reign with an atmosphere of magnanimity, likewise willing to forgive every personal grievance that he suffered all the years of his service.

Tsar Shuisky first dissolved the Senate installed by Otrepyev and re-formed the ancient Boyar Duma as it functioned in the past. He then sent couriers to all of Russia's cities to announce his reign and to announce the death of Otrepyev, and that every citizen would swear loyalty to him and to his future wife and children, should God bless him with any. The directive delivered by the carriers likewise had the subscription of the widow-tsaritza Marina Nagoi, as her validation of Vasili Ivanovich as tsar. In the directive read throughout Russia Shuisky was magnified as the savior of both the country and the national church, Russian Orthodoxy. To further justify his defeat of Otrepyev ,Shuisky distributed Otrepyev's regarding the conversion of Russia to Unia and its subjection to Papal authority and the allocation of the regions of Smolensk and northern Ukraine to Yuri Mnishek in return for his role in providing finances and troops to help Otrepyev ascend the throne of Russia. Included were other letters from high dignitaries of Poland who admitted that they knew Otrepyev was an imposter, but supported him for financial gain should he succeed in his fraud, as well as letters documenting Otrepyev's conspiracy with Polish gentry to execute Russian noblemen and officials beginning May 18, to complete Polish political control of Russia, since the Boyar Duma was already replaced by a Senate filled with Otrepyev's appointees. The evidence justified the riot of May 18, culminating in the death of Otrepyev and his Polish and Russian confederates.

Following the coronation the new tsar began to rectify the political appointments made by Otrepyev and to purge the government. Pr. Vasili Mosalski was exiled to Keksgolm (today known as Priozyorsk) in Karelia near what is now the Finnish border; Mikhail Nagoi was demoted from his rank as Cavalry Master; Afanasi Vlasyev was exiled to Ufa in the Urals; Mikhail Saltykov was exiled to Ivangorod in Livonia (Latvia), and Bogdan Belski returned to Kazan. Every other Russian official promoted by Otrepyev was demoted by Tsar Shuisky and exiled from the Moscow region, their property also confiscated. Some feared a return to the Godunov era of clandestine arrest, but others noted the necessity of removing the harmful elements introduced by Otrepyev into the Russian government. People still felt apprehensive since only a minority of Moscovites approved his ascension and the repercussions of the murder of Otrepyev and his associates were still felt by the nation. The fact that Tsar Shuisky was almost 60 years of age and still a bachelor, with an heir in question, added to the gloomy mood and apprehension of the people.

To confirm the murder of Tsarevich Dmitri Ivanovich and on the very day of his coronation Tsar Shuisky ordered Bishops Filaret of Rostov and Theodosi of Astrakhan along with princes Ivan Vorotinsky and Peter Sheremetev, and Andrei and Grigori Nagoi, to relocate the body of the boy from Uglich to Moscow. The coffin was exhumed and opened to view the contents as a witness. After 15 years the body was still recognizable along with some personal items that relatives had place in the coffin with the boy.

On June 3, the coffin arrived in Moscow. The mother Marina and Tsar Shuisky opened the coffin again and personally viewed the body, again testifying to its contents. Tsar Shuisky then lifted the coffin on his shoulder and carried it personally to the Archangel Cathedral inside the Kremlin. To many it was a pathetic sight, since it was Shuisky who manipulated the investigation at the order of Tsar Godunov to conclude that the murder was an accidental death. For the unconscionable tsar it was a necessity, lest a future False Dmitri again resurrect. The mother wept in the center of the cathedral; she pleaded for the forgiveness of the people for complying with the demands and threats of Otrepyev and testified that the child in the coffin was her son. Only to put the past behind them, prelates and officials pardoned her of her false-witness. The body of Dmitri Ivanovich was entombed inside the Archangel Cathedral.

Patr. Ignatius was defrocked by order of Tsar Shuisky on the day of his coronation. His patriarchal vestments were removed and Ignatius was dressed in a plain monk's frock and confined under lock and a sentry to a cloister at the Chudovski Monastery. The same day a delegation was dispatched by Shuisky to Staritzki Monastery to retrieve the exiled Patr. Job. He was requested to return to Moscow and assume the patriarchate. However, due to loss of eyesight and old age he declined their offer. He suggested Metr. Hermogen of Kazan as a possible candidate, one of the prelates who was willing to confront Patr. Ignatius for his complicity in the coronation of Otrepyev and for performing the royal marriage. Since Hermogen's coerced return to Kazan by Patr. Ignatius he had become somewhat of a hero, and so the choice was unanimous for Hermogen to become patriarch. Upon arrival from Kazan Hermogen was quickly ordained as patriarch by a council of ROC prelates and the staff of Metr. Peter was handed to him personally by Tsar Shuisky. The new patriarch blessed the tsar to inaugurate a new era of close relationship between the church and state.

To remove disgrace from the Godunov family Shuisky ordered that the bodies of Tsar Boris and son Feodor and wife Maria be exhumed from their pauper's grave at the monastery of St. Varsonofei and transferred to the Troitse-Sergieva Monastery for entombment. It was trying for Shuisky who rescued Boris Godunov from his complicity in the murder of Tsarevich Dmitri Ivanovich, but a political necessity. After the exhumation, 12 monks carried the coffin of Boris Godunov on their shoulders, while other Russian officials in a triumphant procession carried the coffins of wife Maria and son Feodor. The disgraced and unfortunate daughter Ksenia rode in an enclosed carriage and wailed at the death of her family. Spectators lining the road also wept as they remembered the prosperity of the early years of Godunov's reign and the years of peace when Godunov was the power behind the throne of his brother-in-law Tsar Feodor. The coffins were entombed at the Troitse-Sergieva Monastery, leaving a place for Ksenia, who would still live another 16 years, at the Pokrovski (Intercession of the Holy Virgin) Convent in Vladimir, without comfort or consolation. As Tsar Godunov was labeled a usurper, Tsar Shuisky hoped to identify him as a legitimate monarch of Russia, and thus route legitimacy to himself, since he was also not of the accepted lineage of Ivan Danilovich of Moscow.

Having affirmed his ascension to the throne with promises to observe the law, justified the execution of Otrepyev, and selected a patriarch to everyone's satisfaction Tsar Shuisky proceeded to install troops on the Oka River and Ukraine to defend them from invasion by Crimean Mongols. Shuisky extended his hand towards Lithuania to execute a peace treaty after all the havoc of the rise of Otrepyev. Further vengeance against Europeans residing in Moscow were curbed, however all the money given by Otrepyev to his wife Marina Mnishek and her family were confiscated and appropriated back to the royal treasury. The pomp of Otrepyev's court was diminished and his bodyguards were relieved of their service as part of Tsar Shuisky's effort to reduce the extravagance that depleted the royal treasury. Polish gentry incarcerated in Russian prisons were freed and escorted out of the country, although the Mnishek family was separated and dispersed to local cities, until final arrangements could be settled with Sigismund regarding the relationship between the two countries. Pr. Grigori Volkonski was the envoy sent to Krakow, Poland, to accomplish this, but Sigismund refused the terms of the treaty or the gifts of consolation offered by the prince on behalf of Tsar Shuisky. He sent Volkonski back to Moscow, upset that the fraud perpetrated by Otrepyev at his expense did not succeed and hoping for another pretender to arise in the future.

Tsar Shuisky did succeed with the Kings of England, Denmark and Sweden. The Crimean Mongol Khan Kazi-Girei acknowledged Tsar Shuisky as his brother, and the Siberian Nogay tribal king Ishterek was willing to accept subjection to Moscow in their best interests. Efforts were also extended to develop a peace treaty with Austria, Persia and Turkey.

Disenchantment with Tsar Vasili and Struggle with the Opposition

The one person inside the trusted court of Tsar Shuisky who would first turn against him was Pr. Grigori Petrovich Shakhovski, a close associate of Otrepyev. He was a military commander at Putivl, the Ukrainian center of Otrepyev's early accomplishments, and where a considerable number of disenfranchised vagrants, criminals and fugitives still resided, former constituents of Otrepyev's volunteer army. Shakhovski harbored spite toward those responsible for the murder of Otrepyev and he also knew the mood of the people of Severski — northwest Ukraine — and the disenchantment of many Russians who were refused part in the selection of the successor to Otrepyev. Aware of the suppressed turbulent mind of Moscow's populace and nation, and the country still in unrest, Shakhovski recognized the government of Tsar Shuisky as unstable and insecure. Shakhovski then gathered the residents of Putivl and boldly told them that Moscovite insurgents had murdered some unidentified German and not Otrepyev; and that Dmitri Ivanovich was alive and clandestinely hiding until he could acquire again the support of his confederates in Severski. Shakhovski supplemented his message with the rumor that Tsar Shuisky was making preparations to arrest and torture all the residents of Putivl for their support of Otrepyev, just as Tsar Ivan the Terrible did to Novgorod for their refusal to subject themselves to his authority. For these reasons, as Shakhovski related, it was to their benefit and security to rise against Shuisky and support the true monarch of Russia.

The residents swallowed his entire propaganda without reservation and initiated a rebellion. Once Putivl was aroused the regional cities followed: Moravsk, Chernigov, Starodub, Novgorod-Severski, Belgorod, Borisov, Oskol, Trubchebsk, Kromni, Livni, and Elezt, all of them severing ties with Moscow in favor of an alliance with a yet-unidentified new Dmitri Ivanovich. Residents, royal guards, landowners and landowners, peasants and riff-raff rallied to the new banner of Shakhovski, including the military commander of Chernigov, Pr. Andrei Telyatevski.

Those who refused to join the rebellion were imprisoned, drowned, murdered, hanged, thrown from towers to their death, and impaled. Among the martyrs were those loyal to Tsar Shuisky: Princes Buinosov in Belgorod, Butorlin in Oskol, Plescheev in Livna and more, and their property was confiscated and distributed among the rebels. Their wives were raped while their daughters were forced into unwanted marriages with the rabble.

As the rebels waded through the blood of their victims they patiently waited for Dmitri Ivanovich and asked each other, "Where is he?" Shakhovski answered them, "The sun will rise upon Russia from Sandomir." This was a city in southeast Poland, the same region where the Mnishek family resided. To provide credible testimony to his claims Shakhovski sent his message to friends resident in Moscow who related to others that Dmitri Ivanovich was still alive and escaped Moscow a few hours before the riot erupted the morning of May 17. Witnesses surfaced immediately, one being a boatman that forded people across the Oka River, who claimed that he was given seven gold ducats to ferry across the river three mysterious persons, one of whom identified the other as Dmitri Ivanovich. Others claimed to have seen him near Tula and Putivl and at other cities wearing a plain monk's frock in transit to Poland. Now he was hiding at Sandomir waiting for an opportune time to return to Russia.

Pr. Volkonski, the envoy of Tsar Shuisky who was in Krakow at the time, was informed that the wife of Yuri Mnishek told others that her son-in-law was living either at Sandomir or Sambor, at her home, or at a nearby monastery. Accompanying him was a Moscovite named Zabolotzki and that many Russian officials living in Poland, including Vasili Mosalski (who migrated there from exile in Ivangorod), had secretly met with him and wished him good fortune. Pr. Volkonski was convinced that the new False Dmitri was Mikhail Molchanov, one of the murderers of young Tsar Feodor Borisovich, and who had been convicted of practicing sorcery during the reign of Tsar Boris Godunov and was publicly whipped. Once Vasili Shuisky became tsar Molchanov vanished from public view. Molchanov had no physical similarities to Grigori Otrepyev, but had black curly hair, large eyes, thick bushy eyebrows, a nose that bent down, dimples on his cheeks, and he was clean shaven. Like Otrepyev, Molchanov spoke Russian and Polish fluently and could understand some Latin. Acting in accord with the premises already published by Shakhovski, Molchanov was able to resurrect Dmitri Ivanovich and fuel the rebels in Severski through some correspondence and envoys, but he was in no hurry to travel there. Too many people knew Molchanov, and he felt his fraud would quickly dissipate and that a more unscrupulous and unrecognizable person would be a better candidate as False Dmitri II than he. As a result, Molchanov withdrew from the fraud.

The initial rumors of the escape of the imposter stirred up the residents of Moscow no sooner than they had finished desecrating the naked body of Grigori Otrepyev and cremating it and blowing his remains from a cannon. Should they believe his escape or not? Others now said that the body that laid in Red Square actually looked more like a young court official who mysteriously disappeared at about this time. Identity exchange, superstition and magic fueled the rumors that circulated in Moscow. All of a sudden the reign of Otrepyev was a benevolent and prosperous one as opposed to that of Tsar Shuisky, whom the rabble labeled a usurper and murderer. Others believing in sorcery related that Tsarevich Dmitri resurrected to the dismay of his murderers. The associates of Shakhovski printed flyers in the name of Dmitri Ivanovich and distributed them on the streets and nailed them on doors, flyers which castigated Shuisky and announced the arrival of Dmitri Ivanovich at the following New Year's Day.[13] As much as Tsar Shuisky attempted to identify the propagandists, it was to no avail.

Tsar Shuisky then dispatched Metr. Pafnuti of Krutitzk to Severski to investigate the matter, but when he arrived the residents refused to listen to him or speak to him. The widow-tsaritza Marina Nagoi, desperate to cover her role in the complicity of Grigori Otrepyev as her son, wrote to the residents of the Ukrainian cities that had rebelled against Moscow, testifying that she personally witnessed the death of her son Dmitri in Uglich as well as the death of the imposter in Moscow. Marina Nagoi also sent a copy of her portrait of the young Dmitri with her brother Grigori Nagoi with the letters, to provide further testimony that this new Dmitri Ivanovich was likewise an imposter. However, neither the letters, nor the portrait, nor the envoy had any success. The revolt simmered and the fury brewed.

Exerting effort vigilantly, Shakhovski summoned all Russia to unite with Ukraine. He wrote letters under the name of Dmitri Ivanovich and imprinted the state seal upon them, which he stole from Moscow during the massacre and confusion of May 17. The regiment of rebels increased under the command of a serf, Ivan Bolotnikov, who may or may not have believed Dmitri Ivanovich to be alive and well. He fervently stirred up the people with his contrived tales of Tsarevich Dmitri's deliverance and the need to deliver Russia from Tsar Shuisky. Bolotnikov became the head of the new rebel army and was able to sway to his side the princes Vasili Mosalski and Mikhail Dolgoruky.

Accepting the unavoidability of combat Tsar Shuisky dispatched troops to Eletz and Kromni, commanded by the nobleman Vorotinsky and Pr. Yuri Trubetzkoy. Once the tsar's army of 5,000 cavalry confronted the army of Bolotnikov, the tsar's army turned and fled. The soldiers taken captive by Bolotnikov were reviled and labeled as murderers, criminals and mutineers. Some were drowned while the rest were taken to Putivl to there be executed. A few were flogged and released to return to Moscow as a sign of the victory of False Dmitri II's new army. Bolotnikov proceeded forward north while cities of central Russia capitulated to his authority: Orel, Tula, Kaluga, Venev, Kahir. More

---

13 March 25, 1607, according to the calendar in use in Russian at the time.

commanders were assigned to the growing number of troops: Istom Pashkov, Grigori Sonbulov and Prokopi Lyapunov. Unlike the volunteer army of Grigori Otrepyev, the new army consisted of more trained soldiers and eager citizens of high standing. Although they swore loyalty to Tsar Shuisky earlier they felt the oath was now void since Dmitri Ivanovich was alive and well and the actual heir to the throne. The zeal of False Dmitri II's army led them to arrest officials who would not join their cause: the Regent of Ryazan Pr. Cherkassky, and princes Trostenski and Karkaginov were chained in fetters and ordered by Lyapunov to Putivl for incarceration or death. The troops became vigilantes as they plundered villages and then burned them, and pillaged churches without consideration for their sanctity. The rebellion further spread like a fire flamed by winds to Smolensk and Tver, with Vyazma, Rzhev and Dorogobuzh capitulating to the rebels to deliver their own villages from destruction by the rebels.

Tsar Shuisky was alarmed by the flight of his troops from Eletz and Kromni and the strength and success of the rebels, but he was far from ready to capitulate. He possessed an inherent courage that continuously propelled him forward against great odds, although he was without a firm strategy at the time. Tsar Shuisky in October 1606 published an account of the development of the rebellion and the absurd account of Otrepyev's deliverance and distributed it to the populace and then assembled a larger army under the command of his nephew Pr. Mikhail Vasilyevich Skopin-Shuisky, sending it to confront the rebels. Of the regiments that were sent by Tsar Shuisky against the rebels, only his nephew Mikhail was able to attain a victory. The balance of the regiments under Princes Mstislavski, Dmitri Shuisky, Ivan Vorotinsky, Andrei Golitsyn and Grigori Nagoi, all retreated shortly after the battles began, most of them to the village Troitzki, about 35 miles from Moscow.

The rebel leaders, with their victory over most of the Russian regiments, having also desolated Kolomna, now were near Moscow at the city Kolomensk. As far as the rebels were concerned, Tsar Shuisky was defeated. They wrote letters to Moscow residents, clergy and state officials that Dmitri Ivanovich again had ascended the throne and demanded from them a new oath of allegiance. The war had ended and the reign of mercy had begun. Meanwhile the rebels were recruiting serfs, rabble and disenchanted peasants and ordering them to attack and stab landowners and merchants, and kidnap their wives and confiscate their property for themselves. The rebels promised them wealth and high positions in the new government.

Tsar Shuisky stationed his troops at the main entrances to Moscow to repel an invasion. The loyal populace of a few of the cities, such as Smolensk and Tver, were able to evict the rebels.

Because there was still no Dmitri Ivanovich, the rebel commanders became anxious and suspicious and refused to further subject themselves to the authority of Bolotnikov. They wanted Dmitri Ivanovich. Lyapunov was the first to recognize a fraud and refused to further be Bolotnikov's pawn and an associate of the rabble that comprised their army. Lyapunov went to Moscow along with soldiers from Ryazan, Kolomna, Tula and other cities. They presented Tsar Shuisky an apology, which he accepted, and Lyapunov was promoted to the rank of royal court officer. Soon others that accompanied Bolotnikov followed the example of Lyapunov and migrated into Moscow, and there Tsar Shuisky extended his hand of friendship to them and hoped for a surrender in order to suppress the rebellion without further bloodshed, willing to offer amnesty. Tsar Shuisky even offered Bolotnikov a high position in his government, should he abandon his rebellion, but he refused.

Another regiment of troops under Mikhail Skopin-Shuisky left Moscow on December 2 and attacked the rebels, who were defeated. They then withdrew with Bolotnikov to Serpukhov. The number of rebels taken captive by Skopin-Shuisky was more than the Moscow prisons could hold and the excess were drowned in the Moscow River. The Cossacks of Bolotnikov's army also surrendered and were incorporated into the tsar's army. For his role in the victory over the rebels Pr. Skopin-Shuisky received the rank of a boyar. For a while Moscow felt the rebellion suppressed.

Bolotnikov thought of remaining in Serpukhov but the residents would not allow him, and he settled in Kaluga. Within a few days he fortified the city with a deep moat and ramparts, gathering 10,000 fugitives and volunteers as his new army. Bolotnikov prepared in case of a siege and wrote letters to the rebel leaders in Severski, telling them that he needed help and especially a Dmitri Ivanovich, either the genuine or an imposter. It seemed that a name without a face was ineffective for a successful campaign and many were willing to sacrifice themselves should a Dmitri Ivanovich surface. But who were the Severski rebels to provide as a Dmitri Ivanovich? Molchanov? Except that he would not be able to pass himself off. A Polish gentry from Sandomir? Or someone else? One person did offer to Shakhovski to take the identity, but after he was given money, the person left for Poland never to be seen again. False Peter — the Volga Cossack Eleika — was another candidate, but after hearing of the murder of Otrepyev he returned to Astrakhan. Shakhovski, desperate for an imposter, recalled Eleika to Putivl and greeted him as the son of Tsar Feodor Ivanovich and nephew of Dmitri Ivanovich and promised him the throne of Russia should an effective False Dmitri II fail to surface. The new fraud had some promise of success as Sigismund sent Polish troops to Severski, who then proceeded to assist Bolotnikov in Kaluga. Other cities abandoned Tsar Shuisky and turned to the yet-unknown and unidentified False Dmitri II, such as Perm, Vyatka and Nizhniy-Novgorod.

Tsar Shuisky dispatched his regiment to Kaluga and on December 3, 1606, began the siege, but rebels attacked the tsarist troops from behind. Tsar Shuisky sent more troops under his commanders: Mikhail Skopin-Shuisky to Kaluga; Vorotinsky to Tula; Feodor Sheremetev to Astrakhan, while he remained in Moscow to guard the city from rebellion. The war proceeded slowly during the winter and a plague decimated the residents of Nizhniy-Novgorod.

To again produce evidence for the death of Tsarevich Dmitri Ivanovich Tsar Shuisky recalled former patriarch Job out of exile. On February 20, 1607, he entered the Uspenski Cathedral in the Moscow Kremlin and publicly read a statement of his complicity in the cover of the murder of Dmitri Ivanovich and repented of his conduct. Job admitted he had concealed the truth from the public and that Boris Godunov organized the murder of Tsarevich Dmitri and was the responsible party. Job also asked the people for their forgiveness, because he violated his patriarchal vows by defending Godunov, knowing well he arranged the murder. Those gathered at the cathedral cried after the statement was read and kissed Job's right hand, glad for his eventual repentance.

Job likewise appended his confession with a plea to the people not to accept any person posing as Dmitri Ivanovich, that they were all frauds. Job returned to Staritzki Monastery and remained there isolated from society and the ecclesiastical world until his death on June 19, 1607. He was buried inside Uspenski Cathedral.

This new testimony regarding the death of Tsarevich Dmitri had little effect in swaying people toward accepting Tsar Shuisky as legitimate monarch or forsaking the inexistent False Dmitri II. The armies sent against the rebels were little successful and the fierce winter weather forced the troops at Kaluga to eat their horses. Nizhniy-Novgorod was the only victory for Tsar Shuisky.

The battles continued to rage south of Moscow between tsarist troops and the rebels, and in the course of a few months. 15,000 troops abandoned Tsar Shuisky and joined the rebels. Such news paralyzed Moscow and agitated Tsar Shuisky. His next defense was to summon all able-bodied Russians to bear arms and under threat of execution for deserters. Monasteries were required to give their store of bread to Moscow in case of a siege. The rebels did not hurry to siege Moscow, waiting for Eleika to arrive, as he was in transit to Tula with supplies and reinforcements. On May 21, 1607, Tsar Shuisky took personal charge of his army, leaving the city under the supervision of his brother Dmitri Shuisky. Near Serpukhov they joined with the armies of Mstislavski and Vorotinsky, for a total of 100,000 soldiers. At this time Eleika arrived with Shakhovski at Tula and was joined by Bolotnikov. The battle began June 5 near the Vosmi River and Tsar Shuisky was able to crush the rebels.

The loyalist Russian army was joined by Mikhail Skopin-Shuisky and moved on to liberate Tula, while occupying the smaller cities in between. The battle for Tula occurred June 30, Tsar Shuisky hoping to capture all the rebel leaders now inside the walls of Tula. During the siege, rebels began to again question, "Where is he for whom we are dying? Where is Dmitri?" Shakhovski and Bolotnikov replied that he was in Lithuania. Messengers were sent by the rebels to Lithuania to find for themselves a False Dmitri, lest all fail for Shakhovski and Bolotnikov. With the intervention of Yuri Mnishek and his family the next False Dmitri surfaced, Matvei Verovkin, a vagrant son of a Polish ROC priest. As with the previous contenders Verovkin had no resemblance to Grigori Otrepyev: he was course, ill-mannered, greedy, although cunning and intelligent and fluent in Russian and Polish. Verovkin knew the Bible well and the protocol and liturgy of the ROC. Another source relates that Verovkin was also a student of the Talmud and Rabbinic writings and also knew Hebrew. The Polish official Mekhovetzki, who was a friend of Otrepyev, now became tutor to Verovkin, informing him of the life and history of Grigori Otrepyev. Mekhovetzki titled himself Ataman to better promote Verovkin and the fraud resurrected, and again with the political and financial support of Sigismund and Polish gentry. News traveled quickly to Ukraine and central Russia that Tsarevich Dmitri Ivanovich was soon to arrive.

On August 1, two men appeared in Starodub informing the populace that Dmitri Ivanovich was not far with his army, and that they were sent ahead to ascertain the mood of the people. They wanted to know: Do the people love their legitimate monarch? Are they willing to serve him zealously? The populace responded, "Where is he? Where is our father? We will lay our heads down for him." One messenger told them, "He is here," and directly their attention to his accomplice, that he was Tsarevich Dmitri. Not one person in the crowd doubted and they threw themselves prostrate to the ground and began to kiss the feet of the stranger, crying, "Praise to God, the treasure of our souls has been discovered." Not far away Mekhovetzki followed with a new army consisting of Polish troops, volunteer soldiers, treasure-seekers, fugitives, peasants and rabble, not much different than the army of his predecessor. The populace of Ukrainian cities Putivl, Chernigov, and Novgorod-Severski, once hearing of the arrival of Verovkin, provided soldiers for his campaign.

Even those who recognized Verovkin as an imposter with no more valid credentials than Otrepyev still rallied behind him as they did behind Otrepyev, and because of their spite toward Tsar Shuisky and the drive to revolt. Ataman Ivan Martinovich Zarutzki, a Cossack chieftain and confederate of Otrepyev, fell down at the feet of Verovkin, promising to continue to serve him as he did in the past, although knowing well Verovkin was not Otrepyev who was not Dmitri Ivanovich. The superstitious and weak minds willingly embraced the new imposter without reservation. One rebel then traveled to Tsar Shuisky at the siege of Tula and delivered to him a letter from the populace of the Ukrainian cities that swore loyalty to Verovkin, advising Tsar Shuisky to yield the throne to Dmitri Ivanovich, and threatened him with execution should he stubbornly refuse. The messenger had the boldness to call Tsar Shuisky right to his face a traitor and usurper. As a result, by order of Tsar Shuisky the messenger was burned at the stake until he was cremated.

Now aware of the appearance of a new imposter and more unrest in Moscow with an increase of rebels in southern Russia, Tsar Shuisky further increased the size of his army, although few recruits were available. The tsar was informed that Mekhovetzki was at Starodub with a large Lithuanian regiment; Zarutzki had summoned several thousand Cossacks and united them with the Severski forces, and announced that Verovkin was soon to arrive at Tula. The siege of Tula continued through the end of summer, until Tsar Shuisky had his troops route the flooded waters of the Yupa River through Tula, to flood the city. Eventually the leaders surrendered, unable to further resist the siege as a result of a lack of food and sanitation and now affected by an artificial flood. On October 10, 1607, tsarist forces entered the city. The rebel leaders Bolotnikov, Shakhovski, Eleika and others were taken in chains to Moscow under guard. But Pr. Telyatevski, as a result of family ties with the Shuisky clan, was freed.

Tsar Shuisky was hailed as a hero on his return from Tula, just as was Tsar Ivan IV after the defeat of Kazan, with three days of celebration festivities in Moscow. Eleika — False Peter — was hanged in public near the Danilov Monastery, while Bolotnikov had his eyes pricked and then locally drowned, while Ataman Feodor Nagib and the more incorrigible of the rebels were taken to Kargopol and there secretly drowned. Shakhovski was exiled to a fortress near Vologda for incarceration, while others were exiled to Siberia. Amnesty was granted by Tsar Shuisky to the lower level of rebel soldiers with the hope of their loyalty to him, rather than to Verovkin. But the victory was short-lived because southern Russia from the European border to the mouth of the Volga River south of Astrakhan had sworn loyalty to Verovkin, along with most of the Ukraine. The new imposter was summoning a larger army and waiting for a more opportune time to again invade and proceed towards Moscow.

The Rise of False Dmitri II and Polish Treachery

During this time of complacency and temporary calm, Tsar Shuisky turned his thoughts toward marriage. Having been deprived of this consolation in life due to his state obligations and political turmoil, he decided to attempt marriage in middle-age, now about 60. Tsar Shuisky married Princess Maria, daughter of Pr. Peter Ivanovich Buinosov of Rostov, whom he had selected to marry some years earlier. Some chroniclers related that the marriage was the end of Shuisky's political and military career. Attempting to make up for lost years now with his new wife he became idle and squandered money on luxuries, while ignoring state affairs. As a result, he lost the support of the Duma, military and clergy. (The royal couple later had a daughter named Anastasia.)

As Moscow was celebrating the wedding of their monarch the civil war proceeded in the balance of the country. An Ataman who was granted amnesty, Bezzubtzev, was dispatched to Kaluga to quell the insurrection, but the residents replied, "We recognize no king but Dmitri. We await him and soon will see him." Verovkin then advanced to siege Bryansk; he had 7,000 Polish troops and 8,000 Ukrainian Cossacks and a few Russians.

Meanwhile, another imposter appeared now that pseudo-Peter had been executed: some vagrant passing himself off as Feodor, another supposed son of Tsar Feodor Ivanovich and Irina. Verovkin refused to recognize the new pretender to the throne as his nephew and quickly ordered his execution.

Tsar Shuisky sent troops from Moscow to Bryansk to deliver the city from the siege. December 15, 1607, loyalist troops crossed the Desna River and attacked Verovkin's army from the rear, while the city pounded them from the walls. Verovkin's army retreated, unable to defend itself in the fierce winter weather and they located to Orel where he spent the balance of the winter. While there he increased the size of his army and agitated the peasants against Tsar Shuisky. Verovkin granted amnesty to criminals, freed oppressed serfs, and assigned land to loyal supporters. Adam Vishnevetzki, his pseudo-brother-in-law, arrived from Lithuania with an additional 3,000 or so cavalry under Pr. Alexandr Lisovski. But it was not as though all was well within the ranks of Verovkin's inner circle. Pr. Roman Rozhinski (Rozynski), an ambitious, arrogant and unrestrained character, in his drive for power personally strangled Mekhovetzki — the self-proclaimed Ataman and advisor to Verovkin — with his own hands. Rozhinski then assumed the position of advisor and second-in-command, although now held in spite by the balance of Verovkin's supporters.

In early spring 1608, the army of Verovkin proceeded to expand in their drive toward Moscow, capturing cities, burning and plundering villages that refused to capitulate to Verovkin as legitimate monarch. Tsar Shuisky, unable to leave his young wife and the capital city, assigned command of his army to his brother Dmitri Shuisky and Pr. Vasili Golitsyn. It was not until April 13, 1608, that the loyalist army had its next crucial battle against Verovkin. The battle occurred at Bolkhov, about 20 miles north of Orel. After several days of mutual slaughter, loyalist troops retreated, while some joined the rebels. As Dmitri Shuisky and Golitsyn retreated to Moscow Verovkin's army was locating to Kaluga, with more of the populace confirmed that Verovkin was genuinely the same person as Otrepyev who was Tsarevich Dmitri. The army of Verovkin increased with more fugitives and volunteers and any disenchanted with Tsar Shuisky joining. On the other hand, landowners and noblemen and state officials with their extended families and servants offered allegiance to Tsar Shuisky, many of them migrating to Moscow from their provincial estates. They feared the loss of their rank and property should the imposter ascend the throne, so hurried to defend their own interests. Pr. Tretyak Sietov, for example, provided 5,000 troops from the peasants of his patrimony. At the same time Tsar Shuisky began an inquisition within his own royal court for traitors. Pr. Ivan Katirev was exiled to Siberia; Pr. Yuri Trubetzkoy to Vologda; Pr. Troyekurov to Nizhniy-Novgorod, while Princes Zhelyabovski and Nevtaev were executed.

By June 1, 1607, Verovkin made the village Tushino his camp. The village was on the road to Voloko-Lamsk, about eight miles northwest of Moscow, and he was hoping with just his presence to intimidate the populace of Moscow into surrendering. Verovkin wrote futile letters to the residents and waited vainly for responses. Pr. Rozhinski wanted to attack Moscow with their full military strength and conquer it at any cost, but Verovkin reprimanded him, saying, "If you destroy my capital, where shall I reign? If you burn the treasuries, how can I reward you?" Verovkin wanted to save the capital as his seat, but was not concerned about the devastation of the rest of Russia. The total military force of Verovkin was 15,000 Polish troops and Cossacks, and 60,000 Russians. Most of them were poorly armed and inadequately trained for battle, Verovkin depending more on the zeal of his supporters and on the reluctance of the tsar's army to fight against him. Tsar Shuisky had in Moscow no fewer than 80,000 well-trained and well-armed troops behind strong walls fortified with a continuous line of cannons. Verovkin knew he was no match militarily and was betting on Moscow betraying Tsar Shuisky.

Tsar Shuisky in the interval of late spring and early summer of 1608 was conducting secret discussions with envoys from Polish King Sigismund to conclude a peace treaty. On July 25, a treaty was signed between Tsar Shuisky and King Sigismund to curb all war for the next 20 years, and that the existing borders between the two countries would remain where they are. Russia in return would liberate any Europeans in custody, including Marina Mnishek who was still in exile. Poland and Lithuania were supposed to withdraw their troops and military support of Verovkin (although this did not occur). The envoys at the same time acted as spies while in Moscow, recording the agitation and fear of the populace to the threat of an advance by Verovkin, as well as the location of troops and arsenals.

It did not take Tsar Shuisky very long to recognize the Pole's treachery, once the Europeans were granted freedom and an escort to the border. Princes Rozhinski and Vishnevetzki or any of the other Poles refused to leave Tushino. At the same time Yan Sapega — nephew of Lev Sapega — brought an additional 7,000 cavalry to Verovkin from Poland. Unrest regarding the manner of concluding the campaign surfaced in Tushino and Yan Sapega separated from Verovkin and his circle of advisors, taking with him 15,000 troops and moving to the Troitse-Sergieva Monastery, 50 miles north of Moscow, to plunder its treasures. Then Lisovski took command of 30,000 troops and defeated

Kolomna, and then turned toward Moscow. Tsar Shuisky dispatched his troops for a turbulent battle at the Medvedev ford of the Moscow River. Lisovski was defeated and Kolomna was again taken by loyalist troops. Yan Sapega on the way to Troitse-Sergieva Monastery was attacked by loyalist troops under Pr. Ivan Shuisky, but Sapega was able to gain this victory and Ivan Shuisky returned to Moscow.

Yuri and Marina Mnishek were being escorted out of Russia according to the terms of the treaty by Pr. Dolgoruky, however, once the military guard reached Smolensk they were overtaken by a regiment sent by Verovkin from Tushino. The Russians were scattered by the rebels, not expecting the attack and Marina was taken captive. The Russians returned to Moscow, while an envoy from Tushino informed Marina that her husband was alive and well and impatiently waiting for her. The father and daughter wasted not a minute and returned with the rebels. Another chance of success as the wife of the tsar of Russia for Marina, and another chance at the acquisition of the wealth of Russia's treasury and the legacy of the promised regions of Smolensk and Severski clouded the clear vision of Yuri and Marina as they journeyed to Tushino to join the campaign. The life of luxury was on the horizon, and treachery — breaking the terms of the treaty — and an alliance with another fraud were insufficient reasons not to pursue it. Marina and Verovkin met in a tent about ½ mile from the camp at Tushino, but without joy or consolation, since she knew well the truth. She had been preparing herself while in exile for a possible involvement in a new fraud, yet the thought of sharing her bed with another imposter was repulsive to her. But it was too late and the ambitious father convinced the daughter to proceed with the renewal of marital vows, which would add credibility to Verovkin's claim of having survived the murder. A pre-nuptial agreement was made between Marina and Verovkin: the renewal of vows would be performed by a Jesuit priest and Verovkin promised not to consummate the marriage until Moscow was defeated and he ascended the throne as legitimate monarch.

On September 1, 1608, Marina Mnishek entered the camp at Tushino and played the part professionally: she wept at seeing Verovkin, embraced him and exchanged words of love with him. The camp was deceived by the display of lovelorn emotion and anyone remaining that doubted, now without reservation accepted Matvei Verovkin as Tsarevich Dmitri.

Matters now became worse for Tsar Shuisky, seeing more of his army migrating to Tushino. He then summoned his nephew Pr. Mikhail Skopin-Shuisky and ordered him to travel to Sweden, to King Charles IX, conclude a peace treaty with him and then recruit Swedish troops to help the struggle against the rebels at Tushino. Tsar Shuisky could no longer trust his own army or officials, and his two brothers were not nearly the capable military commander as was nephew Mikhail. The populace of Moscow had lost faith in their monarch as a result of the calamities of an incessant civil war and the destruction and plunder of so many Russian cities and Tsar Shuisky hoped this intervention would suppress the rebellion. The ROC clergy attempted to instill loyalty into the people during liturgy, reciting prayers on behalf of the tsar and reminiscing of his previous exploits and feats on behalf of Russia, but their effort fell on deaf ears. The populace of Moscow felt barricaded and trapped. Rebel troops would ride up to the city wall to assist fugitives fleeing, even though they knew Verovkin was an imposter. Relatives would meet and discuss who should stay in Moscow and who should flee to Tushino, to take advantage of one or the other place, and to have a relative in the winning camp — whichever it would be — in order to help the other. Devious entrepreneurs would smuggle food, salt, clothing and weapons out of the city and sell it to the troops at Tushino. No one would dare report it to the tsar, lest he be branded as an informer and risk his own life. Tsar Shuisky did not know what to do, but he was reluctant to do as his predecessors Tsar Ivan IV and Tsar Boris Godunov did: arrest those suspicious of collaborating with the enemy and imprison and torture and execute them. Moscow was still secure and so Tsar Shuisky procrastinated until news would return with Skopin-Shuisky.

The Troitse-Sergieva Monastery enticed the rebels due to its wealth, its gold and silverware, store of jewels, and ancient valuable artifacts. It was not as if the resident monks and priests did not expect an attack or siege, and once they heard of the rebel cavalry moving in their direction the residents donned arms. For Yan Sapega it was more of a moral victory than a military, because of the important role of Troitse-Sergieva in the religious life of Russia; the amount of wealth to be acquired would never be enough to compensate for the effort and lives that would be expended in order to occupy the monastery.

On September 23, 1608, rebel leaders Yan Sapega, Lisovski, and Vishnevetzki were in sight of the monastery with 30,000 troops, while inside the monastery, the tsarist commanders were Pr. Grigori Dolgoruky and Alexei Golokhvastov. Quickly the monastery was filled with local residents, who gathered what they could from their homes and fled to the monastery for their safety. What they could not take the residents left in their homes and set them on fire, so not to allow the rebels to plunder. On September 29, Sapega and Lisovski wrote a letter to the monastery military commander to surrender and accept Verovkin as the legitimate monarch of Russia. They emphasized that their rebel army was larger than the tsar's and that Verovkin would grant them amnesty, should they surrender. The prelates and monastery officials refused to surrender. On September 30, the rebels erected camps surrounding the monastery and dug a trench on one side of the monastery (the other side is a river). Beginning October 3 and for six weeks, 63 cannons shot balls at the walls of the monastery, but with minor superficial damage.

On the night of October 19, monastery troops climbed down the walls of the monastery using ropes and attacked unsuspecting guards and then quickly withdrew into the darkness of night back inside, and this was to occur regular through the length of the siege. The rebel soldiers were unable to directly attack the monastery because of the return volleys from the troops stationed on the walls. On the night of October 25, the rebels brought brush up to the walls and set it on fire, but this had little effect on the stone wall. The next ploy was underground passages up to the walls and under the walls; but once the rebels surfaced inside the monastery the residents fought back and barricaded the opening. Winter settled in and the siege was at a stalemate. With spring, due to the unsanitary conditions of the monastery and poor food and water supply, scurvy plagued the residents. From 20 to 50 residents died daily, with that many buried in a single grave.

Archimandrite Joasaf send messengers to Tsar Shuisky asking for an army to deliver them from the siege, stating that only one month's food supply remained in the monastery and complaining of the effects of the plague of scurvy. Tsar Shuisky was still awaiting news from Sweden's King Charles and so sent less than 100 soldiers to assist their plight. The new regiment had little effect against the massive rebel army. The scurvy, which lasted about three months, was finally curbed with the warm weather beginning early May. Over the course of the scurvy, about 3,000 died. Sapega and the rebel army stormed the monastery May 27, 1609, but the balance of residents, women and children included, fought the rebels from the walls with rocks, fire, pitch, plaster and burning brimstone.

Not having enough of a military force to occupy Moscow and after a year of not being able to defeat the Troitse-Sergieva Monastery, Verovkin sent commanders to Suzdal, Vladimir and other cities of the region to attempt to sway them to his support. The ploy worked. Pereyaslavl and Suzdal swore allegiance to Verovkin and sent rebel troops to Rostov to force their allegiance.

Metr. Filaret was held in custody at the time in Rostov and when the city was taken by rebel troops he was taken into custody. Filaret was taken to the camp at Tushino as a criminal, wearing peasant clothing and bare-footed. Verovkin greeted him royally as his False cousin and a victim of Tsar Godunov's purges. Verovkin saw the value of having such a dignified prelate as part of his court and assigned him the title of patriarch, giving him sacerdotal vestments to wear and some fugitive clergy as personal servants. Filaret was too ambitious a person to refuse, as well as not wanting to be foolish to pass up the only possible opportunity of escape from exile and again a rise to power. Nonetheless, Verovkin kept Filaret in custody, fearing that he might use his freedom to motivate the troops to reconsider their loyalty to him and sway them toward Tsar Shuisky. Verovkin likewise utilized the presence of Filaret to flaunt his artificial devotion to the ROC, unlike his predecessor Otrepyev. He had ROC clergy teach Marina the traditions and rites for her to at least superficially appear as a devoted Orthodox. One of the trophies from the capture of Rostov that Yan Sapega presented to Marina was a very valuable icon of St. Leonti. Marina was sly in her ability to impress the Tushino camp of her adherence to the ROC.

More cities north of Moscow capitulated to Verovkin: Uglich, Kostroma, Galich, Vologda; the very cities that Tsar Shuisky was relying upon for military support from the rear should Verovkin attempt a siege of Moscow. As the rebels entered the cities they would shout, "Long live Dmitri," and the residents would respond in like manner, greeting the rebels as friends and brethren. The cities that refused voluntary surrender, such as Shui (the origin of the Shuisky family), Tver, and Kineshma, were stormed and demolished. These cities had little defense because their troops were in Moscow. The next city to fall was Beloye-Ozersk and then Yaroslavl, while the great victory of the rebels was Pskov, the pride of Tsar Shuisky whose uncle Ivan Petrovich Shuisky was acclaimed as the hero of the siege of Pskov against King Batori of Poland some 25 years earlier. But Verovkin did not treat Pskov kindly as the other cities that surrendered to him. He had the tsarist loyalists imprisoned, executed, tortured and impaled. The monasteries were plundered of their valuables. Verovkin also ordered the city to be burned, and during the conflagration rebels killed innocent residents while lauding the King of Tushino. Fortunately, the majority of the city survived the flames. Consequently, few cities refused to acknowledge the validity of Verovkin as legitimate monarch: Kolomna, Pereyaslavl, Nizhniy-Novgorod, Saratov and Kazan, and most of the cities of Siberia.

8. Civil Wars, Invasions and False Dmitri II

Beginning of Civil War, More Imposters, the Rise of Tushino and the Siege of Troitse-Sergieva

By the end of summer 1608, Tushino became a bustling city of 100,000 inhabitants, the new capital of Verovkin's infamous command of his rebel troops. Buildings were constructed, stores opened, and streets and squares were laid out. Who were the residents? Fugitives from justice now wealthy from the spoils of their plunder, Cossack soldiers and hired mercenaries, superstitious people hoping for a monarch with ties to the ancient dynasty, disenchanted free-loaders, vagrants, devious entrepreneurs making fast money with weapons sales, and the same type of riff-raff that earlier followed Otrepyev all over central Russia. Every day was a festivity in Tushino, where wine and honey flowed from barrels and meat, cheese and fruit were in piles up to the chest. All of it was brought by supporters from the various villages and farms of central and northern Russia. Tatars, remnants of the Mongols still residing in Russia, streamed into Tushino along with members of Siberian tribes. Verovkin's residence expanded into a palace filled with Russian officials and Polish gentry. Verovkin had control of European Russia from central Ukraine to the White Sea, and from the Polish border to the foot of the Urals and to the Caspian Sea. Rumors of the successful exploits of Verovkin poured into Moscow, now threatened by famine and betrayal. Patiently Verovkin waited, hoping to defeat Moscow without even one death, just as spies residing in the city would encouragingly relay to him. Nobody — inside or outside of Moscow — wanted any of it destroyed.

Marina Mnishek resided at Tushino and still considered herself tsaritza of Russia although playing the role of a servile hypocrite to her barbarian husband, who lavished her with gifts and luxuries. Yuri Mnishek would kiss the hands of Verovkin hoping he would fulfill the promises for his support and deliver to him Smolensk and Severski and 300,000 rubles in gold from the Moscow royal treasury. Such acts of sycophancy by her ambitious father repulsed and nauseated Marina, knowing well the entire demonstration was a fraud perpetrated on the entirety of Russia. Having attained his goal, or so he thought, Yuri Mnishek left Tushino in January 1609 for Warsaw.

In spring of 1609, matters turned for the better for Tsar Shuisky, as cities that once surrendered to Verovkin were now having second thoughts. Tsar Shuisky wrote to these cities: Galich, Yaroslavl, Kostroma, Vologda, Ustyug, begging them to reconsider their decision and overthrow the rebels. As a result civil war erupted in the major cities of Russia: Kazan, Nizhniy-Novgorod, and Astrakhan, between rebel forces and those loyal to Tsar Shuisky, including the cities mentioned above. Thousands died in violent struggles in each of the cities as the residents attempted to return Russia to stability under Tsar Shuisky. The rebels continued to burn villages and slaughtering all the residents: whether women, children or the elderly. Russia became a desolation. It was not the era of Mongol devastation under Batu Khan, but accomplished by fierce barbarians of their own country who slaughtered their own countrymen. Prelates of the ROC were regular victims. Bishop Fiokist died in prison. Archbishop Galaktion of Suzdal refused to bless Verovkin and so was exiled and died in some unknown place; Bishop Joseph of Kolomensk was tied to a cannon and dragged to his death; Bishop Gennadi of Pskov died while incarcerated.

Moscow itself became a theater of sedition and betrayals. The remaining state officials feared vengeance imposed by Verovkin and his rebels more than the tsar or the law. The government of Russia was a shade of its former might, severed from the balance of the country with little hope for a deliverance from Verovkin and his rebel camp such a short distance from Moscow. The residents were vexed at the inability of Tsar Shuisky to resolve the conflict, not having any one else to blame.

On February 17, 1609, leaders of the conspiracy inside Moscow sounded an alarm and gathered residents in Red Square. Pr. Roman Gagarin, military commander Grigori Sumbulov and court official Timofei Graznoi together brought Patriarch Hermogen along with whatever members of the Boyar Duma were still in Moscow. The three mutineers proposed to the people and officials the overthrow of Tsar Shuisky. Their basis was that he was not selected by a general Estates (Zemski) Duma, but only by a few sycophants and by deceit and coercion, which was the reason for the civil war in Russia. The rebels accused Tsar Shuisky of wanting the position solely for personal ambition, with a lack of intelligence and capability to govern the country. Residents defended Tsar Shuisky and Patr. Hermogen begged the crowd not to participate in such an injustice as turning against the tsar. The balance of the Boyar Duma remained loyal to Tsar Shuisky and gathered the still loyal army to fend off the mutineers and disperse the crowd. The rebels clandestinely left Moscow that evening to Tushino. The few active rebels that remained in Moscow were arrested by order of Tsar Shuisky and then tortured and executed in Red Square as an example to others.

If the seditions in the capital were not sufficient aggravation for Tsar Shuisky, then an increase in the cost of bread made rule for him even worse. Greedy merchants who foresaw a famine in the city in case of a complete siege were hording grain and raising the prices. The merchants of local cities likewise raised their price of wheat to buyers in Moscow. The sale of wheat for bread became a black-market and a person could only obtain it at a high price or being a close associate of the sellers. Tsar Shuisky and Patr. Hermogen attempted to have the sellers open the stores to the general public and lower the prices, but it was futile. The residents blamed Tsar Shuisky, which forced him to open the Moscow state reserves of wheat and this settled the crowds, but only for a while because this store of wheat was a small supply reserved for emergency situations.

As the above was occurring in Moscow and Tushino, Mikhail Skopin-Shuisky was able to successfully acquire the military support of Sweden. On February 28, 1609, Skopin-Shuisky signed a treaty with King Charles IX with the following primary terms: (1) A peace treaty between Russia and Sweden forever; (2) King Charles will provide Tsar Shuisky with 2,000 cavalry and 3000 infantry, while Shuisky will pay their salary; (3) At no time will Shuisky conclude a peace treaty with Lithuania or Poland. Although it was not a grand army, but nonetheless one that would attack Tushino from the rear while the Russians would from the front. On March 26, 1609, the Swedish army under the command of Pr. Skopin-Shuisky and Swedish General Yakov Delagardi entered Russia, to be greeted by 2,300 Russian soldiers. A new camp was established near Novgorod to plan a strategy to rescue Russia from Verovkin and his rebels at Tushino. The spring thaw made roads muddy and difficult to travel, and it was not until May 10, that the army left camp to journey toward Moscow. Novgorod added 3,000 more troops to his army and local cities again vowed loyalty to Tsar Shuisky. Tver was taken on June 11, and Skopin-Shuisky quickly gained a reputation as a natural military leader and hero, perhaps the only one who could deliver Russia from Verovkin and stabilize the country.

Yan Sapega continued his siege of Troitse-Sergieva Monastery, sending regiments of soldiers to burn local villages, plunder their possessions and persecute the residents. He would also interrupt communication between Moscow and cities east and north of it. News of the advancement of Swedish troops reached Sapega and how Tver had renounced Verovkin. The Tushino camp was in turmoil, the rebels wondering what the best course of action would be: stay and defend Verovkin, or leave the camp in the direction of Skopin-Shuisky's army and join it. Verovkin rallied his troops, ordering them to march in the direction of Novgorod to confront the Swedes. Skopin-Shuisky heard that northern Russia from Uglich to the White Sea to Perm had renounced Verovkin and again swore loyalty to Tsar Shuisky. This filled the young commander with hope. The initial battle between Skopin-Shuisky and the rebel army under Yan Sapega occurred at Kolyazin, about 150 miles north of Moscow on the Volga River. Skopin-Shuisky had 10,000 Russian and hardly 1,000 Swedish troops (many abandoned the campaign during the winter), and was able to defeat the larger rebel army over the course of two days: August 18–19, 1609. Sapega retreated back to Troitse-Sergieva. Verovkin realized the dire circumstances of himself and his rebel army with their defeat at the battle of Kolyazin, that Moscow was still undefeated; cities had renounced him while others were mounts of ashes; other cities were executing vengeance on any Europeans that could be taken into custody and the army of Sheremetev was approaching Tushino from the east. The final hope of Verovkin to deliver his campaign from defeat was to attack Moscow, now weak from malnutrition and disloyalty to Tsar Shuisky. Verovkin assigned the task to Polish commander Bobovski, who attacked with a small force, hoping for a surrender and failed. The next attack was led directly by Verovkin in June 1609, but again was repelled by loyalist Russian troops led by Dmitri Shuisky.

Meanwhile, Sheremetev had been gaining victories over cities from Kazan to Nizhniy-Novgorod to Kostroma, and defeating the army of Lisovski. Now Sheremetev was returning to Moscow to boast of his victories. Vladimir likewise, the ancient capital, swore loyalty to Tsar Shuisky and other cities followed. Tsar Shuisky hoped that with the Moscow army and with the return of Sheremetev and the arrival of Skopin-Shuisky with Swedish volunteers, he would be able to finally quash the Tushino camp or at least have them surrender out of despair.

During these upheavals, more pretenders surfaced: another son of Tsar Ivan IV named August, supposedly the son of Tsar Ivan's 3rd wife Anna Koltovskaya; then two grandsons, Osinovik and Laver, surfaced in Astrakhan, who were supposedly sons of the murdered Tsarevich Ivan Ivanovich. No doubt they were hoping for a piece of the royal pie should Verovkin be defeated and again the populace would clamor for a descendent of the royal dynasty. Volga Cossacks supported them, still having fantasies of wealth and luxury as his new army, even after the recent failure of False Peter. Their first attempt at victory was Saratov on the Volga River, but they were defeated. The disenchanted Cossacks killed Osinovik on the banks of the Volga, while Verovkin ordered that

August and Laver be hanged on the road from Saratov to Moscow. Following them in various Ukrainian cities surfaced eight more sons of Tsar Feodor Ivanovich, named Feodor II, Erofei, Klementi, Saveli, Semeon, Vasili, Gavrilo and Martin. But they vanished just as fast as they appeared.

With the recent victories Moscow was receiving loads of food by September 1609, from Pereyaslavl, Vladimir and Kolomna. The size of Skopin-Shuisky's army had now increased to 18,000 Russians plus the 1,000 Swedes, and he was waiting for more reinforcements from the north of Moscow before proceeding to attack Tushino. More important though was the liberation of Troitse-Sergieva. On October 18, Skopin-Shuisky attacked the army of Yan Sapega, which was overrun by sheer numbers. The army of Sheremetev from the east then came in between Tushino and Troitse-Sergieva to block Sapega's retreat to his camp. Sapega returned to Troitse-Sergieva as Skopin-Shuisky moved his camp to Aleksandrovski Slobod, the former residence of Tsar Ivan IV. The battles concluded in a stalemate as winter approached, although the backbone of Verovkin was broken by the three Russian commanders: Pr. Mikhail Skopin-Shuisky, Pr. Dmitri Ivanovich Shuisky and Pr. Peter Nikitich Sheremetev. From this point and to the end of his campaign Verovkin's army was crippled.

Crimean Mongols now took advantage of Russia's civil war and national troubles to appropriate more territory for themselves or even become the victor. Mongols were banking on Russia destroying itself with its civil war and becoming so weak that an easy victory would be provided. During the spring of 1609, Mongols began assembling and training an army. In July 1609, Canibek (Dzhanibek) II, a descendant of Khan Uzbek, and his army crossed into Russia. In previous invasions, the Mongol hordes would attack and pillage and then retreat to their camps in the steppes. This time Canibek's army slowly proceeded north, plundering and burning villages and impressing native Russians into service, since there was no more Russian army controlling the border. They reached as far north as the Oka River in the vicinity of Serpukhov, Kolomna and Borovsk, about 100 miles south of Moscow. Tsar Shuisky attempted to hide from the populace the threat of the Crimean Mongols and their proximity to the capital, but the people of Moscow had heard reports of the infidels' arrival from Kolomna and other cities devastated by the Mongol horde. It was not an envious position for Tsar Shuisky.

Victories and Success of False Dmitri II

Because of the stagnant effort of Verovkin through the autumn 1608 — his procrastination in completing total victory over Russia with the defeat of Moscow — many of the educated and aristocratic Russians who earlier had acknowledged Verovkin were now beginning to consider Pr. Wladyslaw, the young 16-year-old son of King Sigismund, as a better candidate for the throne. Polish aristocrats, hearing the rumors, presented to Sigismund the proposition of going to war against Russia, weak and unstable as it was. The Polish senate approved a decision to void the recent treaty and to go to war. Yuri Mnishek, who had just returned home from Russia, was unable to change the decision or warn his son-in-law. Sigismund became for Tsar Shuisky what Batori was to Tsar Ivan IV, and recruits were summoned to form a new army. In June 1609, Sigismund left Krakow with his army under the command of Polotzki, but not knowing exactly where to attack Russia first: through the Ukraine, or to Smolensk, or directly to Moscow. Consulting with Lev Sapega Sigismund chose Smolensk, being advised that they would surrender easiest to him in order to be liberated from the yoke of Verovkin.

Believing the rumors that Smolensk was impatiently waiting for him as deliverer, Sigismund in September 1609 reached the city with 12,000 Polish cavalry, German infantry, and Lithuanian soldiers, along with 10,000 Zaporozhski Cossacks. They set their camp along the Dnepr River, surrounded Smolensk, and sent a directive to the residents of Smolensk, telling them that God was punishing Russia for Godunov's atrocities and for those of other wicked tsars. Sigismund and his troops were unaware of the fortitude and strength of the city, having at the time a population of over 20,000. The wall was four miles in perimeter and 16 feet high, even though the actual garrison consisted of only 1500 Royal Guards, and the balance were armed residents. Sigismund in his directive informed them that many Russians secretly convinced him — as king of true Christianity — to deliver Russia from both Verovkin and Sweden. As a result, it was to the benefit of Smolensk to surrender to him or else he would destroy the city and kill all its residents. The city military commander Mikhail Borisovich Shein, Pr. Gorchakov and Archbishop Sergei refused his demands. They also sent the directive to Tsar Shuisky at Moscow, asking for military help. The Poles surrounded the city and began the siege.

At night, Sigismund's soldiers would attempt to climb the walls, but were repelled. Tunnels under the walls likewise failed and the siege was at a stalemate when winter arrived. In the process, cities of northwest Ukraine capitulated to Sigismund's army abandoning Verovkin. The advancement of Sigismund alarmed the Tushino camp more than Moscow. Delegates from Sigismund arrived in Tushino in December 1609 to discuss unification of their armies with Verovkin. Their goal, as they explained it, was to join forces with Verovkin and so defeat Tsar Shuisky, but Verovkin was reluctant to do so, figuring this would terminate his effort to attain the throne of Russia and all his effort evolve into a futile campaign, losing it to the Polish king. Verovkin was aware of the rumors circulating that many were inclined to preferring son Wladyslaw as king instead of him. In reality, their purpose was to absorb Tushino into their own army and remove Verovkin in the process. Verovkin asked for time to meditate on a response. What was Verovkin to do, while still surrounded by Russian society and still the head of his military? He could only sit in his mansion and calmly wait for a decision from those he considered his servants and confederates and hope for their loyalty. The envoys invited Russian officials of Tushino camp to a meeting and handed them the directive of Sigismund, explaining that although the king of Poland entered Russia armed, but for the purpose of its peace and prosperity Sigismund wanted to suppress the rebellion, remove the shameless Verovkin, and overthrow the usurper Tsar Shuisky, liberate the people and affirm Orthodoxy in Russia. The attendants could not express their gratitude for such a proposition and their despondent faces brightened. They told each other, "We cannot find a better monarch."

Still enveloped with dreams of majesty, Verovkin feared having to awaken to reality and preferred to close his eyes. Verovkin had suffered the insolence of Polish gentry and the contempt of Russia, not able to be either condescending or strict. Tushkevich, for example, called him an impostor right to his face. Many Russians feigned honor to Verovkin, while behind his back were abhorred by his presence. Such people refused to obey his commands and often reprimanded him insolently and planned behind his back how to rid themselves of both Shuisky and Verovkin. The withdrawal of Verovkin at such a fatal moment would only provide greater benefit for the success of Sigismund's envoys.

In this manner did the intents of Sigismund to appropriate the crown of Monomakh unveil and was triumphantly approved by Russians, but by what Russians? The traitors who abandoned Tsar Shuisky and had no loyalty to Verovkin: Boyar Mikhail Saltykov, Pr. Vasili Mosalski and their associates. Such had no qualms about betraying Russia and Verovkin to Poland, and only to save themselves from Shuisky's vengeance, hoping to gain amnesty from Sigismund at an early stage of the game. Patr. Filaret was also present at the meeting, although against his will, and to protect his own life silently condoned the proceedings by refusing to object. The envoys were convinced of the agreement of the Tushino camp to accept Sigismund as king, and were now ready to begin negotiations with Tsar Shuisky and so entered Moscow to meet with the tsar. Their proposed peace treaty provided for Russia to return either the region of Smolensk or Severski to Poland, which would satisfy the greed of Sigismund, should Russians eventually fail to overthrow Tsar Shuisky. After reading the propositions of the envoys, Tsar Shuisky refused to respond as an indication of his contempt towards them. Moscow was calm, while Tushino fanned flames of revolt.

The envoys were able to gain the support of Pr. Rozhinski and several senior officials of Tushino, but they did not want to yet abandon Verovkin, fearing that the rabble that comprised Verovkin's army would then migrate to Tsar Shuisky. The Russian officials decided to tolerate the rule of Verovkin in order to scare Moscow, eventually to overthrow Tsar Shuisky. But Verovkin ascertained the conclusion of the meeting with the envoys and summoned Rozhinski to his mansion, demanding to know the reasons for the defection. Rozhinski harangued Verovkin and attempted to strike him, but Verovkin fled his residence. He ran to his wife Marina and told her that his Hetman wanted to betray him to Sigismund and he had to flee to save his life. That night, December 29, 1609, Verovkin fled Tushino. He changed into peasant clothing and with his jester Peter Koshelev hid in a pile of boxes on a cart and fled to Kaluga, there to reorganize his campaign. At dawn the Tushino residents discovered that Verovkin had vanished. Many thought he had been killed during the night and the body thrown into the river. The camp was in an uproar, since the majority of his makeshift army were still zealous supporters. The disappearance of Verovkin caused turmoil in the camp and the envoys from Sigismund were considered the initial suspects. Their carriages were searched for the body of Verovkin, but not to be found. The crowds rushed to Rozhinski, demanding to know his whereabouts and at the same time plundering his mansion of its valuable possessions, all of which he left behind. Rozhinski and other officials attempted to suppress the riot, telling them that Verovkin had temporarily secluded himself. Russians of Tushino were perplexed as to what to do: some abandoned the camp, some left to join Sigismund's company, while others left for Moscow.

It was not until after January 1, 1610, a few days later that the Tushino camp was aware that Verovkin had fled to Kaluga, about 100 miles due south. Verovkin had told the residents of the attempt on his life and of the demands of Sigismund. The residents of Kaluga welcomed Verovkin as a champion, where many still had high regard for Bolotnikov. They treated Verovkin as the legitimate monarch of Russia, assigned the best house in the city as his residence and supplied him with clothing and provisions. Crowds of supporters from Tushino began to migrate to Kaluga and a new central headquarter for his command was established. The first order of Verovkin was for his newly-formed regiment of bodyguards to execute Poles and Germans wherever they could be found, as well as Russians who were still loyal to Tsar Shuisky. The former military governor of Kaluga, Skotnitzki, was drowned, suspected of treason by Verovkin. Ivan Ivanovich Godunov, a dedicated servant and brother-in-law of Tsar Shuisky was thrown from the top of a tower; having survived the fall, he was thrown into a river. Floating downstream he attempted to enter a boat, but the boatman cut his hands from his body, causing Godunov to drown. Verovkin unleashed his anger at every foreigner, telling his listeners that once he became tsar in Moscow, not one foreigner would remain in Russia. His bodyguards proceeded on a murder campaign in the neighboring cities: Tula, Peremish, Kozelsk, and others.

Verovkin sent a directive to the Tushino camp, where it was publicly read. He promised his supporters great rewards if they were to again swear loyalty to him and punish those responsible for the recent treason in the discussions with Sigismund's envoys. Verovkin's messengers also told them that only he can make them wealthy and already has millions of rubles in his possession. Some listened, some did not, but the groveling rabble and fortune-seekers were always at the loyalty of any who would throw them a piece of bread. Marina Mnishek worried about losing her title of tsaritza, thinking that Verovkin had abandoned her and his campaign. Psychologically devastated with his abandonment, she went tent to tent seeking support from soldiers, spending the next few nights in their company, leaving aside any shame or dignity. The former attitude of Marina Mnishek toward her False husband quickly changed as she pleaded in distress and tears for the Tushino camp not to abandon him, although her concern was her future, her fantasy of again being tsaritza of Russia. They told her, "The envoys of the [Polish] crown have deceived us and distanced Dmitri from our presence. Where is he for whom we have laid down our life? From whom will we acquire any reward?" A civil war erupted within the Tushino camp, Rozhinski and his confederates surrounded the Verovkin loyalists and killed about a thousand. Not gaining the success she expected with the Tushino camp and fearing she would be the next victim of the vengeance of Rozhinski, Marina Mnishek, deep in the winter night of February 11, left Tushino on horseback with a male and female servant. The flight of Marina caused a mutiny against Rozhinski in the camp, some wanting to kill him and end the strife. They accused him of being bought by Sigismund in order to appropriate the treasuries of Moscow for Poland and not for the troops of Tushino camp. Rozhinski claimed his innocence and was able to quell their anger.

Rozhinski wrote a letter that evening to deliver to Sigismund, informing him that that his effort would be entirely futile if Sigismund did not satisfy the needs of the troops and officials at the Tushino camp. This desire or need of Rozhinski's was delivered to Sigismund through Russian envoys and Tushino Polish gentry. Among the 40 that traveled to meet with Sigismund at Smolensk were Mikhail Saltykov and his son Ivan, Princes Vasili Mosalski, Yuri Khvorostin, Lev Plesheev, and Mikhail Molchanov (the murderer who earlier attempted to become a False Dmitri). On January 31, 1610, Sigismund met with them in the presence of his senators and royal court. The aged and silverheaded Saltykov addressed the group in a lengthy sermon about the calamites of Russia and their trustworthiness to the Polish crown, until he could speak no more. The others continued in the same vein, until Saltykov regained his strength and offered the throne of Russia, not to Sigismund, but to his young son Wladyslaw. The Russian court official Gramotin concluded the envoy's presentation with a list of the advantages that would pertain to both governments, and the safety, security and prosperity which would exist under the reign of Wladyslaw. Lithuanian chancellor Lev Sapega replied with a note of gratitude and acceptance of the proposal, and stated that a committee of senators would be selected to further discuss the manner of transition to Polish rule. The envoys informed the Poles that they should not delay, but hasten to Moscow and with their help be able to defeat Moscow, establish a new government and stabilize the country. Sigismund was reluctant to accept the proposal and proceed too quickly; he wanted the consensus of the Russian army, royal court, Orthodox clergy and populace for his son Wladyslaw to ascend the throne of Russia. Sigismund likewise required an oath of loyalty from the entirety of the Tushino camp, lest some of them continue their support of Verovkin and hinder the effectiveness of the Poles to occupy Russia and a worse civil war then erupt. Further conversations included the requirement of Wladyslaw to covert to Eastern Orthodoxy instead of Catholicism. This would have to be done voluntarily as a prerequisite. Troops that were loyal to the Russian envoys would handle the dismissal or removal of both Tsar Shuisky and Verovkin, so no obstacles would hinder the establishment of the new government. Wladyslaw was only 16 years old and the envoys were well aware that he would be a puppet in his father Sigismund's hands, but the envoys were worried more about their own fate at the hands of Tsar Shuisky, now with the country reversing their allegiance: away from Verovkin — now in Kaluga — and toward Shuisky. The envoys were treated as special guests during their visit with Sigismund, with festivities and banquets, drinking to the health of Tsar Wladyslaw.

Letters were written by the envoys to the military governors of the cities surrounding Moscow, lauding the magnanimity of Sigismund to agree to invading Russia, quashing the civil war, providing his son Wladyslaw as the new monarch, and establishing stability. The letters urged residents to swear loyalty to the new tsar Wladyslaw.

The Tushino Russians were content with the proposal, but the Tushino Poles were not and expected millions of rubles as compensation for their effort as well as estates in the soon-to-be appropriated provinces of Smolensk and Severski. Not wanting to alienate or vex the troops that he needed so badly, Sigismund promised to yield to them estates in Severski and Ryazan, and to magnanimously reward both Verovkin and Marina Mnishek if they surrender to his authority. Sigismund also promised them money, to be brought to Tushino with his troops, who would then remove Pr. Mikhail Skopin-Shuisky from action, defeat Moscow and overthrow Tsar Shuisky. But this response did not gratify the Tushino Poles, not believing any of Sigismund's promises until they see the money in their hands. Sigismund procrastinated as he continued the siege of Smolensk; he sent no money and no troops, not to mention that Sigismund's military commander Polotzki would not budge from the siege of Smolensk because of his private support of Verovkin. Some of the Russians defending Smolensk were deceived and accepted the proposal, such as Rzhev and Zubtzov, but Shein refused. After five months under siege in Smolensk, he still refused to capitulate. Shein was summoned from the city to attend the discussions, which he listened to with contempt, and then returned to the city to continue to endure the siege.

News from Kaluga agitated the new leaders of the Tushino camp, because Verovkin again increased his makeshift army and established himself as False tsar. Marina his wife arrived there and was welcomed as a heroine. The city feasted and celebrated with visions of its officials becoming the new royal court of Moscow and the residents to be blessed with the prosperity and peace as compensation for their support of Verovkin. The supplies lines were now directed to Kaluga and those remaining at Tushino in the winter cold suffered malnutrition and frost bite, as if under siege in their own camp. The Tushino troops attempted to plunder local villages for their survival but were repulsed by tsarist loyalist troops or by regiments of Skopin-Shuisky. They complained that with the departure of Verovkin, so departed their good fortune. Only poverty and death remained in Tushino while honor and wealth resided at Kaluga. What remained of the Tushino makeshift army attempted to pillage their own camp and migrate to Kaluga, but Rozhinski — and his final time to do so — convinced the mutineers to endure a while longer under his command.

Civil War between the Armies of Tsar Shuisky and False Dmitri II

Meanwhile, Pr. Mikhail Skopin-Shuisky was active increasing the size of his army. An additional 3000 Swedes arrived from Vyborg and Narva, and were preparing to proceed against Sapega and Rozhinski. First they were to occupy the area between Smolensk and Moscow and also Tver, in order to severe communication and supplies from Sigismund. The initial result was the abandonment of the siege of Troitse-Sergieva Monastery on January 12, 1610 after 16 months, Sapega fleeing the site and leaving behind many supplies. The monks plundered Sapega's camp and attributed the success to the intervention of Skopin-Shuisky, now hailed more of a hero than before. The residents of Troitse-Sergieva provided Skopin-Shuisky's troops with provisions while thousands of rubles were distributed among the Swedish mercenaries from the monastery treasury. Sapega and the remnant of his makeshift army traveled through snow south-west, meditating whether to unite with Sigismund at Smolensk or Verovkin at Kaluga.

The camp of Yan Sapega at Troitse-Sergieva had been a shield for Tushino, standing between it and Skopin-Shuisky's troops at Alexandrovski Slobod, but once Sapega fled, Tushino had no more defense, and now especially with Verovkin gone and the remaining troops restive. The army of Skopin-Shuisky moved toward Tushino, occupying and purging rebel villages in the process. Rozhinski summoned the entire camp to leave without hesitation and it was set on fire. The smoke and rising flames of Tushino devoured the camp to a field of rubble and ashes, as its former residents departed in different directions. For 1½ years Tushino rivaled Moscow as the capital of Russia, each with its own tsar and Tushino surpassing the population of Moscow, and now was as if it never existed. Residents fled to Moscow hoping for amnesty or the kindness of relatives, or to their home cities hoping to fade into oblivion to escape repercussion. The more vile and desperate migrated to Kaluga to join Verovkin there, still having fantasies of opulence and dignity unearned. Some followed Saltykov, as did the Polish gentry, towards Smolensk, or back to Europe.

Hotly pursued by the troops of Skopin-Shuisky, Rozhinski fled to Voloko-Lamsk. There he was captured and brutally executed.

In five months Skopin-Shuisky was able to summon an army of Swedes and Russians and liberate Troitse-Sergieva and annihilate Tushino. He and his army jubilantly entered Moscow on March 2, 1610, as no other victor has in the history of Russia, residents and officials congratulating him and Delagardi for the deliverance of Moscow and Russia. Skopin-Shuisky was one of the few who retained his loyalty to Tsar Shuisky during this turbulent period. After the festivities of victory ended Skopin-Shuisky began arrangements to develop a larger army, now to rid Verovkin and his camp at Kaluga from Russia, as he did Rozhinski and the Tushino camp. A month passed into the beginning of spring before any further campaigns could be attempted.

Palace intrigues surfaced with the arrival of Pr. Skopin-Shuisky, court officials fearing their own heads should they also be suspected or accused of confederacy with Verovkin. Such envious officials began to discredit Skopin-Shuisky behind his back to his uncle Tsar Shuisky, telling him that his nephew was a risk to his future, that the populace preferred him as tsar and that the military was ready with a coup to replace Shuisky with his nephew. Such gossip and rumor traveled about Moscow and the neighboring villages, that Skopin-Shuisky would be preferable as tsar. The populace compared Vasili Shuisky to Saul who killed his thousands and Mikhail Skopin-Shuisky to David who killed tens of thousands. Even soothsayers and fortune tellers advertised their prognostications that the next monarch of Russia would be named Mikhail (and coincidentally fulfilled in Mikhail Romanov). But the populace prematurely agreed to support nephew Skopin-Shuisky as the successor to Vasili Shuisky and this attitude vexed Dmitri Shuisky, who felt that if anybody was to be heir to the throne it would be him, the younger brother, and not a nephew. Envy flared in the intrigues of the royal court since Tsar Shuisky, now 60 years of age, had no male offspring, save only a daughter recently born, Anastasia. The friction grew between Dmitri Shuisky and his brother the tsar.

Skopin-Shuisky attempted to exonerate himself and mitigate the accusations of uncle Dmitri, but with little success with uncle Vasili the tsar, who was now reluctant to assign nephew Mikhail the army to proceed against Verovkin at Kaluga. Not to curb further action, Tsar Shuisky gave orders to the Boyar Duma to make arrangements with Swedish General Delagardi, for him to be promoted as commander of the Russian military. Delagardi sensed the strife in the royal court and warned Skopin-Shuisky as a friend to be aware of any attempts on his life, and the two proceeded to organize the army for a campaign to rescue Smolensk from siege. On April 23, 1610, Dmitri Shuisky gave a banquet on behalf of his nephew Mikhail. Dmitri's wife — Ekaterina, another daughter of henchman Maluta Skuratov — poured something for Mikhail to drink. He died later that evening. Once the populace heard of the death they immediately attributed it to poisoning by uncle Dmitri Shuisky, following the pattern of execution implemented by his brother-in-law Tsar Boris Godunov during his reign. The populace of Moscow could not be comforted over the death of the 23 year-old Pr. Mikhail Skopin-Shuisky as a result of court strife. He was entombed inside the Archangel Cathedral in the Moscow Kremlin and prelates lauded him as the Russian Achilles at his memorial service.

Dmitri Shuisky took over as military commander and troops reluctantly followed. The Swedish mercenaries wanted money, so Tsar Shuisky had to coercively plunder monasteries for the money, as did Tsar Godunov and Otrepyev before him. Gold and silver cups and bowls were confiscated and melted, which incensed the monks and the populace who labeled it sacrilege. Now General Delagardi was able to organize the Swedes to follow Dmitri Shuisky to liberate Smolensk.

Shuisky's army assembled at Mozhaisk to confront Sigismund, but the Poles did not want to abandon the siege of Smolensk, so Sigismund assigned Hetman Stanislav Zholkevski only 2000 cavalry and 1,000 infantry to confront the 6,500 Swedes and Russians and another 6,000 troops from the camp at Tushino who deserted Verovkin and decided to join Tsar Shuisky's army. Both armies grew with recruits. The battle was fought June 23, 1610, near the village Klushin, between 13,000 Russians and Swedes and 6,000 Poles and Europeans. Even though he was out-numbered, the army of Zholkevski was able to disperse the Russians and Swedes under Dmitri Shuisky and Delagardi. Following the battle Zholkevski was able to get many Russians to swear loyalty to the next tsar of Russia, Wladyslaw. Zholkovski wrote letters to cities, including Moscow, regarding the defeat of Russia's army and for them to swear loyalty to Wladyslaw. Tsar Shuisky returned to Moscow and desperately summoned troops for a final defense against Zholkevski's army, which by now made camp at Mozhaisk to recover from the battle. The cities of central Russia were in upheaval over the events: to whom should they give their loyalty? Wladyslaw? Tsar Shuisky? Verovkin? And who would be the victor? And how would the victor treat the defeated? The populace of Moscow decided that Vasili Shuisky should be tsar no longer, and that Verovkin would be a better choice than Wladyslaw and a Polish occupation.

Verovkin took advantage of the depressed condition of Moscow's populace due to the defeat of Dmitri Shuisky's army, and his camp moved in its entirety from Kaluga to Kolomensk, a village about a mile southeast of Moscow.

The people of Moscow revolted in the streets, demonstrating against Tsar Shuisky, complaining that he had not been selected by the entire country and that all the misfortunes of Russia were due to his inability to reign. The death of nephew Mikhail Skopin-Shuisky was also blamed on brother Dmitri. One group of concerned Kremlin court officials, along with a few officials who returned from Tushino after its devastation, proposed that Tsar Shuisky abdicate, Verovkin be captured and executed, the Poles be driven out of Russia, and a new tsar be elected according to the will of the people. The Tushino fugitives claimed they could capture Verovkin and bring him to justice. The proposal was announced at Red Square by Prokopi Lyapunov and greeted positively by the crowds. Patr. Hermogen was removed from the security of his Chudovski Monastery cloister by the rabble, but he told the crowds that this was treason and it would be of no benefit to them. The rabble with a few remnants of the Boyar Duma decided to overthrow Tsar Shuisky and form a new government that would be led by the Boyar Duma under the direction of Pr. Mstislavski. On July 17, 1610, a letter was composed with the demands and delivered to Tsar Shuisky by members of the Duma. The monarch refused to capitulate. The soldiers loyal to the Duma arrested Tsar Vasili Shuisky and his young wife and daughter and removed them from the palace and to a private house on the Kremlin grounds, there to be held under guard.

Turmoil reigned in the capital and only increased when the people realized that they had been duped by the Tushino fugitives. Lyapunov was assured that the Tushino fugitives were to deliver Verovkin to them for execution, but instead the fugitives replied, "Long live the son of Tsar Ivan. We will die for Dmitri." Again Patr. Hermogen was retrieved from his safe haven and he again begged the people to reinstall Vasili Shuisky as tsar, but his plea was in vain. The people feared more the vengeance of Shuisky upon them, should he again be allowed to ascend the throne. Vasili Shuisky with wife and daughter sat in the same room where four years earlier he had met with conspirators to plan the murder of Otrepyev. The next morning Lyapunov, Pr. Peter Zacekin, some clergy from Chudovski Monastery, and a regiment of soldiers arrived and told him to prepare himself for tonsure, "No," Shuisky hollered, "I will never be a monk, I wanted to do good for you so why do you hate me?" His cries were worthless as a priest read a prayer of confirmation and performed the rite of tonsure. The same was repeated for the unfortunate Tsaritza Maria to take the vow of a nun. After the rites, Maria had to be torn away from her husband: he was led to the Chudovski Monastery and she to the Ivanovski Convent; the history of their daughter ends at this time. The two brothers of the tsar, Dmitri and Ivan, were confined to their homes under guard.

The Boyar Duma, headed by Lyapunov and Golitsyn wrote letters that Tsar Shuisky had voluntarily capitulated and that the government was now in the hands of the Boyar Duma. However, the noblemen were unable to establish order in the capital or countryside, especially with Verovkin just a short distance away. As anarchy flared, residents left the city to Kolomensk to seek safety in the camp of Verovkin. This provided more fuel to Verovkin's fire to attack Moscow and which became the greatest fear of Moscow's populace.

The Polish Army Occupies Moscow

Having only a few supporters with the intent of establishing order, Pr. Feodor Mstislavski was able to take charge of affairs in the Boyar Duma. He consulted with court officials and then announced to the Boyar Duma that in order to save the nation it would be in their best interests to entrust Russia's throne to Wladyslaw. Not wanting to be tsar himself, his humility acquired the consent of all from noblemen to serf. On July 31, 1610, rebel leader Hetman Zholkevski and Ivan Saltykov wrote to the Boyar Duma relating to them the proposal made to Sigismund regarding his son, and who still young could be molded into a Russian Orthodox tsar. The ROC clergy was hesitant to agree to the proposal, still fearing the conversion of Russia to Unia as with the attempt of Otrepyev to do so. Not having the means or power to return Vasili Shuisky to the throne, they proposed Pr. Vasili Golitsyn or the young Mikhail Romanov, son of Filaret. But with the civil unrest in the city and Verovkin almost at the walls of Moscow the verdict of the Boyar Duma was, "Let us accept the advice of Mstislavski," A compromise was reached between the two highest prelates of Russian Orthodoxy and the Russian nobility. Hetman Zholkevski, also ready to attack the city on behalf of Sigismund should they refuse the offer, agreed to negotiations. Princes Mstislavski, Golitsyn, Sheremetev, Mezetzki and Telepnev met with Zholkevski in his tent outside the city walls. They informed him that Russia was ready to recognize Wladyslaw as monarch, but conditionally, and Telepnev read the conditions: that Wladyslaw would be baptized into the Orthodox faith and desist any further communication with the pope or Catholicism in general, and that he would marry a native Russian of the Orthodox religion according to Greek rites, were the two primary concerns, and the balance were incidental as far as Zholkevski was concerned. The Boyar Duma felt they would possess the power behind the throne of Wladyslaw anyway, with the young tsar nothing more than a figurehead. The Hetman sent a messenger to Sigismund for his approval of the conditions, but did not receive any soon reply, so he, not being able to postpone any further the negotiations due to the impatience of the Russians and their fear of attack by Verovkin, on August 17, himself agreed to the conditions. A few more were added such as the fixed boundaries between Russian and Poland-Lithuania and the withdrawal of all European troops from Russia, referring to the siege of Smolensk and other Polish gentry still residing in Russia, and that Verovkin would be captured and executed. Both sides — Russians and Poles — took an oath of obligation to the conditions of the agreement and loyalty to Tsar Wladyslaw. The two groups feasted in celebration, hoping to restore Russia to peace, stability and prosperity. The following day, 10,000 Moscow residents swore allegiance to the new monarch, while prelates of the Orthodox Church swore allegiance at Uspenski Cathedral in Patr. Hermogen's presence.

The festivities were hardly concluded when messengers arrived from Sigismund with a letter ordering Zholkevski to attack and occupy Moscow immediately and in the name of Sigismund, not Wladyslaw. Sigismund was a fervent and dedicated Uniate, ready to have Catholicism replace Orthodoxy just as Otrepyev attempted to do. Zholkevski however felt some guilt about the order, since it would cause him to violate the terms of the agreement he just made with the Boyar Duma.

Hearing of the agreement between Russia and Lithuania-Poland, Verovkin hoped to sway Zhelkovski to his side with bribes: first it was 30,000 gold ducats to him, and then 100,000 more to Sigismund and Russia would cede Livonia and Severski to Poland once Verovkin became tsar. Zholkevski adamantly refused. Having failed with his attempted bribes to secure his own safety, Verovkin and Marina Mnishek along with Zarutzki and regiments of Cossacks, Mongols and Russians, abandoned Kolomensk and fled back to Kaluga on August 26, 1610.

Local cities, such as Kolomna, Tula, Ryazan, Tver, Vladimir and Yaroslavl, swore loyalty to Tsar Wladyslaw, although he was still in Poland. Fugitives from Tushino: Mikhail Saltykov, Pr. Vasili Mosalski, Feodor Mescherski, Mikhail Molchanov, and others, all threw themselves at the mercy of Zhelkovski and declared their allegiance to Wladyslaw and repented of their association with Verovkin. Yan Sapega surrendered to Zholkevski hoping for amnesty, which he was granted.

Zholkevski wrote daily to Sigismund for him not to ruin the achievement that he had worked so hard to accomplish: the civil war finally over with a Pole as the new monarch of Russia. In the interim Zholkovski was elected to head the Boyar Duma, until Wladyslaw should arrive from Poland. What then irritated the members of the Boyar Duma, those who remained in Moscow during the reign of Tsar Shuisky, was that now Zholkevski was granting amnesty to the former members of the Tushino camp and reinstating them in the former positions in the royal court or Duma or government, which the boyars refused to do. This erupted into strife between those earlier loyal to Tsar Shuisky and those that returned from Tushino. As a result many reinstated fugitives left Moscow for Kaluga.

Zholkevski to protect his authority and that of the tsar-designate Wladyslaw sent a delegation from Moscow to King Sigismund at Smolensk, to present the terms of Russia's subjugation. The delegates were Metr. Filaret, Avrami Palitzen of Troitse-Sergieva Monastery, Zakari Lyapunov and Pr. Vasili Golitsyn. In their absence Zholkevski hoped to strengthen his authority and stabilize the government. Their purpose at Smolensk was to discuss the treaty and terms of transition of power to Wladyslaw and so end the siege of Smolensk and for the Polish army to leave Russia. On September 11 they left Moscow. Before leaving for Smolensk, Patr. Hermogen blessed the delegates and Filaret promised him, that he would "Die if necessary for the Orthodox Christian religion."

While the most important figures of secular and clerical authority were in route to Smolensk, Zhelkovski was able to incline Feodor Mstislavski, Mikhail Saltykov and remaining boyars to his idea of inviting the Polish army into Moscow, as if to subdue the civil unrest, those clamoring for the arrival of Verovkin (even though he was by now heading for Kaluga, in the opposite direction). Refusing the advice of the ROC clergy and palace court the boyars agreed to the request and within 10 days, on September 21, the Poles from the camp at Mozhaisk were at the walls of Moscow to occupy the city. The Poles entered Moscow that night and in the morning the residents awoke to find themselves as captives in a Polish-occupied city. Zholkevski told the populace that the Poles were to be servants of the Russians under the reign of Wladyslaw, but soon the entire city, food supplies, munitions, streets and gates, were controlled by the Polish occupiers under the authority of Zholkevski. The Kremlin palaces became hotels for the occupiers with celebrations every night at the expense of what little remained in the Russian treasury. Yan Sapega was given 10,000 gold ducats and sent with a regiment to take Polish control over Severski.

Soon after, former Tsar Vasili Shuisky was taken from his cloister at Chudovski Monastery and transferred under Polish guard to Joseph Voloko-Lamsk Monastery. The Polish Alexandr Gosevski became military governor of the city and was placed in charge of the 17,000 strong Russian Royal Guards. Only Patr. Hermogen spoke against the occupation, but he do could little.

News of the Polish-occupation of Moscow reached Sigismund at Smolensk, and his advisors told him to accept the royal agreement and transfer of power to Wladyslaw, have peace with Russia, and both countries would gain economic prosperity. Sigismund refused the advice and decided that if anybody was going to be tsar of Russia, it was going to be him. Sigismund was ordering Russian officials and nobles to swear loyalty to him while promising them land and money, and patiently awaited the arrival of Golitsyn and Filaret before proceeding on his venture. The envoys on their journey to Smolensk believed the credibility of Zholkevski less and Sigismund even less, and they sent a return message to the Boyar Duma that Polish soldiers were violating the treaty and plundering villages in the countryside. Not only did Moscow suffer from the Poles, but every city they set their foot in was plundered.

On October 7, the envoys arrived at Smolensk, but were not allowed into the city or into Sigismund's camp. They were forced to erect their tents on the banks of the Dnepr River, there to endure the onset of winter and lack of food. On October 12, Filaret, Golitsyn, and Palitzen were permitted to meet with Sigismund and address him. They explained to him the treaty and agreement that was concluded with Zholkevski and which conceded to having son Wladyslaw as their new monarch. Lev Sapega haughtily spoke on behalf of Sigismund, that the will of Sigismund would be executed and not some document created by his subjects. The envoys were told that son Wladyslaw was too young to govern such a massive country as Russia, and so father Sigismund was to ascend the throne of a united three-nation confederacy: Lithuania-

Poland-Russia. The envoys were bewildered and perplexed at the response of Lev Sapega and their defense was to unveil all the devastation caused by Sigismund to Russia beginning with their support of Otrepyev and the subsequent civil wars. Sigismund and his officials refused to listen. The next proposition to change Sigismund's mind was the Russian offer of millions of gold ducats to be paid Poland after all the terms of the treaty and transfer of power to Wladyslaw were concluded. The Polish officials likewise refused, having their minds on the expansion of their territory into Russia.

As news filtered into Moscow about the proceedings at Smolensk, Zholkevski left to personally meet with Sigismund. In order for Poles to have control of Russia, the treaty and agreement had to be accepted by Sigismund or else another civil war would erupt. As hostages, Zholkevski took with him the two brothers of Tsar Vasili, Ivan and Dmitri, and Dmitri's wife. The wife of Tsar Vasili was exiled to the Pokrovski Convent in Suzdal. On leaving Moscow, Zholkevski stopped in Voloko-Lamsk and took into his own custody Tsar Vasili Shuisky, dressing him in plain clothes and fettered him as a criminal, becoming Zholkevski's trophy for his victory over Moscow to display to Sigismund and all of Poland. At their meeting in Smolensk, Sigismund refused Zholkevski's request to endorse the treaty, not wanting to desist the siege of Smolensk and refusing to send Wladyslaw to Moscow. By now it was the end of November, 1610.

With the departure of Zholkevski Moscow was leaderless and on the verge of anarchy. The Boyar Duma under the weakness of the aged and frail Mstislavski was powerless and continually condescending to the Polish occupation, fearing for their safety. Pr. Prokopi Lyapunov of Ryazan, whose brother Zakari was at Smolensk with Filaret and Golitsyn, then arose to provide some leadership, but working outside the city organizing a siege.

General Delagardi, the earlier Swedish military hero, had returned to join the Swedes now occupying Pskov and Ivangorod. Moslems under Shah Abbas took advantage of the weakness of Russia's government and initiated sieges of Astrakhan and Kazan. Mstislavski was convinced that the only manner of stopping the upheavals was the intervention of Sigismund's strong military, and so begged him to abandon Smolensk and march on Moscow. Sigismund, now exhausted with winter at Smolensk, could move nowhere, and so continued his siege, blaming Shein, the Smolensk military commander, for prolonging the siege by not capitulating to him.

Residents were leaving Moscow at night to neighboring cities, afraid of vengeance by the Polish soldiers, who were unrestrained in morality and thought nothing of havoc or crimes against the populace. The people had abandoned hope in Wladyslaw ever arriving or ascending the throne, much less stabilizing the country. The Polish occupation arbitrarily killed Russians with impunity, raped women, desecrated sacred shrines and churches, burnt villages and plundered them, with no defense from even the Russian Royal Guards. If this was insufficient Swedes migrated further into Karelia and northwest Russia, occupying more territory. Cities of the south and east of Moscow, even Kazan, returned loyalty to Verovkin, the people convinced that his power base at Kaluga was again increasing. Bogdan Belski, still residing in Kazan, was thrown from the top of a tower to his death. The officials of Kazan wrote letters to other cities to make Kaluga the new capital under Tsar Dmitri Ivanovich and for all Russia to unite under his banner. In reality Verovkin at Kaluga was nothing more than a scarecrow pointed toward Moscow, although having 5,000 Cossacks, Mongols and Russians as his army, but they were disorganized and already apathetic to the campaign. Living luxuriously with Marina through the autumn of 1610 and into winter, Verovkin was not in a hurry to attack Moscow. While in Kaluga she bore a son to him whom they named Ivan Dmitriyevich after False grandfather Tsar Ivan and father False Dmitri, even though any Tushino soldier could have been the father. If Moscow was to collapse to the Poles, Verovkin had on his mind to escape to Astrakhan.

On December 11, 1610, Pr. Peter Araslan Yurusov, of the Siberian Nogay clan, went hunting with Verovkin. Araslan had on his mind to take vengeance on Verovkin for his makeshift army murdering his best friend, the Khan of Kasimov Yuraz-Magmet. While hunting at some isolated spot Araslan killed Verovkin with his hunting rifle and decapitated him. Araslan and his Nogay tribesmen fled back to Siberia. One witness to the murder, Koshelev, returned as fast as possible to Kaluga and informed Marina Mnishek of the event. It was the middle of the night and she ran into the street half-naked in her sleeping gown. The entire city was alarmed and Marina demanded vengeance. By morning not one Mongol was alive in Kaluga; all were massacred in their beds by blood-thirsty bodyguards at the order of Marina. Cossacks and residents caught in the alarm were also massacred.

The headless body of Verovkin — his head was not to be found — was buried in the local cathedral. Marina immediately attempted to make her son Ivan Dmitriyevich tsar-designate, but the Russians refused. Princes Trubetzkoy, Cherkassky, Buturlin, Mikulin, and others were not about to swear loyalty to a child of dubious legitimacy and his Polish mother as regent. They sent a message to Moscow of their new loyalty to the Boyar Duma, took possession of Kaluga, and placed Marina and son in custody. Such an event was necessary to pull Russia back together.

9. The Liberation of Russia

The Siege of Smolensk and Its Defeat by Polish Forces

A few of the Smolensk envoys returned to Moscow: Sukin, Vasilyev, Archimandrite Evfimi and Avrami Palitzen, to inform them of the treachery of Sigismund. However Sigismund, having heard of the death of Verovkin, wrote on December 13, 1610, letters to the Boyar Duma of the arrival of Wladyslaw to Moscow. But now the Russians no longer wanted or needed Wladyslaw and saw no reason for Sigismund to remain in Russia. Boyars wrote letters to surrounding cities, requesting their help in ridding the Poles from Moscow and restoring Russia to Russians. They warned the cities that if Polish occupation continued then Russia would become Catholic and lose its identity as a nation, and merge into Poland. As a result, cities Ryazan, Vladimir, Suzdal, Nizhniy-Novgorod, Romanov, Yaroslavl, Kostroma and Vologda armed their troops and residents for the liberation of Moscow from Polish occupation. Sigismund heard the directives and ordered the execution of Zakari, brother of Prokopi Lyapunov, and then he informed Filaret and Golitsyn that they would soon be taken to Poland, telling them that they would there discuss the transfer of power with Wladyslaw personally, although his actual purpose was to have them as hostages.

In January 1611, the residents of Moscow rose in rebellion as during the latter part of the reign of Otrepyev, humiliating and discrediting the Poles occupying the city. Merchants began charging them double for goods purchased. The Boyar Duma was divided between those loyal to Part. Hermogen and Prokopi Lyapunov and those hoping for the arrival of Wladyslaw who was still in Poland, probably not even knowing of his selection as tsar of Russia. The Polish occupiers arrested boyars that wrote letters ordering the purge of Europeans from Russia and placed them in custody, while food became difficult to obtain. Moscow residents were ready for a mass slaughter of the Poles in Moscow as soon as the volunteer Russian regiments would arrive from the local provinces.

Outside the city of Moscow, Lyapunov was able to create a makeshift army from a mix of soldiers and residents of the supporting cities, along with fugitives, fortune seekers, vagrants and destitute, all of whom were disenchanted with the interference of Europeans in Russia politics: a wide assortment of types to compose an army. Many of them were members earlier of Verovkin's army, but now they turned against those with whom they once plundered. Some 6,000 Cossacks under Ataman Prosovetzki still in the region from the dispersion of Tushino joined Lyapunov. Over the first three months of 1611, an army was organized and Princes Dmitri Timofeevich Trubetzkoy of Tula, Vasili Litvin and Artemi Ismailov of Vladimir, Prosovetzki of Suzdal, Feodor Volkonski of Kostroma, and Ivan Volinski of Yaroslavl migrated toward Lyapunov outside of Moscow.

The Polish occupation was about 7,000 troops in Moscow under the command of Gosevski, while the population of the city between 200,000–300,000.

Polish troops rested in empty homes in the Eastern Quarter while their officers in the Kremlin debated what to do next. A few Russians attempted to have a semblance of a government, but they worried about the success of the rebellion, also fearing both populace and Poles. The Polish leaders realized their inability to win overwhelming odds against them: outnumbered by the residents of Moscow, a makeshift army organizing and advancing toward them, and their King Sigismund at Smolensk with his fixation on the siege and not concerned with providing them troops. Polish officials occupying the Kremlin gave the order to burn Moscow.

On March 19, 1611, fighting began in the streets of Moscow between Russians and Poles in the Eastern Quarter. The fighting spread in the streets, the two enemies were shooting at each other from rooftops and towers and windows, although Russians far outnumbered Poles. The fighting spread into the White Quarter. Driving forward the residents were pushing the Poles into the Kremlin, their only place of refuge. That evening, 2,000 cavalry of Germans and Poles left the Kremlin and Eastern Quarter and set on fire the buildings of the White Quarter: houses, churches, businesses. The first house set on fire by the retreating Poles was Mikhail Saltykov's, then the Poles set more houses on fire in the city. The residents were terrified and gathered their wives and children to move them to some area safe from the Polish arsons. The Poles herded the people into the streets and from street to street. People died from either smoke inhalation or conflagration, all their possessions reduced to ashes. Over a hundred thousand left Moscow the next day towards Troitse-Sergieva, Vladimir, Kolomna, Tula and other cities, the roads still filled with snow. Many died from exposure to the cold. If any of the fires were extinguished during the night from the cold, Polish troops would restart the fire in the morning. Moscow burned for three days straight, and the rising flames at night lit up the surrounding city as bright as day. As buildings collapsed the flames seemed to reach and touch the sky. Once the fire subsided only rubble and ashes and charred stone walls and church skeletons lay within a perimeter of about 15 miles. The fire consumed the majority of the city including 450 churches; barely one third of the city survived the conflagration, which was the walled areas of the Kremlin and Eastern Quarter. The area smoldered for several more days while the Polish troops feasted, plundering the royal treasury and the valuables of the Kremlin and cathedrals of Moscow. So engulfed in the terror of brutal slaughter, cremation of corpses and pillage that drunk Polish troops began to kill each other as a result of the psychological devastation of their sense of humanity and morality. Other Poles and Germans returned to their homes and enjoyed the spectacle of the flames and smoke. Polish soldier pillaged whatever their hands could grasp that was not consumed by the flames. Hundreds of abandoned stores in the Oriental Quarter were pillaged, all of it the spoils of war.

Even though it was already March, it seemed for 1611 that winter would not end. Strong frost held the country in suspension while snow still covered all of Moscow and the countryside. The Moscow River was not thawed completely with ice still floating in it. Pozharski, leading the loyalist Russians into the burning city against the Poles, died during the battle. His body was taken to the Troitse-Sergieva Monastery. At the same time, Gosevski took advantage of the fire to clandestinely remove some of his foes from action: he order the secret execution of Boyar Andrei Golitsyn.

The Polish garrison occupying Moscow again imprisoned Patr. Hermogen, now in the Kirillov Cathedral, and stripped him of his patriarchal title and vestments. They recalled former patriarch Ignatius — knowing he was Greek — and reinstalled him as patriarch hoping for his loyalty. Ignatius had been confined at the Chudovski Monastery during Patr. Hermogen's cathedra, and so willingly accepted reinstatement and performed Easter liturgy on March 24, 1611, the day after the imprisonment of Patr. Hermogen and after the fire had finished smoldering. For Easter Sunday Patr. Ignatius was dressed in the patriarchal vestments he had not worn in five years, since the overthrow of Otrepyev. He celebrated Easter liturgy with the attendance of the Poles and Russians professing loyalty to Wladyslaw and during the liturgy he extended longevity and prosperity to Russia's Polish tsar. Patr. Ignatius also realized that he could not continue as patriarch under the simultaneous circumstances of Moscow's occupation by Poles and its siege by native Russians. Ignatius took advantage of his liberty and quickly escaped later that day from Moscow, intending to travel to Vilnius in present-day Estonia.

News of the calamities of Moscow, transcending the terrifying, provided new strength for a national movement. Zealous monks at Troitse-Sergieva Monastery, once hearing of what was occurring at the capital, sent their troops to assist the loyalist Russians and wrote letters to the provincial commanders obligating them to recruit troops and sent them also. As the troops drew near to Moscow they incurred on every roads Moscovites fleeing the city, some of whom — the more able-bodied — joined the new military, while leaving their wives and children to the care of relatives.

On March 28, the armies of Lyapunov from Kolomna, Zarutzki from Tula, and the Cossacks arrived together at the walls of Moscow near the Yauzki Gate. They entered the White Quarter, while the Poles and Germans retreated into the Eastern Quarter and Kremlin, both having high walls. Some 100,000 Russians still remained in Moscow. They were joined by other armies of Dmitri Trubetzkoy, Artemi Ismailov, and Litvinov Mosalski as well as the troops of Troitse-Sergieva. More fighting erupted in the streets of Moscow, the European forces led by Gosevski and the vacillating Saltykov. Patr. Hermogen's presence was again request by Gosevski, this time he was threatened with death and ordered to tell Lyapunov and the Russians to retreat. Hermogen replied, "You Poles retreat!" He was returned to cloister.

Unfortunately, the Russian forces, outnumbering the Europeans, were disorganized and leaderless. Every commander gave orders that were not followed by their own troops and the commanders argued one with another regarding the manner of defeating the Europeans without further caused havoc to the residents or devastation to the city. A triumvirate was selected as a council to direct the liberation of Moscow: Prokopi Lyapunov, Dmitri Trubetzkoy and Cossack Ataman Zarutzki. They requested money, provisions and troops from the local provinces. Fugitives from the Smolensk region journeyed to Moscow to join the new army.

The Russian army on May 22, invaded the Eastern Quarter and other suburbs of Moscow, and in fierce street fighting over a period of five days, the Russian loyalists had control of the city, except for the Kremlin. The Europeans lost ¾ of their troops and were left without food.

Sigismund was still concentrating on the siege of Smolensk. The reports of Gosevski regarding the burning of Moscow and the subsequent attack of Russian loyalists did not change his mind. On April 8, 1611, Polish gentry in more conversations taunted Filaret and Golitsyn, whether it would be best to just erase Moscow off the map. The envoys agreed to write to Patr. Hermogen, the boyars and military to desist further bloodshed, but only if Sigismund would immediately depart Russia. This inflamed Sigismund's wrath with his unabated and inflexible obsession to defeat Smolensk and he made arrangements for Filaret's and Golitsyn's exile in Poland. The envoys expressed their courage rather than capitulating to Sigismund's threats. The two were arrested and boated down the Dnepr River to Kiev where they were exposed to public disgrace, and then moved to Warsaw. Sigismund subsequently offered the rule of Russia to Zholkevski, who declined the offer because he was outraged at the conduct of Sigismund for whom he dedicated and sacrificed himself to present the Russian throne to his son Wladyslaw. Zholkevski left the presence of Sigismund and Smolensk and returned to his home in Poland. Sigismund wrote letters to Gosevski, encouraging him with his soon deliverance, promising him and his loyal troops money from the Moscow treasury, as well as the possessions of the wealthy aristocrats of Moscow. Sigismund then returned to the siege of Smolensk.

After 20 months of siege, Shein and the residents were surviving, even with provisions gone and 70% of the occupants having died, more from disease, such as scurvy, than from bullets or cannon fire. One fugitive from the city, Andrei Dedishin, capitulated to the demand of the Polish troops and disclosed to them a weak place in the city wall. On June 3, the Poles invaded Smolensk through the breach and street fighting erupted until the weak residents and troops surrendered to the Poles. The valiant hero of the siege, Shein, was arrested and sent to Poland as a prisoner and Sigismund's trophy of war, along with Archbishop Sergei, while Shein's wife and son remained in the defeated city. About 70,000 residents of Smolensk died during the course of the siege while only 8,000 survived; although 2/3 of Sigismund's army perished (no specific number was recorded.) Polish historians record that if Sigismund would have gone to Moscow with his remaining troops after the defeat of Smolensk, the Russian troops would have surrendered. Joining Yan Sapega and his army, and Gosevski and his army inside Moscow, Sigismund could have occupied Moscow and ascend to throne as tsar and so incorporate Russia into his realm. Russia historians conclude the opposite, that 5,000 troops under Gosevski and the weak armies of Sigismund and the gang of insurgents of Yan Sapega would still have been defeated by the Russians, eager to deliver their capital from the Poles.

Sigismund decided to rest on his laurels and so returned to Warsaw with the trophies of his victory, where the population welcomed him as a war hero. But the greater honor was displayed when Zholkevski entered Warsaw as the hero of Moscow with his trophy, the ill-fated Tsar Vasili Shuisky, held in a cage on a wagon pulled by horses through the streets. On October 19, 1611, a parade was held through the main streets of Warsaw to display the three Shuisky brothers, Tsar Vasili, Princes Ivan and Dmitri, and Ekaterina the wife of Dmitri, Archbishop Sergei and Mikhail Shein. Sigismund and Zholkevski led the parade in decorated carriages while the royal captives were put on display following behind them in open carriages. The next carriage held Vasili Golitsyn and Metr. Filaret. The populace lining the streets lauded Zholkevski as the second Aemilius Paullus, comparing his victory over Perseus at Pydna and bringing him to Rome as a captive to the defeat of Moscow and bringing Tsar Vasili to Warsaw. The city celebrated the defeat of Smolensk and occupation of Moscow, the victory over their immemorial enemies, in great festivity and the celebrations extended to the entire Roman Catholic world and even to the Vatican in Rome, which they viewed as the Jesuit victory over Russian Orthodoxy.

The three Shuisky brothers were incarcerated at Gostinski Castle near Warsaw, continually under guard, where Tsar Vasili died a year later on September 12, 1612, and his brother Dmitri dying their also, five days later. Vasili was between 60-65 years old; his brother a few years younger. None of their relatives attended them the final days of their death. The two brothers were buried secretly, the Poles not wanting to make a shrine of their graves for future devotees. The youngest brother Ivan Shuisky was released from incarceration February 1613 and was allowed to live a semi-public life, except that his name was changed to Ivan Levin and he received a pension from the Polish government of three rubles a month until his death at some unrecorded date.

Filaret was initially confined at the private estate of Lev Sapega and then for balance of this period was incarcerated at the Marienburg Fortress in Aluksne, Latvia. Vasili Golitsyn and Mikhail Shein were also incarcerated at some prison, and the three of them lived to their release nine years later, when they returned to Russia. Ekaterina, wife of

Dmitri Shuisky, was also incarcerated and died somewhere in Poland shortly after.

The Siege of Moscow and the Swedish Invasion

Meanwhile the siege of Moscow under the triumvirate of Lyapunov, Trubetzkoy and Zarutzki continued, Gosevski still retaining control of the Kremlin and parts of the Eastern Quarter. Zarutzki had his eyes on the throne and his Cossacks would roam the region gaining support for him. He likewise made use of Marina Mnishek, now residing in Kolomna, hoping to use her and her son as a means of gaining the approval of the populace (rumor had it that Zarutzki was the lover of Marina during this period). To diffuse the drive of Zarutzki, Lyapunov created an Estates (Zemski) Duma, consisting of soldiers, noblemen and court officials, and delegated to them certain civil authority to begin establishing a form of government. A constitution of sorts was written April 1611, and signed by the civil or military leaders of 25 cities, including Artemi Ismailov, Princes Ivan Golitsyn and Ivan Sheremetev. Lyapunov hoped that after the defeat of the Poles a smooth transition to a stable and recognized government would occur, including the selection and coronation of a new tsar acceptable to the entire nation.

Lyapunov was one person without the ambition of ascending the throne of Russia, although realizing that in his present capacity in the administration, much depended on him in regard to the selection of a tsar. But whom? Mstislavski was too old, and so Lyapunov turned to General Delagardi of the Swedes and began correspondence with him. At the same time, the Swedes would provide the military to remove the Poles from Russia and quench the new rebellion of Zarutzki with his undependable leftovers of the army of Verovkin.

The tide turned against Lyapunov, even though both Trubetzkoy and Zarutzki were earlier associated with the camp at Tushino; they felt they had the precedence in matters of the fledgling government. Zarutzki also was commander of the Cossacks of the Don and Ukraine, the larger military force, but it was Lyapunov who would issue orders for them to desist ransacking local villages. After being reprimanded once too many times the Cossacks sought vengeance rather than desisting their rampages. To escape them Lyapunov attempted to flee to

Ryazan, but was apprehended by Cossacks and returned to the camp outside Moscow and placed in custody. Gosevski more than Zarutzki wanted Lyapunov dead, and so he counterfeited some documents that were discrediting to Cossacks and had one of his spies leave the Kremlin and distribute them in the camp outside Moscow. Although Lyapunov denied composing the letter it flamed the anger of the Cossacks and they killed both him and Ivan Nikitich Rzhevski with their sabers. Rzhevski had attempted to defend Lyapunov from the Cossack vigilantes and their anger turned against him likewise. For three days the butchered bodies of Lyapunov and Rzhevski laid in public watched by sentries. At night dogs were allowed to eat at the corpses. On the 4th day after their murder their remains were thrown into the back of a wagon and taken to the nearest church for a requiem and then to Troitse-Sergieva for burial in the commoner's cemetery. The murderers were never tried or sentenced for their crime.

All this was occurring outside Moscow while the Swedes were marching on Novgorod. The Swedish army under General Delagardi had been able to occupy areas of Karelia, but they were unsuccessful in their attacks and siege of Ladoga and Oreshek (later known as Schlesselburg). In March 1611, the Swedish army camped four miles from Novgorod at the Khutinski Monastery. They camped until summer, poor weather hampering their efforts at an attack or even effective siege. Vasili Ivanovich Buturlin arrived from Moscow, supposedly for a meeting, but turned his loyalty against Lyapunov, now, with his death, and in favor of the Swedes. (Delagardi and Buturlin had become friends earlier outside of Moscow.) On July 8, 1611, the Swedes attacked Novgorod and after a siege of eight days, entered the city on July 16. However, Buturlin fled the city fearing the vengeance of the residents. The leaders of Novgorod, Metr. Isidor and Ivan Nikitich Odoyevski, agreed to surrender to Delagardi and enter into a peace treaty. The primary concern of Delagardi was the allegiance of Novgorod to King Charles IX, which they agreed to, and to allow one of the sons of Charles to reign over them as king, either Gustav Adolf or Phillip. Delagardi also extended the terms of the treaty to Moscow, otherwise their army would continue to Moscow and force an occupation upon them. Charles — much like Sigismund — did not have any intention of allowing one of his sons to go to Russia to become tsar, but intended to occupy the throne himself. If the Swedish campaign against Moscow was to fail, then Charles made sure that Novgorod and Karelia would be annexed to Sweden, but as a semi-autonomous state.

The fortune-seeker Yan Sapega, the defeated leader of the siege of Troitse-Sergieva, left Ukraine with his gang of insurgents and appeared in Moscow on August 17, 1611, advertising himself as a Russian loyalist, offering his help. His help was refused. In vengeance, Sapega moved toward Pereyaslavl and began to plunder and burn villages. The following month Yan Sapega returned to Moscow and was providing supplies and provision for the Poles inside the Kremlin and Eastern Quarter. On September 14, Yan Sapega became ill and died while residing at the abandoned home of Tsar Vasili Shuisky.

The Lithuanian Hetman Yan Khodkevich (Chodkeiwicz), living in Livonia (Latvia), a distinguished soldier and leader, was nominated by Sigismund to lead the troops of Smolensk against Moscow. On October 6, 1611, Khodkevich arrived at Moscow with only 2,000 troops; the journey from Livonia (Latvia) had taken its toll on the troops, especially those remaining from the siege of Smolensk. Winter set in soon after his arrival and he withdrew to Rzhev to the Rogachev Monastery, taking with him some of Sapega's troops. The Polish troops remaining in Moscow for the winter were in dire circumstances, and so in October they sent envoys Yuri Nikitich Trubetzkoy and Mikhail Glebovich Saltykov to Sigismund begging for provisions and supplies.

As the army of Nizhniy-Novgorod assembled to drive toward Moscow the Poles ordered Patr. Hermogen to write to them for them to desist and remain in Nizhniy-Novgorod. Patr. Hermogen refused and instead cursed the Poles. As a result, the Poles had Patr. Hermogen kept under guard and in isolation in his cell for the next 9 months until his death on January 17, 1612 at age 81. He was buried at the Chudovski Monastery. Some chroniclers sense that Patr. Hermogen was deliberately starved to death in his cell for refusing to order the siege to be lifted. Now with Patr. Hermogen gone, Russians inside the Kremlin selected Arseni, a Greek, as his successor. His role as patriarch was short-lived and for the most part he was a puppet of the Poles who were Catholic.

Rise of False Dmitri III and Russia's Capitulation

In Ivangorod on March 23, 1611, a third pretender nick-named Sidorka appeared claiming to be Dmitri Ivanovich, stating that others were killed in his place, which was the reason he survived the attempts on his life. Sidorka was deacon or monk Isidor from some unidentified monastery in Moscow who fled when the Poles entered the city and he migrated to Novgorod. He attempted to start an arms business with the needs for weapons at a high demand, but failed. All of a sudden he announced himself to the residents of Novgorod as Dmitri Ivanovich having survived his murder at Kaluga, but the people knew he was a vagrant monk and failed merchant, and so laughed at his claim. Nonetheless a few dozen swallowed his bate and Sidorka left Novgorod with them to Ivangorod. There he regurgitated his story: his torso was carved apart at Uglich as a child, but he survived; then he survived his murder and cremation in Moscow, and then survived his decapitation at Kaluga, and now here he was alive and unharmed. Sidorka on December 4, 1611, migrated from Ivangorod with his small circle of social outcasts to Pskov where he established himself, hoping to expand further east into Russia. The miracle of his survival spread in the region, and the suffering and despondent population of the war-torn city welcomed him as legitimate monarch.

Much as with the previous false Dmitris, many divined Sidorka as an adventurer and imposter, but were willing to acknowledge him hoping this would curb the civil war and bring stability to Russia. Letters were sent throughout Russia of the reappearance of Dmitri Ivanovich, and so impressed the uneducated and suffering masses of common people that on March 12, 1612, Sidorka was declared tsar of Russia by Cossacks. The leaders of Russia's defense: Zarutzki, Trubetzkoy, and others, remembering what occurred to Lyapunov due to his altercation with Cossacks, accepted the declaration as valid. The camps outside Moscow all swore loyalty to Sidorka as Dmitri Ivanovich and a celebration was held, while the leaders Ivan Zarutzki and Dmitri Trubetzkoy were powerless against the elements. To further save their own skin they sent a message to Marina Mnishek who was residing at Kolomna with her son. The former supporters of Bolotnikov all rallied to the banner of Sidorka. This action further divided the Russian loyalist forces and weakened their offense against the Poles occupying Moscow.

The superstitious and desperate Russians, overwhelmed by the siege of Smolensk by the army of the Polish Sigismund, by his commander Khodkevich sent to siege Moscow, by the invasion of the Swedish army of Delagardi, by the report of the burning of Moscow, by the capture and exile of Tsar Vasili Shuisky, by the murder of Lyapunov, by their oath of loyalty to Wladyslaw — who never left Poland — and by the fiery annihilation of Tushino, were drawn toward the latest False Dmitri, Sidorka of Pskov. Although a year passed since his proclamation, by March 1612, a greater portion of Russia stretching from Pskov to Moscow were communicating with Sidorka regularly. One official from the camp outside Moscow, Kazarin Degichev, traveled to Pskov, took one glance at Sidorka and confirmed him as the same person as Verovkin, the hero of Kaluga. Another report was brought to the camp outside Moscow by Ivan Plesheev, and he was able to convince the army of Sidorka's authenticity and acquire another of loyalty from them. Other cities, such as Kaluga, Serpukhov, Tula, Ryazan, Tver, Rzhev, refused the validity of Sidorka, and still had favor toward Wladyslaw as tsar.

To counterpoise the western Russian populace throwing their support behind Sidorka the cities of the east — Kazan, Nizhniy-Novgorod, Vladimir, Yaroslavl and Kostroma — refused to acknowledge him as Dmitri Ivanovich and selected Prince Dmitri Pozharski as their military commander to liberate Moscow and Russia from the Poles and other Europeans. Yaroslavl became the new center of Russian loyalist forces, those who would not recognize Sidorka as Dmitri Ivanovich, and Pozharski gathered troops from Tver, Rostov, Kasimov and other cities. Provisions and supplies flowed into Yaroslavl, along with merchants and artisans and the city grew in size. Former boyars and princes who abandoned Moscow earlier streamed into Yaroslavl: Andrei Kurakin, Vasili Morozov, Semeon Golovin, Nikita Odoyevski, Peter Pronski, Ivan Cherkassky, Boris Saltykov, Ivan Troyekurov, Dmitri Cherkassky, the Sheremetev brothers and others. Yaroslavl became what Tushino was two years earlier, except now with a large population of Russian loyalists and plenty of provisions from spring harvests to support it. On April 7, 1612, Dmitri Pozharski sent a letter from his Russian camp at Yaroslavl to as many cities as possible telling them of the betrayal of Dmitri Trubetzkoy and Ivan Zarutzki, that they had now sworn loyalty to the newest imposter, Sidorka, and his False wife Marina and her son (although fate would not allow the two to ever meet in person). Pozharski pleaded with the population to rise against the traitors, against the Poles and promoters of Sidorka. Along with the signature of Pozharski were 34 princes and nobles who were Russian loyalists. The purpose of both Trubetzkoy and Zarutzki was now to manipulate the imposter and Marina to their own advantage, for them to be the real power behind the throne of Russia. Ivan Presheev then acquired a change of mind after discussing the issue of the survival of Verovkin with Pozharski and other Russian nobles. He returned to Pskov on April 11, 1612 with a copy of the directive of Pozharski, declaring Sidorka an imposter.

Matters turned against Sidorka in late April 1612, as loyal Russian troops were reorganizing for another assault on Pskov. On the night of May 18, 1612, Sidorka escaped an attempt on his life and fled Pskov. Soldiers captured him some distance from the city two days later, placed him in fetters and chained him to a horse as he was brought back into the city on May 20. Quickly the country turned against Sidorka and he was sent caged in a wagon and under heavy guard to Moscow from Pskov on July 1.

This resulted in the embarrassment of Zarutzki who had earlier claimed Sidorka's validity as Dmitri Ivanovich and led his Cossack troops to believe so. Zarutzki sent a letter of apology to the council at Yaroslavl, but instead of gratitude Zarutzki received a reprimand, which he felt was unwarranted after his efforts in fighting and leading Cossacks to fight the Poles. This inflamed Zarutzki's wrath and jealousy of Pozharski — who refused Sidorka's validity — and led him to take vengeance.

Defeat of the Polish Occupation of Russia and Their Withdrawal

At the end of September 1611, Khodkevich defeated a small military camp south of Moscow. His military strength increased when Yan Sapega annexed his army to Khodkevich's, but their combined army was still unable to wrestle the main Russian army from the walls of Moscow. To not have to withdraw Khodkevich had his troops infiltrate the city and subsidize the Kremlin with additional troops, now increasing the amount to 2,500, while many already exhausted left the city and returned home. Autumn arrived and the heavy rains caused Khodkevich to withdraw from Moscow to the village Rogachev, where he set up winter camp. Russians still residing in Moscow suffered immensely, especially with only the Eastern Quarter and Kremlin having survived the fire and provisions in short supply. The Russian fortifications under Trubetzkoy and Zarutzki organized for a winter assault on the city while Polish morale was low and snow was high. In December 1611, they again stormed the Eastern Quarter, but were repulsed by the Poles. Gosevski was able to defend the garrison and the assault failed. Prosovitzki, who commanded the Cossacks, argued over the defeat with Zarutzki and then withdrew his troops to Semeonov Monastery on the road to Kolomensk, while Zarutzki's troops moved to Uglich for the winter.

In April 1612, a new Council laid plans for the liberation of Moscow from the Poles and selected a new military commander who would be acceptable to all the troops, Pr. Dmitri Cherkassky. The regiments remaining in Kashin likewise migrated to Yaroslavl and Cherkassky was able to convince many of Zarutzki's troops to join him.

Khodkevich was having problems in Rogachev due to brigands who were stealing his forage during the winter, although by March 1612, some supplies began to arrive. A Lithuanian, Captain Struve, and his regiment joined Khodkevich in March, and with a total of 3,000 troops they began making arrangements to assault the Russians and acquire control over all of Russia. By April they were maneuvering toward Moscow. The harsh winter caused heavy losses for Gosevski in the Kremlin and they were hardly able to recover as spring arrived. In June, Commander Zborovski abandoned the Kremlin along with a large portion of Polish troops. They left supplies for the city and headed toward Smolensk. The remaining soldiers pillaged the royal treasury and palaces: royal regalia, furniture, art, utensils, tableware, clothing, curtains, murals, kitchenware and whatever the destitute troops could pilfer was appropriated. The monasteries lost icons and frames and all ecclesiastical paraphernalia and vestments. The soldiers' claim was that this was their compensation, since money from Poland to pay their wages was yet to arrive, and they felt it probably would not arrive.

Sometime that summer of 1612, Gosevski and more Polish soldiers stealthily fled the city, now left in ruins, rubble and destitute. Especially pilfered were the jewels on the crowns of early tsars, and the gold and silver that embellished royal robes. Then they stole the equestrian gear: saddles, bridles and blankets. They even removed the gold encased as part of the décor on the sepulchers of the early tsars. The Germans likewise, deprived of wages, loaded what was not destroyed by fire or exposure into carts and wagons. Their migration out of Moscow did not get very far as brigands attacked the convoy to retrieve the looted valuables. The only Europeans that remained in Moscow after the departure of Gosevski were Struve, who had entered the city with his small regiment, and a small garrison of soldiers. Khodkevich now had the responsibility to provide supplies and provisions for the garrison and his army moved to Voloko-Lamsk.

As Pozharski was making an inspection of cannons and artillery a few days later, and while walking through the crowd with a smith named Roman who had been working with the artillery, an assassin attempted to knife Pozharski. He missed and knifed Roman instead. He fell in a pool of blood and died. The attacker was quickly apprehended and tortured to gain information. He divulged the names of two Cossacks who had hired him to kill Pozharski: Stepan and Obrezkov. The Yaroslavl council sent Stepan with an armed guard to Moscow to settle the matter with Zarutzki, as the organizer of the attempted assassination. The other accomplices were imprisoned. On the night of July 28, 1612, Zarutzki fled Moscow to Kolomensk taking with him 2,000 exhausted and disenchanted Cossack troops.

Arriving outside of Moscow late July and early August were some 7,000 loyalist Russian cavalry with an immense amount of artillery under commanders Mikhail Dmitreyev and Pozharski's nephew Prince Lopata-Pozharski. Further reinforcements arrived later from Yaroslavl and surrounding cities. On August 18, the entire military stood three miles from the walls of the city, and then was joined by the army of Trubetzkoy, the size of the army is estimated at 10,000. The army of

Khodkevich left Kolomensk the early morning of August 22, aiming toward the army of Pozharski in order to defend Moscow and the Poles
right to the city. Khodkevich's army was estimated at between two and
three thousand. For 7 hours the battle waged until a stalemate drew the
two armies apart. On August 23, both armies reorganized.

The morning of August 24, Pozharski attacked, but was again unable to gain a victory. The armies retired, but Khodkevich withdrew
his army completely from the battlefield and left the garrison inside the
Kremlin to fend for itself. By morning Khodkevich was on the road to
Smolensk far from the city. The defeat of Khodkevich could hardly have
been called a victory as the Russians began to fight among themselves.
For one and a half years Trubetzkoy's troops were carrying the siege of
Moscow while in trenches with no money to pay them and little food to
eat. Provisions were supplied quickly for Pozharski to avoid more strife
and so avoid complete anarchy. A new triumvirate was created for the
assault directly against the city, now that Khodkevich had fled and no
army remained to defend the city from the outside. The new leadership
consisted of Trubetzkoy and Pozharski as earlier and now including
Kuzma Minin from Nizhniy-Novgorod.

At the beginning of September, Pozharski sent correspondence
to Struve inside the Kremlin, telling them that surrender would be in
their best interests. Now with Khodkevich gone and no indication of
Prince Wladyslaw traveling to Moscow or any further military reinforcements from Poland, the siege would force the city to die of malnutrition and disease. In response the Poles inside the city affirmed their
allegiance to Wladyslaw, assured of his soon arrival with troops and
provisions. Rather than accepting the generous terms offered them by
Pozharski — their life — the response was sarcastic and arrogant and
the remnant of the Polish military occupation placed their hopes on
Wladyslaw.

Inside the Kremlin matters were different and the Polish troops
now pillaged the regalia and valuables that were reserved for Wladyslaw for his coronation and reign. Russians were also migrating from the
Eastern Quarter and devastated White Quarter outside the city now
that the army was at the walls. Food supplies dwindled and Struve ordered the expulsion of superfluous people to decrease the number of

months that would need to be fed during the upcoming winter. Aged men and women and children were expelled from the Kremlin, and so Mstislavski sent letters to Pozharski and Minin begging them to accept the homeless now driven from the city. The Russians greeted the expelled residents at the gates and gave them food and shelter in their camp before sending them to local villages to reside with friends and relatives. The women complained of rape by the unrestrained Polish soldiers.

By mid-September the famine in the Kremlin reached a catastrophic scale. Russians who remained or were forced to remain died first, deprived of food by their captors. As the bread was consumed the occupation army and residents ate dogs and cats until every stray animal was consumed; then every blade of grass and weed, and every leaf that grew in the city; next they ate the bark of the trees. The Polish soldiers were next to die. Snow fell the beginning of October due to an early winter and this destroyed any remaining plants or edible trees in the city. Even a mouse could not be found in the city. The Polish soldiers turned to cannibalism to survive. They took prisoners out of their cells, killed them, and ate them. Of the remaining 3,000 Polish troops in the Kremlin after the departure of Khodkevich at the end of August, half died over the months of September and October. The remainder was demoralized and malnourished.

It was not until October 22, that Struve permitted any envoys of Pozharski to enter the city to negotiate surrender. The Russians demanded surrender without reservations, but the Poles seemed to prefer to die under the conditions than betray their honor, and so demanded concessions. The Poles procrastinated, still hoping for the arrival of Wladyslaw with reinforcements and provisions. But the Cossacks could no longer be patient with the futile efforts at negotiation and so attacked the city a couple of days later, making a break through a wall. They killed every European they saw until the defenders withdrew into the Kremlin. This attack devastated any remaining morale in the Poles.

The next day October 25, Struve and Mstislavski met with Pozharski and Trubetzkoy. The aged Mstislavski first apologized for his betrayal of Russia. The Boyar Duma — what was left of it in the Kremlin

— annulled their oath of loyalty to Wladyslaw and agreed to desist all communication with Sigismund. The remaining Poles were allowed to go free provided they not take anything with them from the Kremlin. On October 26, 1612, the gates to the Kremlin were opened after a Polish occupation lasting over two years. The following day the Polish garrison officially capitulated to the Russians, and the Poles were immediately disarmed. As the Russian troops entered their capital, they saw the abomination of desolation: square miles of ruins, ashes and rubble and corpses covered by snow and stripped of all possessions. Nonetheless, a victory parade was organized by the Russian troops, starting at the Arbat and though the Eastern Quarter and then gathering at Red Square before entering the Kremlin through the Spasski Gate.

More Invasions by Poland and Sweden

By April 1612, Swedish troops in Novgorod had their eyes on expanding toward Kirillov and Beloye-Ozero, across the Russian north. As a result Pozharski in Yaroslavl sent a regiment to Beloye-Ozero to defend it from Swedish troops. Meanwhile Khodkevich, the Polish commander, concluded a peace treaty with Delagardi, the Swedish commander. The two perennial enemies made an agreement with the intent of dividing Russia in half after the victory over Russia's forces in Yaroslavl: the northern half to Sweden, the southern half to Poland. This placed Pozharski in a difficult situation, wanting to move toward Moscow but unable to defend two fronts at the same time: Sweden and Poland. To attempt to restrain Swedish expansion, Pozharski sent a delegation from Yaroslavl to Novgorod, hoping to conclude a peace treaty with minimal losses so he would not have to worry during his assault on Moscow.

The delegation was headed by Stefan Tatischev, and his intent was to convince the Swedes at Novgorod that the Russians were almost ready to accept Charles' son Phillip as monarch, but some time was needed to study the agreement made between Novgorod and Sweden and discuss the conversion of the Lutheran Phillip into Russian Orthodoxy. Tatishev was successful and Pozharski invited the Swedes to Yaroslavl; they arrived June 10. Procrastination was the key. Pozharski was able to establish a prerequisite to Swedish rule, that they had to the end of that year 1612 for Prince Phillip to arrive and settle in Novgorod in order for Russia to acknowledge him as monarch, and until that time the Swedes would make no further expansion into Russia. The Swedes left Yaroslavl July 26. Envoys were sent to Sweden to retrieve instead the older son of King Charles, Gustav II Adolf, to ascend the throne over Novgorod and northwest Russia, but they were retained in Stockholm for six months. Swedish King Charles IX did not succeed in tasting the fruit of his success in the Russian campaign. About three months after the defeat of Novgorod, he died. His son, the 17-year-old Gustav ascended the throne in his place and Pskov and Novgorod were quickly annexed by Sweden.

Trubetzkoy now organized another army of 15,000 and attempted a siege against the Swedes at Novgorod, but was unsuccessful. Sweden only withdrew when they were threatened with war by the German Hapsburgs and abandoned occupation of Novgorod, Staraya Russ and Ladoga, but they retained Karelia and Narva, which isolated Russia from access to the Baltic Sea.

During the early summer 1612, King Sigismund of Poland decided to wage a new campaign and again invade Russia, hoping to enthrone his son Wladyslaw this time. Realizing the mistake he made after the defeat of Smolensk and now knowing how bad of a condition Russia was in due to the civil wars, Sigismund felt it would be easy to defeat Moscow. On August 18, 1612, Sigismund's second Russian campaign began. His army consisted of 4,000 soldiers and he joined with the returning Khodkevich at Vyasma at the Russian–Polish border. The road to return to Moscow was in disrepair and Sigismund and his army had problem after problem along the way until arriving at Voloko-Lamsk at the end of October. Sigismund still had no knowledge of the events at Moscow with the famine and capitulation of the garrison to the Russians. He likewise failed at gaining the trust of any Russian cities or villages during his invasion.

On November 16, Sigismund reached the city Rzhev, about 60 miles east of Moscow, where he made camp for the winter. Sigismund had taken former Patr. Ignatius with him, expecting him to perform the coronation of his son to make it official. Prior to beginning another siege of Moscow envoys were sent to Moscow to discuss the possible surrender of Moscow, but the new leadership refused to discuss any matters with Sigismund and imprisoned the two envoys that he sent. The early winter and successive failures took its toll on Sigismund and his army and so he ordered retreat on November 27. Sigismund's retreat foretold the retreat of Napoleon in 1812 and the Germans in 1944: bodies and baggage were scattered and abandoned in the snow all along the road from Moscow to Smolensk.

Mikhail Romanov is Crowned as Tsar

The population of Moscow toward the end of 1612 was a fraction of its earlier size; only 2,000 upper class, 1,000 Streltzi, 4,500 Cossacks and a few thousand commoners inhabited the city. Russia in general at this point was on the point of total collapse: military, economic, social and government.

After the retreat of Sigismund back to Poland in late November, a popular assembly of nobles and landowners was summoned by Pozharski, now assured that a new government could be formed. The first item on the agenda was the selection of a new tsar, one who would be acceptable to the populace as well as from a noble genealogy. The discussions and assembles were random due to the harsh winter and poor communication. One candidate that was quickly rejected was the so-called Ivan Dmitriyevich, son of Marina Mnishek and Verovkin, whom Zarutzki was fervently promoting as the next tsar. Zarutzki had already made Kolomensk his new home in close proximity to Marina and gathered a rag-tag band of brigands.

Among the candidates were Dmitri Pozharski, Dmitri Cherkassky, Ivan Golitsyn and Filaret Romanov (still in exile in Poland). The aged Mstislavski withdrew his name from consideration due to his alliance with the Poles during their occupation of Moscow. A distant choice was the 16-year old son Mikhail Feodorovich Romanov, son of Filaret and great-nephew of Anastasia, the first wife of Tsar Ivan IV, but his age was not in his favor. The first meeting of the popular assembly was held December 6, 1612, but little was accomplished. Many from outlying cities could not attend because of winter cold and snow.

A second meeting was held in January 1613, but the issue resolved was the return of property that was not legitimately appropriated by landowners. Verovkin earlier, while at Tushino, gave tracts of land and estates to his supporters. Now the popular assembly decreed that his action was illegal and so all the property had to be returned to its previous owner or to the state. Another issue settled was the liberation of the serfs that were part of the Russian loyalist army. The next session began February 2, 1613, and the Romanov faction again proposed young Mikhail as fitting all the qualifications, but the assembly was still undecided and hoped for someone older and with experience. The same indecision plagued the next meeting February 7, until an assembly on February 21, 1613 finally agreed on Mikhail Romanov. The primary role in selecting Mikhail was his uncle Ivan Nikitich Romanov and his relatives, noblemen who were active in the newly-formed popular assembly and outspoken in their concern for a new Russian government: Vasili Petrovich Morozov, Ivan Borisovich Cherkassky, Boris Saltykov, and Ivan Feodorovich Troyekurov. Prelates from the Troitse-Sergieva Monastery, such as the hero Avraam Palitzen and archimandrite Dionysi, advocated Mikhail along with prelates from other monasteries. They were betting that Mikhail would be more benevolent to ROC monasteries in regard to finances and property than someone else as tsar. The opposing faction were the militant leaders of the campaigns, who felt that one of their own should ascend the throne, thus creating a military state, but the popular assembly was quick to notice this and not permit it. The advocates of Mikhail foresaw or fantasized the return of Moscow aristocracy and royalty to a new height, as during the initial peaceful reign of Tsar Ivan IV or his son Feodor Ivanovich, with the splendor of the royal court and festivities and respect of nations. It was this vision that carried the approval of Mikhail Romanov by the popular assembly.

Now the noblemen had to find Mikhail and inform him of his selection and prepare him for coronation and reign. He and his mother Ksenia Ivanovna Shestova had been kept in Moscow in seclusion by the Polish garrison until they were expelled before or during the burning of the city. They migrated to Yaroslavl and remained there under the protection of Pozharski until the army moved to Moscow to continue the siege. The family, now including two nephews of the mother: Boris and Mikhail Saltykov, found shelter at the Ipatiyevski Monastery near Kostroma. The final arrangements were concluded at the popular assembly and Prince Feodor Sheremetev was delegated the responsibility to find the young Mikhail and handle his coronation along with Avraami Palitzen and Archbishop Feodorit. The delegates arrived at Ipatiyevski Monastery on March 14, 1613 and informed Mikhail of their decision.

A month and-a-half passed before Mikhail arrived at Moscow as the delegates had to impress on the young man the serious circumstances behind his selection and need for a person such as him to ascend the throne. The young Mikhail was bewildered but condescended to their request, and he was also assured by his relatives that they — as long-standing noblemen and prelates — would assist him in creating a new government under the auspices of the Boyar Duma. During the journey to Moscow a few days were spent by the family at Troitse-Sergieva, and they arrived in Moscow May 2, 1613. Mother Ksenia Ivanovna was housed at the Voznesenski Convent.

The documents composed by the popular assembly justified their selection of Mikhail. A portion of the text included the right of Feodor Nikitich Romanov (Filaret) to the throne when as if Tsar Feodor Ivanovich on his deathbed bequeathed the throne to his cousin (mentioned earlier in this history). The dubious statement was now rewritten to apply to his son, the old lie disseminated 16 years earlier now modified and so recorded as official doctrine. Even the events that earlier occurred surrounding the request of Boris Godunov as tsar by Patr. Job and his sister Irina at the Novo-Devichi Monastery were re-written to match the request of young Mikhail by Archbishop Feodorit and mother Ksenia at the Ipatiyevski Monastery. Truth was not needed to justify the selection, but embellishments were for the national acceptance of the new tsar. A few selected members of the popular assembly signed the documents April 14, 1613, as the bone fide proceedings.

The coronation was held Sunday, July 11, 1613, performed by Metr. Efrem of Kazan. The actual hero of the day was Prince Feodor Mstislavski as the most distinguished of all the boyars present; his tie to both the earlier Moscow and Suzdal princes, and his service under Tsars Vasili III, Ivan IV and Feodor provided him the respect due a dedicated national statesman. The next place of honor was given to Dmitri Pozharski, the hero of the siege and defeat of the Polish garrison to regain Moscow.

How did the Time of Troubles conclude? With a Russia that was a wasteland of ruins, rubble and corpses from the Arctic Ocean to the southern steppes of Astrakhan and into Ukraine, and from the eastern European border to the foot of the Urals. Cities and villages were burned and depopulated and desolate. Crimean Mongols had also taken advantage of the upheavals in Russia, now without an army controlling the borders, and had occupied several of the provinces in southern Russia. Thus ended the era of Russia's upheavals, but it would take 50 years before Russia would recover from the desolation it was now in and establish its place again among the nations and return to the economic, political, geographic and religious condition it was in during the reign of Tsar Feodor Ivanovich.

EPILOGUE

Once Mikhail Romanov ascended the throne, his family settled matters with the final False Dmitri, Sidorka. Brought from Pskov to Pozharski's camp outside Moscow (before that city was liberated), he was chained inside a cage that was set in a cart. After the liberation of the city, Sidorka was carted around Moscow on public display and people would walk up to him in the cage and spit at him. The records vary regarding Sidorka's demise. One account states that he was executed by Russian soldiers shortly after arriving at the camp outside the city. Another says that Sidorka was publicly hanged in Moscow shortly after the coronation of Tsar Mikhail. Others record that Sidorka just disappeared without a trace after the coronation, no doubt executed in secret and permanently removed from public view.

During the popular assemblies of late 1612 and early 1613, the Cossack army of Ataman Zarutzki left Kolomensk and made its camp just south of Ryazan, and he took Marina Mnishek and her son with him. The Cossacks hoped that the son would ascend the throne as Tsar Ivan V Dmitriyevich, but the selection of Mikhail Romanov dashed their hopes. Fearing vengeance, Zarutzki with mother and son left Ryazan for the Don basin in western Ukraine while his Cossacks abandoned him and returned to their homes. But the Cossacks in that region refused his asylum and refused to support Marina or her son. Then the fugitives migrated to Astrakhan, which also rejected them. The next course was asylum in Persia. During his stay at Astrakhan, Zarutzki had an altercation with the military governor Ataman Khorostinin and killed him. This forced the fugitives to flee again, now north, hoping Volga Cossacks would accept him, but they took Zarutzki and Marina and son into custody and handed them over to Russian troops and they were taken to Moscow. Sometime in 1614, Ataman Zarutzki was impaled in public display by order of the Romanov family. The child named Ivan Dmitriyevich — age about three — was hanged. Marina Mnishek was incarcerated in a cell at the Tula Fortress to live out the balance of her life in solitary confinement. She died shortly from malnutrition and disease.

With the flight of Patr. Ignatius to Livonia and the death of both Patriarchs Job and Hermogen, a temporary form of administration surfaced within the ROC after the liberation of Moscow to keep order and progress continuing in the church. The closest administrator to the previous patriarchs was Metr. Pafnutie of Krutitzk, a suburb of Moscow, who was then designated by the Boyar Duma to preside over patriarchal matters at ecclesiastical councils. After his death the position of interim administrator was assigned to Metr. Isidor of Novgorod, but because his diocese was now under Swedish occupation he was unable to travel to Moscow, so the next in line was Metr. Efrem of Kazan. He held the reigns of the ROC until his death a year after the coronation of Tsar Mikhail Romanov and then the responsibility was assigned to Metr. Jonah of Krutitzk. Russia was officially without a patriarch during this interim until the return from Polish exile of Filaret — Feodor Nikitich — the father of Tsar Mikhail Romanov, who was then ordained as patriarch.

After the ascension to the throne of Tsar Mikhail, the military commanders Minin and Pozharski strove to avoid simultaneous war with Poland and Sweden, attempting to utilize diplomatic means, but with limited success. Sigismund did not desist in his attempts to defeat